ADVANCED LOGIC PROGRAMMING FOR LANGUAGE PROCESSING

ADVANCED LOGIC PROGRAMMING FOR LANGUAGE PROCESSING

Patrick Saint-Dizier

Institut de Recherche en Informatique de Toulouse (IRIT),
Toulouse, France

Academic Press
Harcourt Brace & Company, Publishers
London   San Diego   New York   Boston
Sydney   Tokyo   Toronto

ACADEMIC PRESS LIMITED
24-28 Oval Road
LONDON NW1 7DX

U.S. Edition Published by
ACADEMIC PRESS INC.
San Diego, CA 92101

This book is printed on acid free paper

A catalogue record for this book is available from the British Library

ISBN 0-12-614860-0

Printed and bound in Great Britain by Hartnolls Limited, Bodmin, Cornwall

Table of Contents

Chapter 3
Logic-Based Grammars 47

Chapter 4
Feature Systems in Logic Programming

Chapter 5
Constraint Logic Programming for
Language Processing

Chapter 8
Higher-Order Logic Programming for
Language Processing

Introduction

The use as a programming language of first-order logic, or more precisely of a substantial subset of it, emerged as a challenging new paradigm in the early seventies. The development of symbolic logic has introduced the notion of logical consequence which can be given a formal definition. If a problem and the knowledge relevant to the solution of that problem can be represented in a suitable form as a set of premises, then one or more solutions can be found and mechanically constructed from them.

For example, within the framework of language processing, a relevant subset of a language can be described as a set of premises, providing morphological, syntactic and semantic constraints. Then, the determining of whether a certain string of words meets the constraints imposed by these premises can be solved by the construction of a proof.

Logic programming offers more than just providing the response 'True' or 'False' to a problem. Under certain conditions, it can indeed be productive, i.e. given a problem to solve with a finite number of unknowns, it can provide the values of these unknowns for which the answer to the problem is true. The set of premises is then viewed as a program specification and the problem to solve as a call to this program, with input and output parameters.

One of the main principles of logic programming, as explained by Kowalski (1979a, 1979b), is to have a clear separation between on the one hand the logical specification of a certain knowledge related to a problem, and on the other hand the mechanical specification of the means to solve the problem, in other words, the control. The former specification describes what the knowledge relevant to the problem is, while the latter describes how proofs can be constructed (constructive proofs) from that knowledge to solve the problem. Clearly, both specifications for a given problem are not necessarily unique. Also, in most logic programming languages, only the first specification is really accessible to the programmer.

Prolog is certainly the most well-known programming language of the Logic Programming paradigm. It has very nice properties, in particular for natural language processing. Morphological, syntactic, semantic and pragmatic information is often expressed by means of symbols (e.g. to represent gender, number, category), structured objects (e.g. trees, graphs) and laws (e.g. syntactic rules, semantic composition rules). Contrary to most programming languages which manipulate functions, logic programs, and in particular Prolog, manipulate relations among entities. A higher degree of freedom is thus introduced for the specification of variable values in tuples. Finally, it should be noticed that variables representing entities, possibly structured, play a very different and often a much more important role than in other programming paradigms. Variables may indeed stand for terms.

Prolog permits the description of information in a non-deterministic way. As a consequence, Prolog's search strategy must be capable of computing all the solutions to a given problem. In other words, all the branches must be fully explored. These search branches must be elaborated in a way such that useless ones (i.e. those which are of no interest to the current problem being solved) are discarded as early as possible. All these requirements make the construction of a computational device a difficult task. This task becomes less difficult when the logical system is weakened. Horn clauses is such a weaker system, but there are many other systems such as the disjunctive Horn clauses. More elaborate strategies than the one found in standard Prolog also enable some fundamental computation problems like completeness to be overcome. Among these strategies, let us mention the class of parallel logic programming languages and the class of constraint-based programming languages.

In Prolog, the knowledge associated with a problem is expressed by means of Horn clauses, composed of basic elements called terms. In a number of cases, the use of terms is felt to be too general or too constraining and programmers have to imagine unnatural and indirect ways of describing knowledge. This situation has motivated the emergence of more specialized logic programming languages, most of them preserving the basic computational properties of Horn clause logic.

The aim of this book is precisely to motivate and to present in detail, at both formal and practical levels, classes of relevant advanced logic programming languages which contribute to the problematics of representing and of processing natural language in all its dimensions.

In this volume, we introduce most logic programming areas relevant to natural language processing. Great care has been taken to present exhaustive programming examples of a moderate complexity, ready to run on most machines. The programming languages we have introduced are easily available and most of them run effectively on a number of machines. We have avoided refering to too many different languages and syntaxes in order not to puzzle the reader. The absence of some languages does not, in any case, constitute a judgement *a priori* on their interest.

In this volume, examples are essentially of two types. First, we have simple, naive examples, used throughout the whole volume, whose goal is to introduce programming techniques (e.g. compilers, interpreters, parallel programming, etc.) where the importance of the linguistic data is relatively minor. The other type of example is the presentation of a fragment of a linguistic system or of an application (e.g. machine translation), where all aspects relevant to the problem being addressed are taken into account. These examples are more elaborate and are meant to show the reader how a real situation can be treated. Hints are often given as to how to extend these programs. These examples address a number of fields and theories such as: morphology, syntax (GPSGs, GB) and semantics (boolean semantics, situation semantics, Montague semantics).

It should be noted that all the areas of logic programming presented in this book are completely compatible and could nicely co-exist, although the complexity of programs could be somewhat high.

Chapter 1 of this book introduces the foundations of logic programming. Notions such as clauses, interpretations, substitution and unification, fix-point semantics, declarative and procedural semantics of logic programs, SLD-resolution and negation are addressed. These notions will be used and extended in the chapters that follow.

Chapter 2 presents the most important basic formalism in logic programming for natural language processing: *definite clause grammars* (DCGs). Besides a formal presentation, different parsing and generations strategies for DCGs, either compiled or interpreted, either top-down or bottom-up, are proposed. Methods for automatically computing syntactic and semantic representations are also presented and illustrated.

Chapter 3 is devoted to the family of logic-based grammars. Among these grammars, we have focused on the most important ones, either from a practical or from a theoretical perspective. Metamorphosis grammars, extraposition grammars, restriction grammars, gapping grammars and discontinuous grammars are successively presented, with their motivations and the way they are interpreted in Prolog.

Chapter 4 deals with an important topic in natural language processing: the foundations, the use and the implementation of typed feature systems. After a detailed presentation of a simple feature-based system in Prolog and the way it can be implemented in various forms, including a bottom-up parser, we present the notion of hierarchy in feature-value systems and show how linguistic knowledge can be encoded according to this approach. Next, we introduce Login, which is an extension to Prolog that models feature-systems as type constructors defined in type hierarchies. It also proposes an extended definition of unification which computes greater lower bounds according to a predefined type lattice. This chapter ends by describing an implementation of an inheritance system, which handles monotonic as well as non-monotonic forms of inheritance.

Chapter 5 introduces a research domain in logic programming which is of much interest to language processing: *constraint logic programming* (CLP). CLP specifies a set of interpreted predicates called constraints, which operate on domains such as booleans, arithmetic numbers, strings and finite domains of various kinds. We focus on three major types of constraints: boolean constraints, which are very convenient for modelling disjunctions and negation in feature structures, constraints on finite domains, which introduce specific resolution algorithms, and linear precedence constraints, for manipulating strings, either in a parsing or in a generation process.

Chapter 6 is devoted to parallel logic programming and its applications to language processing. This area has not yet been very much explored and this chapter presents the main advantages and hints for using a parallel logic programming language such as Parlog in natural language processing applications. Programming techniques for processing features in feature-based systems in parallel are presented as a direct application of this paradigm. Finally, concurrent constraint programming is presented, in which features of constraint systems and parallel systems are merged.

Chapter 7 deals with object-oriented logic programming (OOLP). After a presentation of the basic concepts of object-oriented programming, we introduce Parlog++, an extension to Parlog which handles objects in logic. Different applications are then proposed such as parsing and modelling inheritance between objects. We then show how OOLP and parallel logic programming can be merged and propose as an example a producer-consumer system for machine translation.

Chapter 8 introduces higher-order logic programming in the area of language processing. The language λ-Prolog is presented and a few applications are introduced: modelling semantic respresentation computation in λ-Prolog and its relations with Montague semantics, a DCG interpreter in λ-Prolog and, finally, a treatment of filler-gap dependencies in GPSGs.

These chapters are almost independent from each other, except for Chapters 1 and 2 which are prerequisites for the other ones. Chapters 3 to 8 can be thus read independently or in almost any order, except for the cross-references they contain.

To end this introduction, let us briefly summarize the enhancements with respect to language processing offered by the different logic programming paradigms presented in this volume. In the diagram below, nodes represent the different paradigms studied in this book and the arcs represent the situations where there is a real enhancement.

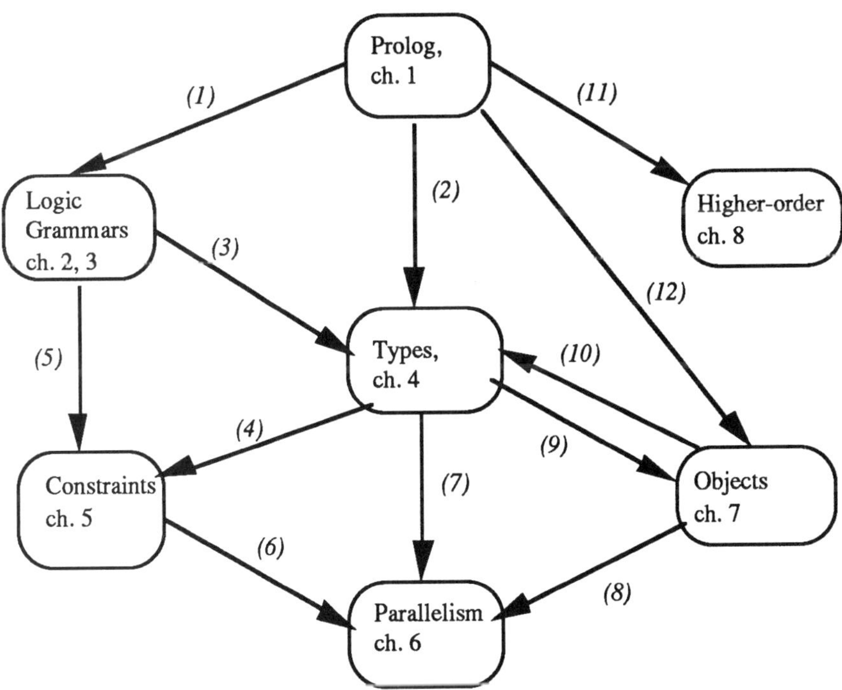

Let us now comment on the arcs in this diagram. Most of the comparison elements introduced in these comments are developed and illustrated in the different chapters of this book.

(1) Logic grammars introduce an automatic treatment of a number of characteristics which are hidden to the grammar writer such as, for example:

- the representation and the percolation in the proof tree of the sentence to parse, represented by a list of words,
- the construction of a syntactic tree,
- aspects of the treatment of long-distance dependencies.

Logic grammars introduce a slightly higher degree of declarativity and of linguistic adequacy in the linguistic descriptions. A better independence from the strategy imposed by Prolog is also attained. Logic grammars indeed permit the definition of various forms of parsers and generators, either in compile or in interpreted mode.

(2) The introduction of types and of typed feature structures (TFS) in logic programming allows a much greater flexibility in the definition and the specification of feature structures. Prolog terms are indeed very rigid and each argument bears a specific, predefined type of information. In TFS, it is possible to specify only the relevant information, and in any order, due to the introduction of a feature labelling system. Furthermore, types are often hierarchically structured, for example by means of a lattice of types. This approach permits a better organization of the linguistic knowledge and also an enhancement of the unification system which can compute greater lower bounds of two terms directly from the type lattice. Finally, properties, expressed by feature structures, can be associated with types. These properties may then be inherited by sub-types, according to different strategies (e.g. single or multiple inheritance, default inheritance).

(3) The introduction of typed feature structures in logic grammars allows a very flexible representation of features, as explained in (2). The elements that logic grammars can handle in an automatic way can also be represented by means of feature structures. The philosophy underlying logic grammars, i.e. providing grammar writers with a declarative framework in which the treatment of some structures are hidden, can also be used within TFS, for example to automatically organize or reorganize feature structures.

(4) Constraints manipulate typed objects such as boolean, rational numbers and finite domains. With respect to type structures, whose treatment is based on

unification, constraints permit the introduction of different modes of interpretation of feature values, depending on their type. For example, boolean values will be associated with a boolean constraint solver, strings of words representing sentences may be associated with a linear precedence constraint solver which would encode the specific treatment of linear precedence in a direct way and which also would incorporate the properties of linear precedence (e.g. transitivity). The introduction of constraints permits treatments of feature values to be defined which are better adapted to represent these values. The use of constraints introduces a better linguistic adequacy, a greater modularity, and a higher degree of re-usability of resources. They also provide a more intensional response to queries since a response is no longer a set of substitutions for variables but a set of constraints.

(5) Logic grammars can be fruitfully paired with constraints. With respect to typed feature structures, there is a loss in flexibility in the specification of feature structures, but there is a gain in efficiency since unification is simpler and faster. The arguments of the terms used in logic grammars are then typed when they are used in constraints, the others may remain untyped.

(6) Parallelism is of much interest to constraint systems and to constraint resolution in particular. Constraint systems (e.g. boolean constraints, constraints on a specific finite domain) are postulated to be independent from each other; it is thus appropriate to have the different constraint resolution mechanisms executed in parallel. Moreover, the resolution mechanisms themselves can be partly executed in parallel, in particular when several constraint resolution or simplification procedures can be used equivalently. As a result, efficiency and completeness are improved in a substantial way.

(7) For similar reasons, it is of much interest, and more natural from a linguistic point of view, to treat certain feature structures in parallel since they deal with aspects of language which have little in common. Information between elements executed in parallel is exchanged at the appropriate time and level by means of synchronization mechanisms. Parallelism can also be used in derivations (or type constructions) when several solutions are possible. Each solution can be explored in parallel with the other ones. The first that succeeds is then kept in committed-choice strategies. Parallelism introduces new parsing and generation strategics, which have in essence some similarities with breadth-first search strategies; they also introduce a higher degree of completeness and a greater efficiency.

(8) Given a set of objects, it is of much interest to have different, independent actions which can be executed in parallel and which may use portions of these objects, either data or methods. Communication between objects often being realized by means of a message-passing mechanism, messages corresponding to different tasks can then be exchanged in a totally unsynchronized way. Moreover, given a message, it is of much interest to be able to explore in parallel the methods (or definitions) activated by this message, either in the same object or in independent objects. Finally, parallelism introduces the notion of synchronization between processes; it may then be of much interest to model processes by objects (such as parsers and generators) and to define synchronization procedures between these objects (for example, to exchange in an optimal way different types of information).

(9) Types and objects are very close. Types introduce a linguistically adequate way of structuring linguistic knowledge. Objects go beyond this possibility: they allow data to be more modular and to be private to certain processes. Objects also allow the programmer to structure processes, to isolate them in different modules, to model task delegation between processes and to define processes which use only certain types of private data. Finally, the inheritance facilities offered by a number of object-oriented languages are more refined than those offered by TFS since different methods in an object may inherit information (or delegate tasks) from different other objects.

(10) Conversely, it is of much interest to incorporate the notions of unification used in TFS into object-oriented approaches. Types allow the structuring of linguistic knowledge at a more primitive level than objects; for example, types enable syntactic and semantic labels to be organized according to lattices. These types of structures could then be incorporated into objects where dedicated methods could compute greater lower bounds while others could attempt to unify terms or to perform inheritance. In general, object-oriented methods permit the structuring of linguistic knowledge at a more global level than TFS.

(11) Higher-order logic programming introduces a much more powerful unification procedure by allowing λ-terms and variable predicate identifiers. The notion of the most general unifier is no longer appropriate since higher-order unification can produce unifiers which cannot be compared. Higher-order logic programming languages also introduce λ-operators which can appear at any place in a clause, and universal quantification, explicit existential quantification and

implication in clause bodies. The different λ-operations are incorporated into the resolution mechanism. Finally, higher-order languages introduce a more refined notion of scoping, in which three levels of scoping are identified relating to λ-abstractions, quantification and control.

(12) The introduction of objects in logic programming offers several advantages, among which are: the definition of modules with private data and procedures, a clearer and more explicit specification of the communication between procedures in different objects, a very refined notion of inheritance and the notions of prototype and instances of that prototype.

Chapter 1

Formal Aspects of Programming in Logic

In this chapter, we present the foundations of logic programming focusing on issues relevant to natural language processing. The elements presented here will serve as a basis for the next chapters where they will be further elaborated. Most of the elements presented here refer to the current literature on the domain, and in particular to Lloyd (1987).

In this chapter we give the definition of *first-order logic* (hereafter referred to as FOL), then of *clausal forms* and *Horn clauses*. The major aspects of the declarative semantics of Prolog procedures are then examined, and Prolog's basic mechanism of resolution (*SLD resolution*) clarified. The chapter ends with some remarks on the meaning of a Prolog program.

1. First-Order Logic

First-order logic (FOL), as with all languages in general, consists of two complementary aspects: syntax and semantics. Syntax characterizes the forms of expressions and formulas of a language. Semantics assigns meaning to the symbols used in these formulas.

We now define a first-order theory. It is composed of an alphabet, a first-order language, a set of axioms and a set of inference rules. The first-order language consists of the well-formed formulae of the theory.

An alphabet consist of seven classes of symbols:
- variable symbols,
- constant symbols,
- function symbols,
- predicate symbols,
- connective symbols,
- quantifier symbols,
- punctuation symbols.

Let us now introduce the notion of a first-order language. It is based on the notion of *term*, which is defined inductively as follows:

(a) a constant is a term,

(b) a variable is a term,

(c) f is an n-ary function symbol and t_1 ... t_n are terms, then $f(t_1, ..., t_n)$ is a term.

In the remainder of this chapter, variables are represented by capital letters, constants by small letters or numbers, predicate symbols by letters such as p, q, and r and function symbols by letters such as f, g and h.

A *well-formed formula* of FOL is traditionally defined in a recursive way, as follows:

(1) $p(t_1, t_2, ..., t_n)$ is a formula (or an *atom* because of its elementary form) if p is a predicate of arity n and if every t_i is a term.

(2) if A and B are formulas, then so are:

$\neg A$ (negation of A)

$A \wedge B$ (A and B)

$A \vee B$ (A non-exclusive or B)

$A \Rightarrow B$ (A implies B)

$A \Leftrightarrow B$ (A is equivalent to B)

(3) if X is a variable and A a formula, then:

($\forall$X A) (A is true for all values of X) and

($\exists$X A) (there exist some X for which A is true) are formulas of FOL.
Parentheses may be used whenever there is a risk of ambiguity.

The semantics of the logical operators in (2) above is the standard one. For example, for the symbol $\vee$, A $\vee$ B is true iff either A or B is true; A $\wedge$ B is true iff both A and B are true; for the symbol $\Rightarrow$, A $\Rightarrow$ B is true iff, whenever A is true, B is true; B may also be true when A is not. Finally, A $\Leftrightarrow$ B is true iff A and B are either both true or both false.

In ($\forall$X A), the formula A is in the scope of the universal quantifier, and X is bound by this quantifier. A variable which is not bound by any quantifier is called a free variable.

A *closed formula* is a formula with no free occurrences of any variable. Thus, for example, the following formula is closed:

($\forall$X (h(X,t(a,b)) $\wedge$ f(4,7))

whereas the following formula is not closed because X is not bound:

f(4,X) $\wedge$ (($\exists$Y) h(Y,t(a,b)))

Notice that the following formula is not closed because the first occurrence of X is unbound:

f(4,X) $\wedge$ (($\forall$X) h(X,t(a,b)))

In the rest of this chapter we only consider closed formulas.

Finally, a term or an atom are said to be a *ground* if they do not contain any variable.

2. Clausal Forms and Horn Clauses

Most actual automatic proof techniques are based on a restricted form of FOL. Prolog itself is based on one of the most restricted clausal forms, *Horn clauses,* so that the required calculations can be efficiently performed on a computer. A clause is a formula of the following form:

(a) $\forall$ X_1, X_2, ..., X_n ($A_1 \vee A_2 \vee ... \vee A_p$)

where each A_i is an atom or the negation of an atom (here called a literal) and X_1, X_2, ..., X_n is a set of variables that appear in the disjunction:

($A_1 \vee A_2 \vee ... \vee A_p$).

Here are two examples of formulas that are clauses:

$\forall X,Y\ (\ f(X,2) \vee g(h,Y,7) \vee (\neg p(X)\ ))$

$\forall X\ (\neg p(X)\ ).$

The following formula:

$\forall X, Y\ (f(X,2) \wedge (\neg g(h,Y,7)))$

is not a clause because it uses the logical AND ($\wedge$).

In logic programming, it is traditional to group together positive literals before the negative ones; this does not change the meaning of the clause because disjunction is a commutative operation. The formula (a) becomes (b):

(b) $\forall X_1, X_2, ..., X_n, (A_1 \vee A_2 \vee ... \vee A_n \vee \neg B_1 \vee \neg B_2 \vee ... \vee \neg B_m)$

with $p = n + m$ and the same conditions as above. This formula is logically equivalent to (c):

(c) $\forall X_1, X_2, ..., X_n (A_1 \vee A_2 \vee ... \vee A_n <= B_1 \wedge B_2 \wedge ... \wedge B_m)$

because:

$(\neg B_1 \vee \neg B_2)$

is equivalent to:

$\neg (B_1 \wedge B_2)$

and

$(B_1 \Rightarrow B_2)$

is equivalent to:

$(\neg B_1 \vee B_2).$

This can be checked with the help of truth tables.

In this formula, $(B_1 \wedge B_2 \wedge ... \wedge B_m)$ is called the antecedent of the implication and $(A_1 \vee ... \vee A_n)$ is the consequent. The B_is are sometimes called *negative literals* and the A_i's *positive literals*.

This leads us to a definition of *Horn clauses*. A Horn clause is a clause with at most one positive literal. Thus, a Horn clause has one of the following forms:

(1) $\forall(X_1, X_2, ..., X_n) (A <= B_1 \wedge B_2 \wedge ... \wedge B_m)$: *a definite program clause,*

(2) $\forall(X_1, X_2, ..., X_n) (A<=)$: *a unit clause,*

(3) $\forall(X_1, X_2, ..., X_n) (<= B_1 \wedge B_2 \wedge ... \wedge B_m)$: *a definite goal.*

Intuitively, form (1) corresponds to a Prolog rule in which A is the head and $B_1 \wedge B_2 \wedge ... \wedge B_m$ is the body. Form (2) is a unit clause (or a fact), possibly containing some variables. Finally, form (3) corresponds to a question (or goal) in Prolog. Forms (2) and (3) are particular cases in which the body or the head (respectively) of the clause is empty.

Forms (1) and (2) are universally quantified; this is implicit in a Prolog program. A rule is indeed read as follows:

For all assignments of values to $X_1, X_2, ..., X_n$, if $B_1 \wedge B_2 \wedge ... \wedge B_m$ is true, then A is true.

Form (3), which corresponds to a question (also called a goal) in Prolog, requires additional explanation. We have seen that such a clause may be put into the form:

(4) $(\forall X_1, X_2, ..., X_n) B_1 \wedge B_2 \wedge ... \wedge B_m \Rightarrow .$

This clause, with an empty consequent, gives the conditions under which $B_1 \wedge B_2 \wedge ... \wedge B_m$ is false. This approach is called a refutation; it will be developed in sections 7 and 8. Formula (4) above is equivalent to:

(5) $\forall X_1, X_2, ..., X_n (\neg B_1 \vee \neg B_2 \vee ... \vee \neg B_m)$

and also to:

(6) $\neg \exists X_1, X_2, ..., X_n (B_1 \wedge B_2 \wedge ... \wedge B_m)$

The negation of this expression:

(7) $\exists X_1, X_2, ..., X_n (B_1 \wedge B_2 \wedge ... \wedge B_m)$

permits the characterization of situations where this expression is true. This is the underlying form of a question in Prolog. Each B_i, which is a conjunct of the question, is a subgoal to be proved.

Finally, a *definite program* is a set of definite program clauses and of unit clauses. In a definite program, the set of all program clauses with the same predicate symbol p is called the *definition* of p.

3. Domains of Interpretation

The values that variables may be instantiated to in a program P can be recursively defined by the notions of Herbrand universe and Herbrand base.

Let L be a first-order language on which P is based. The *Herbrand universe* U_L for L is the set of all ground terms which can be constructed out from all the constants and function symbols in L. For example, if P is the following program:

```
has(X):-  near(f(X),f(Y)).
object(a).
object(b).
```

it has the predicate symbols object, has and near, the constants a and b and the function symbol f. The Herbrand universe is then:

$$U_L = \{ a, b, f(a), f(b), f(f(a)), f(f(b)), f(f(f(a))), \dots \}$$

The *Herbrand base* B_L for L is the set of all ground atoms which can be constructed from the predicate symbols in L with ground terms from U_L as arguments. For the above example, we obtain the following Herbrand base:

$$B_L = \{ \text{object}(a), \text{object}(b), \text{has}(a), \text{has}(b), \text{near}(f(a), f(a)), \text{near}(f(a),$$
$$f(b)), \text{near}(f(b),f(a)), \text{near}(f(b),f(b)), \text{near}(f(f(a)), f(f(a))), \dots \}.$$

From these definitions follows the notion of interpretation which maps constants and function symbols of L into appropriate elements of U_L.

4. Substitution and Unification

Variables are bound to terms by the mechanism of variable substitution. Two terms are compared by means of the unification mechanism, which is based on the notion of substitution. In this section, our aim is not to explore all the details of unification, but only to state general definitions.

A *substitution* θ of terms t_i for variables X_i is a finite set $\{X_1/t_1, \dots, X_n/t_n\}$. The X_i are assumed to be all different variable symbols. The terms t_i can be ground (i.e. fully instantiated) or not; they can also be variables (in this case, this is simply a variable renaming procedure). Each t_i must be different from X_i. Each pair X_i/t_i is called a binding for X_i.

A substitution is applied on an expression by simultaneously replacing all the variable occurrences X_i concerned by the term t_i.

For example, the substitution:

$$\theta = \{ X / p(a,b), Y / a, Z / p(T,U) \},$$

where small letters are constants and capital letter are variables, applied to the term:

$$g(X, f(X, Y, Z), Y)$$

gives the following result:

$$g(p(a,b), f(p(a,b), a, p(T,U)), a).$$

$X / p(a,b)$ and Y / a are ground substitutions because the term substituted for the variable is ground. Notice that, in order to avoid infinite terms, it is not advisable to have similar variable symbols on both sides of a substitution, e.g.

X / f(X,Y) would result in an infinite term of the form:

   f(f(f(... f(X) ...)), Y).

A substitution θ is called a *unifier* for a set of terms T if the application of θ to each element of T yields the same new element.

A *most general unifier* (noted as mgu) is a unifier which is minimal, i.e. where useless or redundant substitutions have been eliminated.

5. Fixpoint Semantics

Fixpoint semantics is used to construct in a certain number of steps the set of all ground predicates which can be proved from a set P of clauses. This defines a monotonic mapping between a definite program P and a set of ground predicates.

Let R be a partial order on a set S of elements. For each subset S_i of S, there is an upper and a lower bound. A least upper bound (noted lub) is the smallest element which is an upper bound and a greater lower bound (glb) is the largest element which is a lower bound. R defines a *complete lattice* on S if for every subset S_i of S, there exist $lub(S_i)$ and $glb(S_i)$.

Let S be a complete lattice and T be a monotonic mapping from S into S. $\alpha \in S$ is a fixpoint of T if $T(\alpha) = \alpha$. α is the least fixpoint if for all β fixpoints of T, $\alpha \leq \beta$.

Let us now characterize the fixpoint semantics for logic programs. Let S_0 be the set of ground instances of unit clauses (i.e. clauses with empty bodies). Unit clauses with variables are transformed into all possible ground unit clauses where variables have been replaced by the elements of the Herbrand universe U_L. Let us now consider the clauses of the program P. Among these clauses, let us consider the ground instances of those clauses where all the literals B_i of their bodies are elements of S_0. Let $T(S_0)$ be the set of heads of these ground clauses. $T(S_0)$ is the set of all ground terms constructed in a single step from the clauses of the program P.

We have the result that:

   $S_0 \subseteq T(S_0)$.

$T(S_0)$ indeed includes the elements S_0 which are the ground unit clauses and is constructed from it. Let us now define $T \uparrow n$ as the result of n applications of T to S_0. Since at each step new clauses of P are used, possibly producing new ground instances, we have the following result:

$$\forall\, i,\ T \uparrow i \subseteq T \uparrow (i+1)\,.$$

Let lfp be the least fixpoint of T, such that:

$$\text{lfp} = \text{glb}\ \{x \mid T(x) = x\ \}.$$

It is also the smallest set such that $T(S) = S$. $T \uparrow \omega$ results in the application of T till no more ground instance is produced. This application may be infinite.

From the construction of the fixpoint of T on P follows an important result established by Van Emden and Kowalski (1976):

Q is a *logical consequence* of P if and only if all the elements of Q (if Q is composed of several literals) belong to $T \uparrow \omega$ of P, and conversely.

This result has been generalized to queries with variables.

We can now characterize the cases where $\neg$ Q is a logical consequence of P (i.e. the query Q will yield a *no* response). The *completion* of a predicate p in a program P (Clark 78) is a formula which is the disjunction of all the bodies of p. Then a *no* answer to Q will be provided if and only if $\neg$ Q is a logical consequence of the completion of p.

This result can be characterized in more depth. Let us consider the Herbrand base B_L for the program P. $T \downarrow n$ is the result of n applications of T to B_L. We have the result that:

$$T \downarrow (i+1) \subseteq T \downarrow i$$

since, at each step i, only the use of clauses is considered. After a certain number of applications of T, possibly infinite, we obtain $T \downarrow \omega$. Then, the following property follows:

$\neg$ Q is a logical consequence of the completion of P if and only if some literal in Q is not a member of $T \downarrow \omega$.

The complement of $T \downarrow \omega$ with respect to B_L is the *finite failure set* for P.

6. Declarative and Procedural Semantics of Prolog

Prolog is composed of two aspects, logic (Horn clauses) on one hand and control on the other hand. The logical aspect describes facts relevant to the solution of a problem and how they are interrelated, apart from any computational preoccupation. The control part states precisely how a proof can be mechanically carried out. Ideally, these two parts should be independent and complementary. This is unfortunately not the case. There are some important divergences that make the writing of programs and, more generally, the elaboration of a methodology for programming in Prolog very delicate.

For now, we consider Prolog to be a set of facts and rules, as well as goals to be proved. The declarative semantics of Prolog is based on that of Horn clauses. More precisely, let us consider a program P and a goal B:

$$B_1, B_2, ..., B_n => .$$

to be proved. The goal is then to find bindings for the variables in B that make it a consequence of P. A proof technique, which uses contradiction, consists of showing that P and $\neg$ B are inconsistent. Thus, B must be true since P, the program, is by convention a set of true axioms. With this method, we obtain the enumeration of the values for the variables $X_1, X_2, ..., X_n$ in B for which B is true.

The negation of B has the form:

$$\forall X_1, X_2, ..., X_m, \neg (B_1, B_2, ..., B_n).$$

A constructive proof of the inconsistency of $\neg$B with P will provide counter-examples of the universal formulation of $\neg$B given above. As a consequence, the constructive proof gives the values:

$$T_1, T_2, ..., T_m$$

for the variables $X_1, X_2, ..., X_m$ for which $P \wedge \neg B$, with each substitution of T_i for X_1, is false.

The declarative semantics of Prolog is, therefore, that a goal B is deduced from a program P if $P \wedge \neg B$ cannot be proved. This method is called *refutation* because the proof uses the negation of the statement to be proved.

The procedural semantics of Prolog appears to be a specification of its declarative semantics with the automation of the mechanism of proof by refutation. The proof strategy that has been adopted is top-down, depth-first, and left to right. This strategy is associated with the mechanism of resolution and, in particular, with SLD resolution. This is discussed in the following section.

7. SLD Resolution

The fundamental principle of *SLD resolution* is a method of rewriting modulo substitutions. A goal of the form:

$$B_1 \wedge B_2 \wedge \ldots \wedge B_i \wedge \ldots \wedge B_m \Rightarrow .$$

associated with the clause:

$$C_1 \wedge C_2 \wedge \ldots \wedge C_p \Leftarrow B'_i .$$

with θ being the minimal set of substitutions (the mgu) such that $B_i\theta = B'_i\theta$ is rewritten as:

$$[B_1 \wedge B_2 \wedge \ldots B_{i-1} \wedge C_1 \wedge C_2 \wedge \ldots \wedge C_p \wedge B_{i+1} \wedge \ldots \wedge B_m] \theta \Rightarrow .$$

This expression is called the *resolvant* of the goal and of the previously given clause. The rewriting process presented here is called *goal reduction*. This process is applied recursively a finite number of times, starting from the original goal B.

The termination condition applies either when the resolvant is empty (B is proved) or when it is no longer possible to apply the rewriting techniques (in which case B is false). The general schema of SLD resolution given above shows a resolvant that is longer than the goal. In fact, a resolvant gets shorter when unit clauses are used.

This can be illustrated as follows, from the goal:

$$B_1 \wedge B_2 \wedge B_3 \wedge \ldots \wedge B_n \Rightarrow .$$

and the fact:

$$B'_2 \Leftarrow . ,$$

modulo the substitution θ_2, we obtain:

$$[B_1 \wedge B_3 \wedge \ldots \wedge B_n] \theta_2 \Rightarrow .$$

The mechanism of SLD resolution that we have just described is derived directly from the inference rule of *modus ponens*. Replacing the head of a rule by its body or removing facts from a goal comes from the fact that in a program the rules and the facts play the role of axioms.

8. SLD Resolution in Prolog

The mechanism of SLD resolution allows for many automatic implementations; the choice of which goals to reduce and which clauses to use in the program remains to be specified. The choices are specified through a computation rule R associated with SLD resolution. This defines a strategy. The rule R has no fundamental influence over the result. However, depending on the rule R, the size of the proof tree (and thus the global efficiency of the system) may be very different. Some difficulties may also appear with recursion resulting in infinite loops.

In the well-known example that follows, two computation rules are considered:

(1) R_1: The reduction of subgoals in a goal proceeds from left to right.

(2) R_2: The reduction of subgoals in a goal proceeds from right to left.

Consider the program path(X,Y) which gives true as a result if there is a path from X to Y:

```
(1)  path(X,Y):-  arc(X,Y).
(2)  path(X,Y):-  arc(X,Z),  path(Z,Y).
(3)  arc(a,b).
(4)  arc(b,c).
(5)  arc(c,d).
```

for the call:
```
?-  path(a,d).
```

The use of the computation rule R_1 gives the following proof tree, in which branches are labelled with the rule number and the substitutions used to apply the rule:

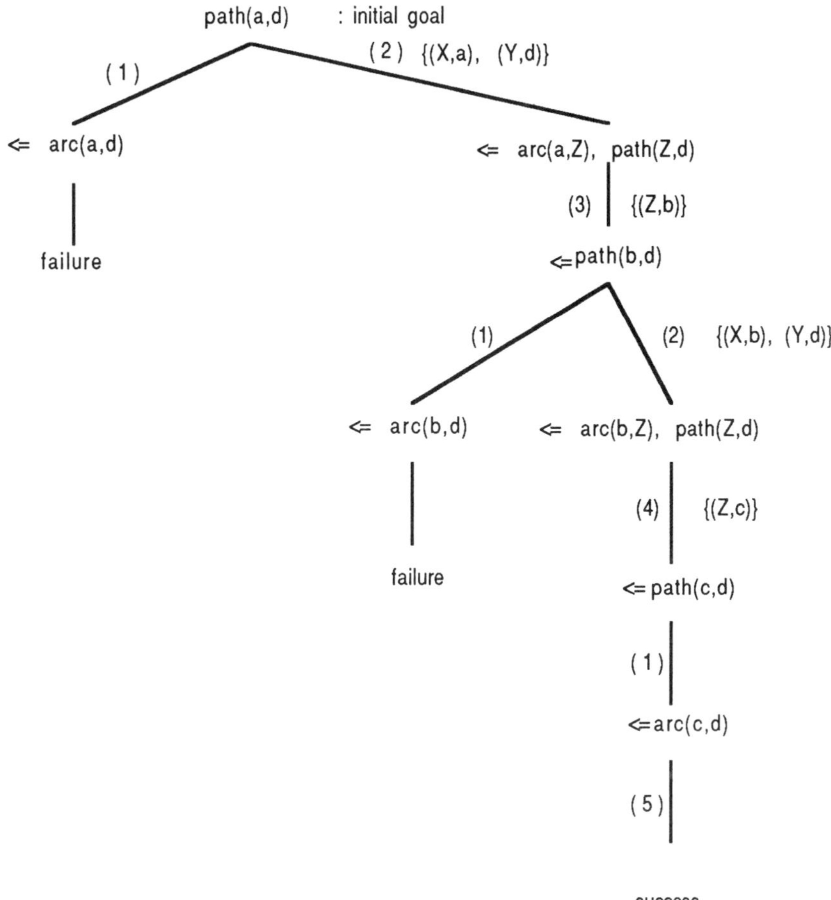

On arcs are represented the substitutions which are applied. The number indicates the clause in the above program which has been selected.

For the same goal, with computation rule R_2, the following proof tree is obtained:

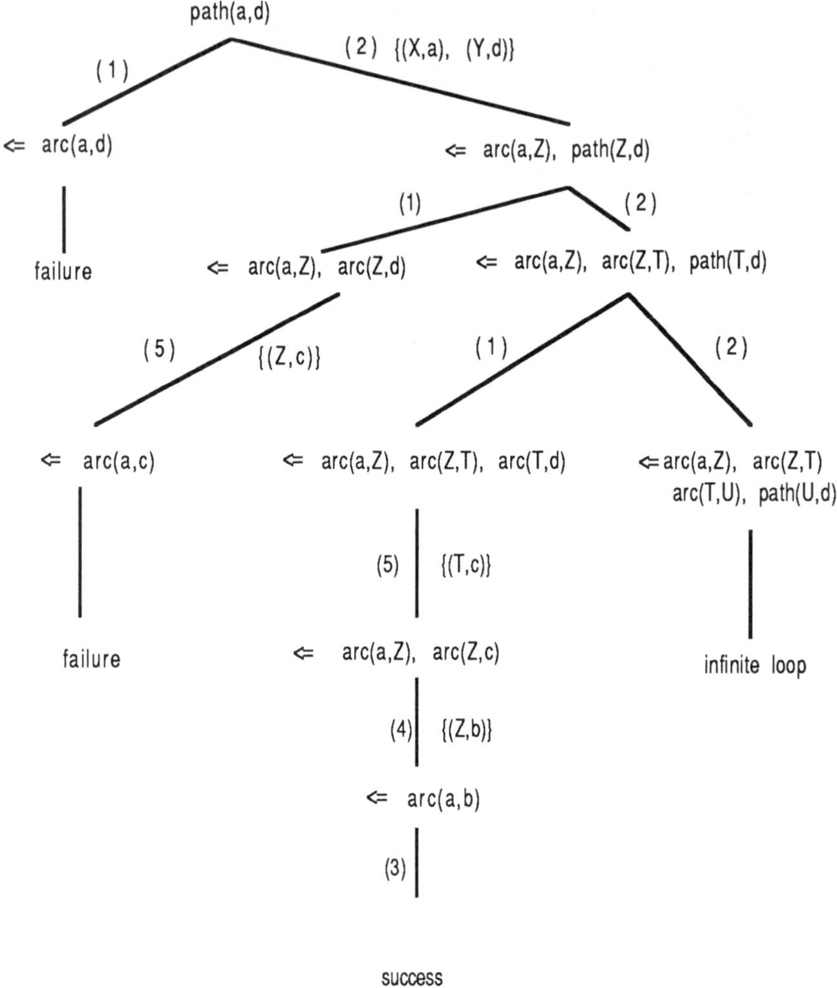

The path that results in a success is longer with R_2. Moreover, the program enters into an infinite loop in the last branch of the proof tree.

Prolog uses calculation rule R_1, which reduces subgoals from left to right.

9. Meaning of a Program

From a formal point of view, the meaning of a program is the set of elementary completely instantiated goals (ground atoms) that can be deduced from the program. This set may be infinite, particularly when recursive definitions are used.

The meaning of a program must coincide with the meaning the programr wishes to express. If this requirement is difficult to meet, it is advisable at least that the meaning of a program be contained within the meaning the programr wishes to confer to it.

Ideally, the meaning of a program should be independent of the underlying automatic proof mechanism. In reality, because of the compromises that have been made, in particular, those to make the system efficient, this independence is not attained. Programming in Prolog is therefore a delicate task. Nevertheless, Prolog's properties make it very attractive for numerous applications, as will be seen in the next chapters.

10. Negation in Logic Programs

The elements we have presented so far only permit us to show that a query Q is a logical consequence of a program P. We are not able to prove that $\neg$ Q is a logical consequence of P, for reasons of non-satisfiability.

To be able to treat negative queries, we need to add to the system a new inference rule, called the *closed world assumption* (CWA) Reiter (1978). This inference rule says that we can infer that $\neg$ Q is a logical consequence of P if Q is not.

In a program, the CWA amounts to postulating that any information which cannot be proven to be true is necessarily false. This rule has several interesting practical applications, but also several shortcomings, in particular in knowledge bases with incomplete knowledge.

The CWA also raises computational problems. There is indeed no algorithm which can say in a finite amount of time whether Q is or is not a logical consequence of P. This situation has motivated a less powerful inference rule: the negation as failure rule Clark (1978). This rule says that if a literal of Q is in the (SLD) finite failure set of P, then we can infer $\neg$ Q. This inference rule can furthermore be easily and also efficiently implemented.

Chapter 2

Processing Language with Definite Clause Grammars

The goal of this chapter is to present a basic formalism for processing language in logic programming: *definite clause grammars* (hereafter noted as DCG) (Pereira and Warren 1980). After introducing the foundations of DCG, we summarize the main techniques which permit the construction of different representations such as syntactic trees or semantic representations. Next, we present an interpreter and a compiler which permit an execution of DCGs in Prolog and show how a bottom-up parser for DCGs can be designed on top of Prolog. Finally, a simple bottom-up natural language generator is presented which generates natural language sentences from semantic representations.

DCGs are not the first logic-based formalism for language processing. Metamorphosis grammars were first introduced in the early seventies (Colmerauer 71, 75, 78), but their complexity made them somewhat difficult to use for simple natural language applications. They nevertheless constitute the formal basis from which most of the logic-based grammar systems are derived. The most relevant of these systems are presented in the next chapter. DCGs can be viewed as a special case of metamorphosis grammars.

1. An Introduction to Definite Clause Grammars

We now informally introduce definite clause grammars. A more detailed presentation and comparison with *augmented transition networks* (ATNs) is given in Pereira and Warren (1980).

Consider the following simple structural description of a sentence. A sentence (s) is composed of a noun phrase (np) followed by a verb phrase (vp). A noun phrase is composed of a determiner (det) followed by a noun (n); a verb phrase is a verb alone or a verb (v) followed by a noun phrase. If we leave out the term 'followed' and simply say, for example, that a sentence is composed of a noun phrase and a verb phrase, we can express the structure of a sentence by means of a set of logical statements:

$$(1) \quad np \land vp \Rightarrow s.$$
$$det \land n \Rightarrow np.$$
$$v \lor (v \land np) \Rightarrow vp.$$

To prove that a certain sentence is well formed, we have to prove that it satisfies the axiom s, i.e. we have to prove np and vp, etc. The above logical statements can easily be encoded in Prolog:

```
(2)    s:- np,  vp.
       np:- det, n.
       vp:- v.
       vp:- v, np.
```

This translation is not however fully satisfactory: since the comma in Prolog represents the conjunction, nothing says that the np has to precede the vp for a sentence to be well formed. This difficulty illustrates one of the technical difficulties of translating grammars into Horn clauses.

The precedence problem can be solved by the introduction of difference lists to the symbols of the above grammar. A symbol then has the following form:

```
g( Arguments ...,X, Y )
```

where g is any grammar symbol, Arguments represents the list of arguments related to linguistic descriptions associated to that symbol, and X and Y denote a string of words. The difference between X and Y is a string of words representing a possible 'surface' realization of the grammar symbol g, with the constraints imposed by the argument values in Argument (e.g. morphological constraints). X and Y are often called the input and the output lists of strings of words or the difference lists for the symbol g. The data structures associated with X and Y are lists. The elements of these lists are terminal elements, namely words potentially forming a sentence. Notice that the way a list is interpreted in DCGs imposes a total order on the elements of that list.

To illustrate this definition, if

g = np

and:

X = [the, student, has, a, computer],

then:

Y = [has, a, computer].

Following the grammar given in (2), Y is the output string of words associated to the np and it is also the input string of words of the vp symbol which is expected after the np. At the level of the np, the difference between X and Y, namely [the, student], has to denote a noun phrase for the predicate np to be true. Similarly, the string denoted by Y has to be a vp, for the sentence to be well formed.

The Prolog program given in (2) then becomes:

```
(3)   s(X, Y):- np(X, X1),  vp(X1, Y).
      np(X, Y):- det(X, X1), n(X1, Y).
      vp(X, Y):- v(X, Y).
      vp(X, Y):- v(X, X1), np(X1, Y).
```

The first clause above can be paraphrased as follows: there is a sentence, and no more, in the list X - Y, if there is a noun phrase in the list X - X1 and a verb phrase in the list X1 - Y. For the sentence to be well formed, there should be no more words after the verb phrase has been processed; in other words, Y in s(X, Y) has to be the empty list. This grammar needs to be paired with a lexicon which describes the lexical entries of the system. Lexical entries obey the same format (more elaborated forms can be found in the literature, but they really express the same phenomenon). For the above example, we have the following lexical entries:

```
(4)   det( [the | X ], X ).
      det( [a | X ], X ).
      n( [student | X ], X ).
      n( [computer | X ], X ).
      v( [has | X ], X ).
```

We now have a full program. A call to parse the above example is:

s([the, student, has, a computer], [ ]).

The program given in (3) and (4) is written in Prolog. The transformations applied to go from (1) to (3) are very regular, simple and purely syntactic. One of the main motivations of DCGs is to avoid grammar writers doing these transformations by hand. The idea behind DCGs (and also behind most logic-based grammars) is to make transparent to (or to hide from) the grammar writer those purely technical implementation details, in order to preserve the clarity of the linguistic description as much as possible. The DCG formalism is thus a simple extension to basic Prolog. Grammar rules written in the DCG format are interpreted or compiled into Prolog in a way transparent to the grammar writer. To be more precise, DCGs make the difference list notation transparent and replace the Prolog operator:- by the classical rewriting operator -->. Terminal elements are written between square brackets. The grammar given in (3) and (4) becomes in DCG form:

```
(5)   s --> np, vp.
      np --> det, n.
      vp --> v.
      vp --> v, np.
      det --> [ the ].
      det --> [ a ].
      n --> [ student ].
      n --> [ computer ].
      v --> [ has ].
```

The comma used to separate symbols in the right-hand side of the rule is a precedence symbol.

2. Definite Clause Grammars with Restrictions

Linguistic systems usually impose constraints on the morphological, syntactic and semantic nature of the words forming a sentence. There is a large variety of possible restrictions, which may differ from one language to another. For example, the agreement restriction requires that a constituent agrees in certain characteristics with one or more other constituents in the sentence. For example, in most Romance languages the subject noun phrase must agree in gender and in number with the verb. The same restrictions apply to nouns and their determiners. Another type of restriction is semantic agreement, often called selectional restrictions. A verb imposes certain semantic restrictions on its subject and on its immediate complements. For example, some verbs require their subject to denote an animate entity.

In DCGs, as in Prolog, each argument of a predicate represents precise information, for example syntactic and semantic features. Since positions in a predicate are fixed and defined once and for all in a program, feature labels, identifying the nature of each feature value, are implicit and thus need not be mentioned.

2.1 Features and controls

Most of the restrictions which can be treated by DCGs can be expressed by means of two predicates:

- *identity*: a certain feature must have identical values for two different words or structures,

- *inclusion*: the value associated with a certain feature for a constituent must be included into a set of values required by another constituent, often represented by a list.

Equality is usually expressed in DCGs by using the same variable identifier for the two concerned feature values while inclusion is usually expressed by the predicate member_of(X, Y) which is true if the element X is a member of the list of elements Y. Besides membership of a set, inclusion can also be expressed in more elaborate systems by subsumption. For example, the feature value animate subsumes the feature value human. This is developed in Chapter 4, which covers typed feature structures in logic programming.

Let us now illustrate the expression of agreement restrictions in DCGs. Let us consider again the DCG grammar given in (5), to which we add the number agreement restriction and the verb semantic restrictions on the subject and the object:

```
(6)   s --> np(Number, Sem),
            vp(Number, Sem_subj),
            {member_of(Sem, Sem_subj) }.
      np(Number, Sem) --> det(Number),
                          n(Number, Sem).
```

```
vp(Number, Sem_subj) --> v(Number, Sem_subj, _ ).
vp(Number,Sem_subj)-->v(Number, Sem_subj, Sem_obj),
                      np(_ , Sem),
                      {member_of(Sem, Sem_obj)}.
det(_) --> [the].
det(sing) --> [a].
n(sing, human) --> [student].
n(sing, object) --> [computer].
v(sing, [human], [object, property]) --> [has].
```

In this grammar, the calls to Prolog predicates are indicated between brackets in order to differentiate them from grammar symbols. Indeed they do not receive any difference list arguments. Useless features in a given rule are represented by the empty variable _ . Notice how information is represented in lexical entries and how this information is percolated up in the grammar rules by means of logical variables.

DCGs is a computational formalism which has the advantage of simplicity and which can be efficiently processed. It lacks flexibility, however, and its expressive power is somewhat limited from a linguistic point of view. At the level of flexibility, the argument positions are rigid and their meaning is implicit. It would be preferable to be allowed to specify only those arguments which are of interest for the present grammar rule, and to be allowed to specify them in any order. As a consequence, updating such a grammar, e.g. adding or withdrawing an argument, is a rather delicate task. At linguistic expressiveness level, this type of grammar, which is basically of type 2 in the Chomsky hierarchy, with arguments expressing a certain context dependency, makes it difficult to express phenomena such as coordination and long-distance dependencies.

DCGs have, however, proven to be very convenient and efficient in a number of simple applications; they also remain the basis of most logic-based grammars which have been elaborated on from the DCG formalism. These grammars are presented in the next chapter.

2.2 General form of DCGs

The general form of a DCG rule is the following:

$$\alpha \mathrel{-\!\!>} \beta.$$

where:

$\alpha \in V_N$ and $\beta \in (V_N \cup V_T \cup P)^*$

V_N and V_T represent respectively the non-terminal and the terminal vocabulary. P is a set of calls to Prolog programs. These calls are usually included between brackets to avoid any confusion with terminal and non-terminal grammar symbols. β contains a finite number of symbols and Prolog calls.

3. Structure Building in DCGs

So far, we have been concerned with grammars for testing whether a sentence is acceptable with respect to the grammar and a given lexicon. DCGs are also a very convenient tool for building structures from sentences. Two main kinds of structures can be built: syntactic trees and semantic representations. They involve similar general construction techniques but the way these techniques are used is quite different.

These techniques are based on Prolog's unification mechanism and the properties of logical variables, which is a simple, powerful and natural tool for incrementally constructing representations.

3.1 Automatic construction of syntactic trees

A syntactic tree is expressed in Prolog by a term whose nodes represent the different syntactic categories involved in the structure of a sentence. For the example given in (4):

the student has a computer

and with respect to our grammar, we have the following syntactic tree:

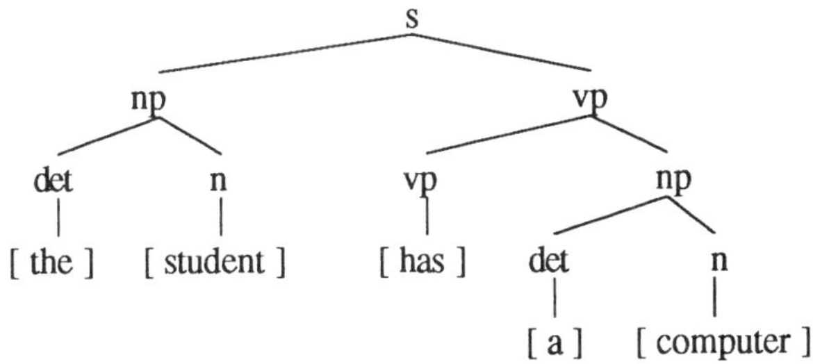

This tree is represented by the following Prolog term:

```
s(np(det([the]),  n([student]))),
  vp(v([has]),
      np(det([a]),  n([computer]))))).
```

The grammar given in (6) can be modified so that it can produce a syntactic tree. The technique consist in adding an argument to each symbol in the grammar which represents its associated syntactic tree. At the level of each rule, the contribution to the construction of a syntactic tree of that rule is expressed in the symbol to the left-hand side of the rule. The new DGC grammar is the following:

```
(7)   s(s(NP,VP)) --> np(Number, Sem, NP),
                        vp(Number, Sem_subj, VP),
                        {member_of(Sem, Sem_subj) }.
      np(Number, Sem, np(Det, N)) --> det(Number, Det),
                                      n(Number, Sem, N).
      vp(Number, Sem_subj, vp(V))-->
                        v(Number, Sem_subj, _ , V).
      vp(Number,Sem_subj, vp(V, NP))-->
                        v(Number, Sem_subj, Sem_obj, V),
                        np(_, Sem, NP),
                        {member_of(Sem, Sem_obj)}.
      det(_, det([the])) --> [ the ].
      det(sing, det([a])) --> [ a ].
      n(sing, human, n([student])) --> [ student ].
      n(sing, object, n([computer])) --> [ computer ].
      v(sing,[human], [object, property ], v([has])) --> [has].
```

As can be seen from this grammar, the construction of a syntactic tree is realized by a simple and very regular process. The introduction of the construction of a syntactic tree in a DCG grammar can be done automatically. This is presented in section 4.3 of this chapter.

3.2 Automatic construction of semantic representations

Semantic representations of a sentence may differ in a substantial way depending on the kind of semantic theory being considered. For our present purpose, we consider a simple representation system based on first-order logic. More complex systems are presented in later chapters.

The semantic representation we consider here, the three-branched quantified tree representation, was designed by A. Colmerauer (1982) and subsequently developed in different works (see Dahl (1981) and Saint-Dizier (1986)). Other works by McCord (1982) and Pereira (1983) have developed representations which have the same expressive power, but emphasize different aspects such as the representation of focus.

In the three-branched quantified tree representation, nouns, verbs and some adjectives are represented by predicates. Determiners introduce a kind of meta-predicate whose arguments are partial representations. The whole structure is a tree in which most nodes are labelled by determiners. Other nodes are labeled by logical connectors such as NOT, AND and OR. Nodes representing determiners have three daughters respectively, representing the variable introduced by the quantification, the restrictions on the quantification and the remainder of the representation:

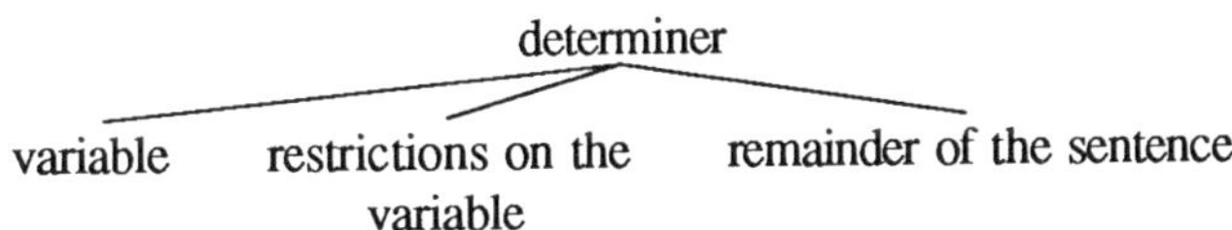

A sentence is usually represented as follows: the root node introduces the subject noun phrase, then we have the verb's complement noun phrases representation and finally we have the verb representation. Relative clauses and adjectives are represented internally at the level of noun phrases, in the second argument of the determiner representation. For example, the sentence given in (4) is represented as follows:

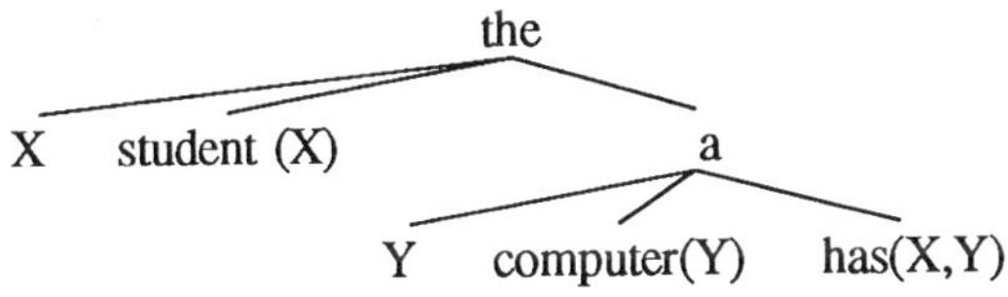

The use of an adjective, for example as in:

The young student has a computer

further restricts the denotation of the variable X; it is therefore represented by the following tree:

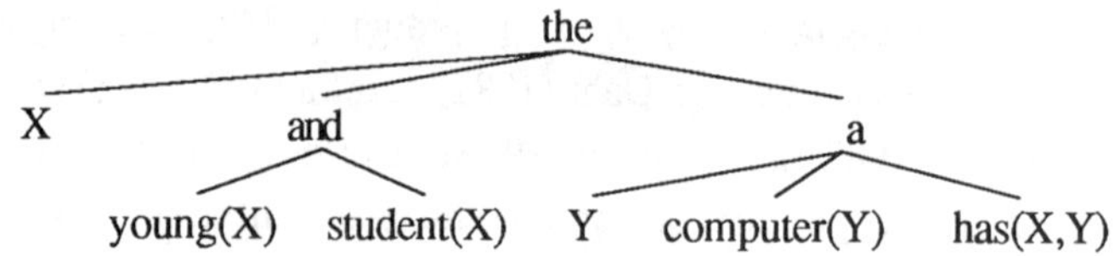

Our goal is here not to present this semantic approach in depth; we therefore limit ourselves to examples and show how this representation can be computed. The same method applies to more complex constructions. This representation can also be subject to a number of restructuring, which are no longer strictly derived from the sentence and are also no longer strictly compositional. In this category fall treatments such as quantifier raising to produce appropriate quantifier scopings, and the determination of the scope of modal operators and negation.

We now give a simple and general method for computing the above semantic representations. This computation is based on two kinds of data:

(a) The representation of each word, given in the lexicon, introduces the predicate (or the formula) representing this word, and, whenever appropriate, the variables occurring as arguments of this predicate, which may potentially be bound to other variables occurring as arguments of predicates when constructing the representation of a sentence.

(b) The semantic composition rules, given at the grammar rule level, which express how to combine the semantic representations associated with the grammar symbols on the right-hand side of the rule to form the semantic representation associated with the symbol on the left-hand side of the rule.

This description is modular since, for each rule, only the contribution of that rule to the determination of a semantic representation is given. The computation of a semantic representation is fully declarative: the use of logical variables permits the specification of structures at an abstract level and to have them instantiated at a later stage of the process.

At the lexical level, an appropriate number of arguments is added to lexical entries in order to represent the variables which can potentially be bound to other representations. The use of logical variables is a very simple illustration of the introduction of λ-calculus techniques within logic programming (see chapter 8, devoted to higher-order logic programming).

For example, for the lexicon given in (5) we have the following structures:

(8)   det(X, Y, Z, the(X, Y, Z)) --> [the].
       det(X, Y, Z, a(X, Y, Z)) --> [a].
       n(X,student(X)) --> [student].
       n(X, computer(X)) --> [computer].
       v(X,Y, has(X,Y)) --> [has].
       a(X, young(X)) --> [young].

Nouns have only one external variable, while transitive verbs have two external variables associated respectively with the subject noun phrase and to the object noun phrase. Finally, determiners have three external variables, reflecting the three daughters that they have in a three-branched quantified tree. Represented as λ-expressions, these representations would be written as follows:

λX computer(X)

λX λY has(X,Y)

λX λY λ Z the(X,Y,Z)

The operation of λ–reduction on predicate arguments is directly realized by Prolog's unification mechanism.

Let us now consider the grammar. Its main goal at this level is to combine semantic representations of the right-hand side symbols to produce the representation associated with the left-hand side symbol. The grammar given in (5) becomes:

(9)

s(R) --> np(X, R1, R) , vp(X, R1).

np(X, R2, R) --> det(X, R1, R2, R), n(X, R1).

vp(X, R) --> v(X, R).

vp(X, Y, R) --> v(X, Y, R1), np(Y, R1, R).

n(X, and(A, R)) --> a(X, A), n(X, R).

The representation produced can then be evaluated, for example, in a deductive database Dahl (1981); Gal *et al.* (1991).

The computation of a semantic representation of a sentence is described in a fully declarative way. This means that the grammar can be used bi-directionally:

(1) to parse sentences and to produce semantic representations,

(2) to generate sentences from semantic representations.

However, the generation process may enter into infinite loops in a number of situations. Also a much more deterministic process can be used for generation; this is presented in section 6 of this chapter.

4. Interpreters and Compilers for DCGs

In this section we present methods for building a DCG interpreter and a DCG compiler. We then show how the specification of the construction of a parse tree can be automated. These points have been extensively treated in the literature, so we limit ourselves here to presenting the fundamental methods and tools.

4.1 A DCG interpreter

A DCG interpreter takes the grammar and the lexicon as data and constructs a representation from the input sentence. The technique we introduce here is of much importance since it is used in most applications involving interpretation. The grammar is the grammar given in (7), repeated below for the reader's convenience:

```
(7)
s(s(NP,VP)) --> np(Number, Sem, NP),
                vp(Number, Sem_subj, VP),
                {member_of(Sem, Sem_subj) }.
np(Number, Sem, np(Det, N)) --> det(Number, Det),
                                n(Number, Sem, N).
vp(Number, Sem_subj, vp(V))-->
                                v(Number, Sem_subj, _ , V).
vp(Number,Sem_subj, vp(V, NP))-->
                v(Number, Sem_subj, Sem_obj, V),
                np(_, Sem, NP),
                {member_of(Sem, Sem_obj)}.
det(_, det([the])) --> [ the ].
det(sing, det([a])) --> [ a ].
n(sing, human, n([student])) --> [ student ].
n(sing, object, n([computer])) --> [ computer ].
v(sing,[human], [object, property ], v([has])) --> [has].
```

The interpreter is the following:

```
(10)
:-  op(1100,xfy,-->).
parse(X, X1, Axiom):-  (Axiom --> Body),
```

```
                                parse(X, X1, Body),  !.
    parse(X, X, {P} ):-  !, call(P).
    parse([M|X], X, [M]):-    !.
    parse(X,X1,(C1,C2)):-     parse(X, X2, C1),
                             parse(X2, X1, C2).


    member_of(X, [X| _ ]):- !.
    member_of(X, [_| Y] ):-  member_of(X,Y).
```

The first clause *parse* calls a new DCG rule, the second clause deals with calls
to Prolog, the third one treats terminal elements and the last clause recursively
processes the body of a rule. The symbol: --> is declared as an operator, it is
given here the priority 1100. The call to parse a sentence is:

```
    ?- parse([the,student,has,a,computer], [ ], R).
```

which produces the following result:

```
    R = s(s(np(det([the]), n([student])),
          vp(v([has]),
            np(det([a]), n([computer]))))))
```

which is the predicate s (also axiom of the grammar) with its argument
representing the syntactic tree.

4.2 A compiler for DCGs

Similarly, we can write a compiler for DCGs which directly transforms the
grammar into a set of Prolog clauses. The transformation consists in introducing
the two appropriate difference list arguments into the symbols of the grammar,
as shown in (3). This is realized by means of the Prolog built-in predicate '=..'.
The compiler is the following:

(11)

```
transf((T --> [C], T3):-              !,    T =.. T1,
                                    conc(T1, [[ C | Body], Body], T2),
                                    T3 =.. T2.
transf((T --> C),(T3:- Body)):-    T =.. T1,
                                    conc(T1,[X,Y],T2),
                                    T3 =.. T2,
                                    transf_body(C,Body,X,Y).
transf_body(({C},Cs),(C,Cs),X,Y):-
```

```
                                    transf_body(Cs,Body,X,Y).
    transf_body((C,Cs),(C3,Body),X,Y):-     !,
                                    C =.. C1,
                                    conc(C1,[X,X1],C2),
                                    C3 =.. C2,
                                    transf_body(Cs,Body,X1,Y).
    transf_body({C},C,X,X):-  !.
    transf_body(C,C3,X,Y)  :-  C  =.. C1,
                                    conc(C1,[X,Y],C2),
                                    C3 =.. C2.
    conc([X|Y],Z,[X|T]):-  conc(Y,Z,T).
    conc([],Z,Z).
```

When describing a grammar, it is convenient to have it in a separate file and to refer to it as an input file when calling the DCG compiler. Similarly, in order to avoid re-compiling the same file several times, it is convenient to store the resulting Prolog clauses in an output file. This is realized by means of the Prolog built-in predicates see(Input_file), and seen on the one hand and tell(Output_file) and told on the other hand. The program that manages the input and the output files is the following:

```
    compile(Finput,Foutput):-  see(Finput),
                                    tell(Foutput),
                                    execute,
                                    seen,
                                    told.
    execute:-  read(R),
               exec(R).
    exec(R):- R = end , !.    % 'end' is placed at the end of the DCG file
    exec(R):-  transf(R,  Clause),
               write(Clause),
               execute.
```

The main call is compile with appropriate identifiers for the input and the output file.

We now have an interpreter and a compiler for DCGs. The compiler obviously produces the most efficient implementation, since it does not have any additional level of processing as it is the case for the interpreter, which has a meta-level of control, represented here by the predicate 'parse'. Interpreters turn

out to be easier to develop and to modify; their use is particularly interesting
when testing a new formalism. There are also cases where it is not possible to
directly translate a formalism into Prolog, and thus an additional level is required.
This is the case, for example, for bottom-up parsing, which requires an additional
level of control to handle its bottom-up strategy (see section 5).

4.3 Automated construction of a parse tree

In a similar way, it is possible to augment the above compiler so that it adds
to the grammar symbols the necessary argument to construct a parse tree, as
shown in section 3.1. The new DCG compiler is the following:

(12)

```prolog
:-  op(1200,xfx,-->).


dcg_tree(( T --> [C] ), T3 ):-
      !,
      T =.. T1,
      conc( T1, [X, Y, C], T2),
      T3 =.. T2.
dcg_tree((T  -->  C),(T3:-  Body)):-
      T =.. [TT1|T1],
      dcg_body(C,Corps,X,Y,List_of_subtrees),
      TT2 =.. [TT1|List_of_subtrees],
      conc([TT1|T1],[X,Y,TT2],T2),
      T3 =.. T2.


dcg_body((({C},Cs),(C,Body),X,Y,L):-
      !,
      dcg_body(Cs,Body,X,Y,L).
dcg_body((C,Cs),(C3,Body),X,Y,L):-
      !,
      C =.. C1,
      conc(C1,[X,X1,L1],C2),
      C3 =.. C2,
      dcg_body(Cε,Body,X1,Y,L2),
      conc([L1],L2,L).
dcg_body({C},C,X,X,[]).
```

```
dcg_body(C,C3,X,Y,[L]):-
    C =.. C1,
    conc(C1,[X,Y,L],C2),
    C3 =.. C2.
```


5. Bottom-Up   Parsing

The strategy imposed *a priori* by Prolog and which is used *a priori* for parsing
DCGs when they are translated into Prolog is top-down, depth-first and from left
to right (defined in Prolog by a computation rule; see chapter 1). Backtracking is
used to explore all the branches. This strategy is driven by the grammar: a
fragment of a parse tree is built and an attempt is made to match the terminal
symbols of that parse tree with a portion (usually the left-most one) of the
sentence to parse. This strategy amounts to making predictions based on the
grammar and then trying to match these predictions with the data about the
sentence to be parsed. If these predications fail, then another attempt is made,
with different grammar rules.

Another strategy is data-driven parsing, whose main idea is to start from the
data, i.e. the words forming the sentence to parse, and to build from it a well-
formed parse tree. This strategy is said to be bottom-up since the words of the
sentence form the terminal vocabulary of the grammar. Different strategies are
possible here, as in top-down parsing. In order to preserve as much as possible
Prolog's computation rule, we show here a bottom-up strategy which is 'depth-
first' and from left to right. This strategy intoduces the well-known method of
left-corner parsing. As shall be seen, this strategy is mainly bottom-up, but it
also has some top-down aspects.

Besides the grammar-driven and data-driven parsing distinction, bottom-up
parsing from left to right also permits the avoidance of infinite loops to which
top-down strategy is exposed with left-recursive rules. Although it is possible to
convert a rule with left recursion into one without left recursion, the result is
less natural and the extra symbols introduced have no linguistic motivation.

As bottom-up parsing has been extensively studied in the current literature
(Pereira and Sheiber 1987; Gazdar and Mellish 1989), we limit ourselves here to
giving the general principles and the basic program.

Left-corner bottom-up parsing first attempts to find a grammar rule whose left-most symbol in the right-hand side of the rule is a terminal element corresponding to the left-most word to parse in the input string. It then attempts to check that the subsequent symbols in the right-hand side of that rule can be derived in such a way that the leaves of the subtrees, the production of which those subsequent symbols entail, match the next words in the input string. From that point of view this strategy mixes bottom-up and top-down strategies. If there is a success, then the left-hand side symbol of the selected rule becomes the left-corner of another rule and the process goes on until, for example, the symbol s is reached.

For practical reasons, the grammar has to be rewritten in a slightly different way so that it can be directly accessed. There are several variants (see Pereira and Shieber (1987)). In our case, we create a fact gram(X,Y) where X is the left-hand side of a rule and Y is its right-hand side, in the form of a list. Calls to Prolog remain unchanged. Terminal symbols are represented by the predicate term(X,Y) where X is the description of the lexical entry and Y is the word itself. The grammar is as follows:

(13)

```
gram(s(s(NP,VP)), [np(Number, Sem, NP),
                vp(Number, Sem_subj, VP),
                {member_of(Sem, Sem_subj) }]).
gram(np(Number, Sem, np(Det, N)),
                [det(Number, Det),n(Number, Sem, N)]).
gram(vp(Number, Sem_subj, vp(V)),
                [v(Number, Sem_subj, _ , V)]).
gram(vp(Number,Sem_subj, vp(V, NP)),
                [v(Number, Sem_subj, Sem_obj, V),
                np(_, Sem, NP),
                {member_of(Sem, Sem_obj)}]).


term(det(_, det([the])),the).
term(det(sing, det([a])),a).
term(n(sing, human, n([student])),student).
term(n(sing, object, n([computor])),computer).
term(v(sing,[human], [object, property ], v([has])),has).
```

The bottom-up parsing program is then the following, written in DCG form to avoid mentioning difference lists:

```
(14)
bup_parse(String) --> leaf(Substring),
                leftcorner(Substring,  String).
leaf(Term) --> [Word], {term(Term,Word)}.
leaf(String) --> {gram(String,[])}.


leftcorner(String,String) --> [].
leftcorner(Substring,String) -->
                {gram(Partstring, [Substring | Rest]) },
                bup_rest(Rest),
                leftcorner(Partstring,String).


bup_rest([]) --> [].
bup_rest([{Prologclause} | Rest]) -->
                {call(Prologclause)}, bup_rest(Rest).
bup_rest([String | Rest]) -->
                bup_parse(String), bup_rest(Rest).
```

The left-corner parsing technique is the most usual strategy; however, for some languages (e.g. those which are head-final) it may be preferable to have a right-corner strategy because the right-most symbol is the symbol that will determine most efficiently the rule to select in the grammar. This strategy is the same except that right-most symbols have to be considered first instead of the left-most ones.

6. Generating with DCGs

While parsing in general and with DCGs in particular has been investigated in great detail, very little has been done on its counterpart, generation. Generation has its own problems, which are substantially different from those of parsing. The major point that parsing and generation have in common (or should have in common) is that they use the same grammatical and lexical descriptions. Parsing starts with a surface sentence and produces either a parse tree or a semantic representation. The input to a generator is usually a semantic representation. This semantic representation may be more or less deep, i.e. it may be more or less remote from any syntactic realization. The deeper the representation is the more complex the generation procedure usually is.

The generation of a sentence or a text is usually organized in two steps: the elaboration of *what to say* and then the generation of a surface form, the *how to say*. We will be concerned here only with the second step and we will consider the generation of isolated sentences only. The method we present is simply a strategy; it can however be used in the same way to generate texts.

The general technique, that we have exemplified in Saint-Dizier (1989) consists of:

- writing a formal grammar of the semantic representation from which the generation process starts,
- identifying the phrasal units and the lexical units (and intermediate units if necessary) which can be associated with the symbols of that formal grammar,
- associating generation points to these symbols (terminal and non-terminal) which will generate natural language fragments based on a consultation of the grammatical and the lexical system. Generation points will here be direct calls to the grammatical system. The grammatical system will itself be in charge of assembling the partial strings of words to form phrases and sentences.

This method is general and can be used for most current semantic representations, such as, for example, discourse representation theory or conceptual graphs.

Let us consider the formal grammar of the three-branched quantified trees given in section 3.2. This representation is neither very deep semantically speaking nor too close to a surface form.

Since Prolog does not allow *a priori* variable functors, let us use a terminal symbol for nodes representing a quantifier, and let the quantifier name be an argument. The formal grammar of the semantic representation of quantified noun phrases is:

(15)

```
quant_np -->  det([quant, var], np, rest_of_sentence).
np --> and( np, modifier ).
np --> [n].
quant --> [det].
rest_of_sentence --> quant_np.
rest_of_sentence --> [v].
```

```
modifier  --> [adjective].
```
Between square brackets are the representations found in the lexicon; they are considered as terminal representations.

The call:
```
genere(quant([the,X], and(young(X),student(X)),
        quant([a,Y],computer(Y), has(X,Y))), Tree, String, []).
```
produces the sentence:

The young student has a computer.

The grammar and the lexicon remain basically the same as above. Terminal symbols have an additional argument which stands for their semantic representation:

(16)
```
gram(s(s(NP,VP)), [np(Number, Sem, NP),
                vp(Number, Sem_subj, VP),
                {member_of(Sem, Sem_subj) }]).
gram(np(Number, Sem, np(Det, N)),
                [det(Number, Det, Sem1),
                n(Number, Sem, N, Sem2)]).
gram(n(Number,Sem,n(A,N),_),
                [a(Number, A, Sem1),
                n(Number, Sem, N, Sem2)]).
gram(vp(Number, Sem_subj, vp(V)),
                [v(Number, Sem_subj, _ , V, Sem)]).
gram(vp(Number,Sem_subj, vp(V, NP)),
                [v(Number, Sem_subj, Sem_obj, V, Semant),
                np(_, Sem, NP),
                {member_of(Sem, Sem_obj)}]).


term(det(_, det([the]),the),  the).
term(det(sing, det([a]),a),  a).
term(n(sing, human, n([student]), student(X)), student).
term(n(sing, object, n([computer]), computer(X)),
                computer).
term(a(sing,a([young]),young(X)),  young).
term(v(sing,[human], [object, property ], v([has]),
                has(X,Y)),has).
```

The generation procedure is handled by the predicate:

```
generate(Semantic_tree, Grammar_symbol_treated)
```

The semantic tree is parsed step by step as given by the grammar in (15). The second argument of generate represents the grammar symbols and associated arguments of the root of the tree which has been built so far. The generation program which contains calls to the grammar rules (they form the generation points) is the following:

(17)

```
generate(quant([Det,Var],N,S), T)   -->
   generate(Det, T1),
   generate(N, T2),
   { gram(H1, [T1,T2]},
   generate(S,T3),
   { gram(T, [H1,T3,{App1}]),
   call(App1) }.


generate(quant([Det,Var],N,S), T)   -->
   generate(S,T3),
   generate(Det, T1),
   generate(N, T2),
   { gram(H1, [T1,T2]),
   gram(T, [T3,H1,{App1}]),
   call(App1) }.


generate(and(N,Mod), T) -->
   generate(N, T1),
   generate(Mod, T2),
   { gram(T,[T1,T2]) }.


/* Lexical insertion rules */
generate(P, det(X,Y,P),[W|S],S) :-
   term(det(X,Y,P),W), !.
generate(P, n(X,Y,Z,P), [W|S],S) :-
   term(n(X,Y,Z,P),W), !.
generate(P, a(X,Z,P), [W|S],S) :-
```

```
term(a(X,Z,P),W),  !.
generate(P, v(X,Y,Z,T,P), [W|S], S) :-
    term(v(X,Y,Z,T,P),W).
```

This generation system is still very simple, but its principles can be used unchanged for more complex natural language systems such as those presented in following chapters. It should be noted that this generator first parses the semantic representation and then produces the surface sentence. As a consequence and due in particular to the way calls to grammar rules are stacked by Prolog, the surface sentence is produced in a bottom-up fashion and, to a certain extent, from right to left, since the last semantic element processed, i.e. the right-most part of the tree describing the verb phrase, will be generated first. Next, the subject noun phrase is generated.

This generator is also much more deterministic than its corresponding parser since it is guided very precisely by the semantic representation, which is already a structured representation, as opposed to a surface sentence which is absolutely flat.

7. Conclusion

In this chapter, we have presented the formalism and different applications of DCGs. We have then presented a bottom-up parser and a method for generating sentences from semantic representations. The tools and methods presented here are basic and general. They can indeed be used in a number of applications and for several natural language processing approaches.

DCGs can be viewed as a basic formalism, which has a direct interpretation in Prolog. It contains *a priori* all that is required for language processing, from a syntactico-semantic perspective, even if the programming of some phenomena is not as transparent, principle-based and efficient as one would wish. Several logic-based grammars have been designed on top of DCGs which allow the expression of some specific phenomena in a more linguistically motivated way. These are presented in the next chapter.

Chapter 3

Logic-Based Grammars

In the past decade several computational grammatical systems have emerged under the denomination of logic-based grammars, whose declarative and procedural foundations are those of logic programming. As a consequence, a grammar which is simply encoded in Prolog is not necessarily a logic-based grammar. The emergence of the various logic-based grammars has been motivated by different reasons: computational (e.g. enhancement of modularity, transparency, introduction of meta-levels of control) and linguistic (e.g. expression of long-distance dependencies).

In this chapter we present the most well-known logic-based grammar formalisms which are of theoretical interest and have led to the development of applications. Other types of computational grammar systems such as those related to unification grammars and those using typed descriptions or constraints are presented in subsequent chapters.

The first logic-based grammar system was *metamorphosis grammars* (Colmerauer 1973, 1978), which mainly had a theoretical interest. Then, definite clause grammars were introduced (see Chapter 2). Next, more elaborate grammatical formalisms emerged: *extraposition grammars* (Pereira 1981) aiming at expressing in a more flexible way left-extraposition; *restriction grammars* (Hirschman and Puder 1986) in which derivation and constraints on arguments are treated separately; *gapping grammars* (Dahl and Abramson 1984), which are a generalization of extraposition grammars allowing more flexibility at the level of gaps; and finally *contextual discontinuous grammars* (Saint-Dizier 1988) which handle long-distance dependencies in a more declarative way. Other logic-based grammars which have a more historical or implementational interest, such as the *definite clause translation grammars*, are mentioned in the conclusion of this chapter.

1. Metamorphosis Grammars

The general form of a metamorphosis grammar (noted as MG) is represented by a quadruple (V, T, P, S) where V is the non-terminal vocabulary, T is the terminal vocabulary, P is a set of production rules and S the axiom (or a set of axioms). The rules in P have the following form:

$$A_1, A_2, ..., A_m --> B_1, B_2, ..., B_n$$

where:

   $m > 0, n \geq 0,$

   $A_i \in V \cup T,$ and

   $B_j \in V \cup T.$

Metamorphosis grammars are more general than definite clause grammars; they are of type 0 in the Chomsky hierarchy. The possibility of having more than one symbol on the left-hand side of the grammar rule allows the specification of restrictions without systematically using arguments as in DCGs. Using symbols instead of arguments may in some circumstances be linguistically better motivated.

   The result of a parse with MGs is not a tree but a graph, as can be seen on the following example. Let us consider the grammar which recognizes the following language:

$$L(G) = \{a^n\ b^n\ c^n, n > 0\}.$$

It can be defined as follows using the MG rule format:

   p --> [a], [b], [c].

p --> [a], p, b, [c].
[c], b --> b, [c].
[b], b --> [b], [b].

In this example, the last two rules are in a strict MG format. The first one of these two rules permits the memorizing of how many c's have been found or should be found, taking into account the number of b's which have or will be found in the input string. The last rule expands the b's. For the string:

$$a^2b^2c^2$$

we have the following derivation graph :

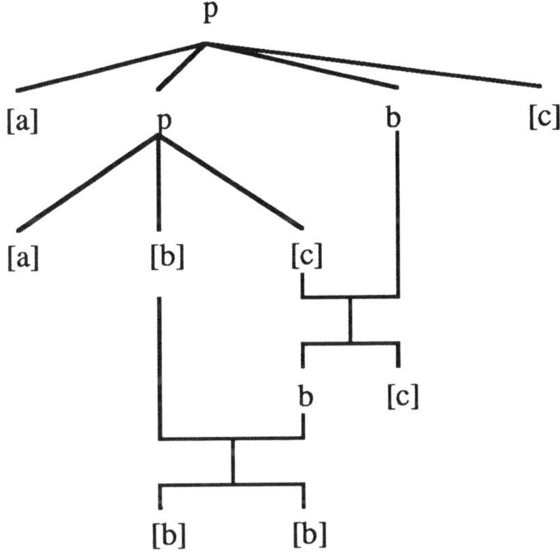

MGs are not very easy to implement efficiently. In order to facilitate their implementation without losing too much of the power of the formalism, A. Colmerauer introduced the notion of normalized MGs where rules of P have the following form:

$$A_1, A_2, ..., A_n --> B_1, B_2, ..., B_n.$$

where:

$A_1 \in V,$

$A_2, ..., A_m \in T,$ and

$B_i \in V \cup T.$

The symbol A_i is then called the head of the rule. There is a simple method to transform a MG rule into an equivalent normalized MG rule (Colmerauer 1978).

Let us consider a MG rule of the form:

$$A_1, A_2, ..., A_m \rightarrow B_1, B_2, ..., B_n \, .$$

The transformation procedure is as follows:

(1) if A_1 is a terminal symbol, it is replaced by a new non-terminal symbol $nt(A_1)$ and the following rule is added to the grammar:

$$nt(A_1) \rightarrow A_1 \, .$$

(2) for all A_i, $i \in [2, m]$, if A_i is a non-terminal symbol, then it is replaced by a new terminal symbol $te(A_i)$ and the following rule is added to the grammar :

$$A_i \rightarrow te(A_i).$$

(3) for all B_j, $j \in [1, n]$, if B_j is a terminal symbol and if it is the head of another MG rule, then it is replaced by $nt(B_j)$ and the following rule is added to the grammar :

$$nt(B_j) \rightarrow B_j.$$

For example, the rule:

[c], b --> b, [c].

is translated into the following set of rules:

nt(c), te(b) --> b, [c].

nt(c) --> c.

b --> te(b).

Normalized MGs can then be directly transformed into Prolog clauses. As an example, after the three stages described above, the general normalized MG rule:

$$A_1, A_2, ..., A_m \rightarrow B_1, B_2, ..., B_n \, .$$

becomes the following Prolog clause:

```
A1(X,[A2, A3, ..., Am|Y]) :-
         B1(X, X1),
         B2(X1, X2),
         ... ,
         Bn(Xn-1,Y).
```

2. Extraposition Grammars

Extraposition grammars (Pereira 1981), henceforth XGs, are essentially motivated by the need to express left extraposition in natural languages in a simple and transparent way. The implementation of XGs in Prolog have led to the development of a very interesting, general programming method for dealing with non-contiguous dependencies in a sentence. XGs have been used in several natural language processing applications.

Left extraposition of a constituent in a sentence is a very common linguistic operation (Radford 1981). It consists of moving a constituent in a sentence to the left. Two main types of movement are usually considered: NP-movement and Wh-movement. After introducing some basic facts related to NP- and Wh-movement, we present the formalism of XGs and their implementation in Prolog.

2.1 NP-movement

NP-movement mainly occurs in two main situations: passive constructions and raising operations.

Let us first consider the passive construction:

This story was believed by the children.

This sentence is derived from a more basic representation, usually referred to as D-structure (and said to be generated by lexical projection), which may be represented as follows:

$[_{IP}$ e $[_{I'}$ was $[_{VP}$ believed $[_{NP}$ this story] by the children]]]

using X-bar syntax. This representation can be equivalently represented by a tree :

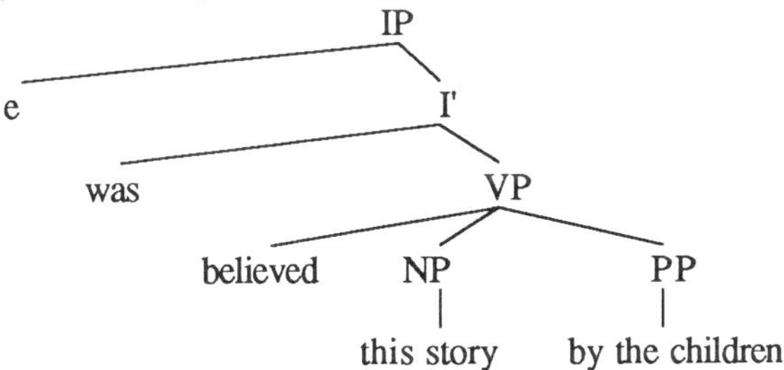

The NP *this story* is moved to the left and inserted at the empty position under IP, noted here as e. We then have the following syntactic representation:

$[_{IP}$ $[_{NP}$ this story$_i$] $[_{I'}$ was $[_{VP}$ believed c_i by the children]]].

The moved NP leaves a trace *e* at its original position, which is co-indexed with it by means of the index i. The moved NP becomes the subject of the verb *believed*; it is also assigned an abstract case at the IP level. The resulting tree, after movement, may be represented as follows:

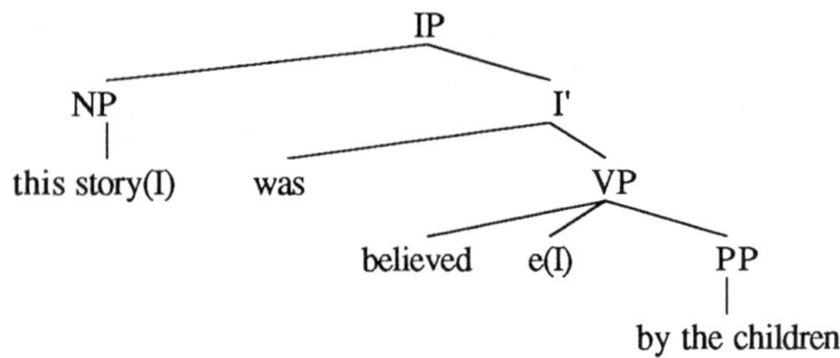

The NP raising operation occurs with raising verbs like *seem*, as in:

Edith seems to have written the story.

This sentence is derived from the sentence:

[IP e seems [IP [NP Edith] [VP to have written the story]]].

The subject of the lower clause is raised out of the clause and moved to the left into the empty position of the higher clause in subject position. The representation of the syntactic structure of the sentence after NP-raising is then:

[IP [NP Edith$_i$] seems [IP e$_i$ [VP to have written the story]]].

Another perspective is to say that the fact that the verb of the inner clause is infinitival forces NP movement.

2.2 Wh-movement

Wh-movement permits the construction of Wh-clauses such as interrogatives and relative clauses. Let us illustrate it here with interrogative constructions.

To give a complete account of interrogative sentences, we have to first consider the construction of a yes-no question. Such a question is derived from its affirmative counterpart, as in:

Edith will write the story.

Will Edith write the story ?

The structure of the affirmative sentence is as follows :

[$_{CP}$ [$_{C'}$ [$_C$ [$_{IP}$ [$_{NP}$ Edith] [$_{I'}$ [$_I$ will] [$_{VP}$ write the story]]]]]]

It can also be represented by the following tree:

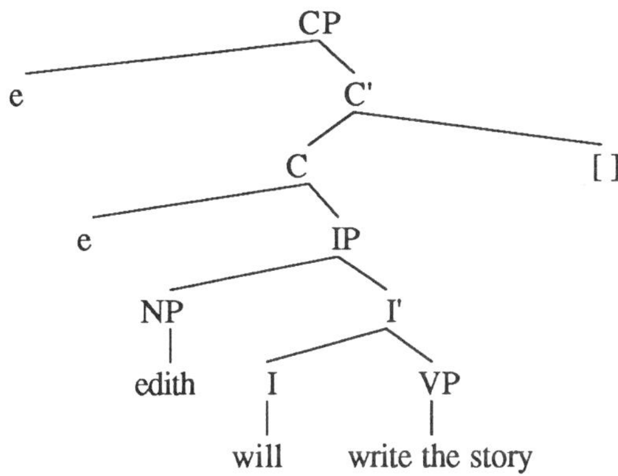

The modal auxiliary *will* is moved out of its D-structure position into the empty category directly dominated by C. It leaves behind an empty position e which is co-indexed with the category of its landing site:

[$_{CP}$ [$_{C'}$ [$_C$ Will$_k$ [$_{IP}$ [$_{NP}$ Edith] [$_{I'}$ [$_I$ e$_k$] [$_{VP}$ write the story ?]]]]]].

Let us now consider Wh-questions that query an argument of the verb of the main clause. Suppose we want to know what Edith will write. We would then ask the following question:

What will Edith write ?

Roughly speaking, the NP *the story* is made pronominal, yielding the following D-structure:

Edith will write what ?

The pronoun is then moved to the left at the specifier position of the CP. As in the other cases, it leaves a trace behind which is co-indexed with the interrogative pronoun *what*:

[$_{CP}$ [$_{spec}$ What$_i$] [$_{C'}$ [$_C$ will$_k$ [$_{IP}$ [$_{NP}$ Edith] [$_{I'}$ [$_I$ e$_k$]

[$_{VP}$ write e$_i$?]]]]]].

Wh-constituents are always moved to the specifier position of CPs. This position is often called the target of the movement or the landing site. Notice also the movement of the auxiliary verb will, which is a kind of 'side-effect' of the Wh-movement operation.

This movement can be represented by the resulting tree:

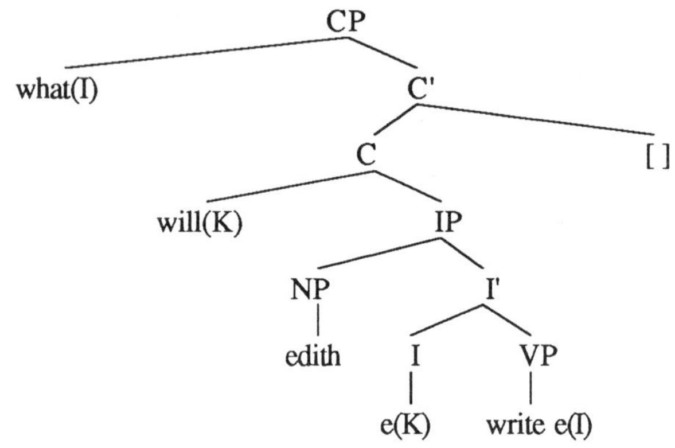

2.3 Introduction to extraposition grammars

XGs are a simple and efficient formalism to deal with NP- and Wh-movements. An XG grammar is represented by a quadruple (V, T, P, S) where V is the non-terminal vocabulary, T is the terminal vocabulary, P is a set of production rules and S the axiom. The rules in P have the following form:

$$s_1, ..., s_2, ..., \text{etc}..., s_{k-1}, ..., s_k \text{ --> r.}$$

where:

$$s_i \in V \cup T, i > 1, \text{ and}$$

$$r \in (V \cup T)^* .$$

The three dots '...' represent finite substrings which are of no present interest for the rule and which will be processed by other grammar rules. These dots are said to denote gaps (not in the linguistic sense, however).

Let us represent the gaps in the above rule by variable symbols X_i:

$$s_1, X_1, s_2, X_2, \text{etc}..., s_{k-1}, X_{k-1}, s_k \text{ --> r.}$$

Then the informal meaning of an XG rule is that the sequence:

$$s_1, X_1, s_2, X_2, \text{etc}..., s_{k-1}, X_{k-1}, s_k$$

is rewritten into:

$$r\ X_1\ X_2\ ...\ X_{k-1}.$$

In other terms, the s_i symbols are rewritten into r and the gaps are rewritten after r, in the same order as they appear in the left-hand side of the rule.

Let us consider now a grammar which recognizes the following language:

$$L(G) = \{a^n\ b^n\ c^n, n > 0\}$$

it may defined as follows using the XG rule format:

p --> [a], bs, [c].

p --> [a], p, b, [c].

bs, ..., b --> [b], bs.

bs, ..., b --> [b], [b].

In the last two rules, the introduction of the symbol b permits the counting of occurrences of b. This technique can be generalized to all elements a, b and c and a more uniform grammar can be obtained (with $n \geq 0$):

p --> as, bs, cs.

as --> [ ].

as, ..., xb --> [a], as.

bs --> [ ].

bs, ..., xc --> xb, [b], bs.

cs --> [ ].

cs --> xc, [c], cs.

Extraposition grammars also incorporate a well-formedness constraint which guarantees that two pairs of extraposed elements will not overlap. This constraint is a simplified version of bounding constraints or subjacency constraints. It turns out to be relatively efficient and satisfactory in a number of cases.

Let us illustrate this constraint. For example, if a constituent A1 and a constituent A2 have traces e1 and e2 respectively then the sequences:

[A1   -   [A2   -   e2] - e1]   and

[[A1 - e1]   -   [A2   -   e2]]

are well-formed, whereas the sequence:

[[A1   -   A2]   -   [e1   -   e2]]

is ill-formed because the links A1-e1 and A2-e2 intersect.

Let us now consider the examples given in section 2.1. The sentence:

Edith seems to have written the story

is treated by the following XG rule:

pro(dummy, l) , ..., np   --> np(l).

Similarly, the example given in section 2.2:

What will Edith write ?
is accounted for by the following XG rule :

```
np(subj), aux, ..., np(obj, I) --> np(+pro, obj, I), aux, np(subj).
```

2.4 Implementing extraposition grammars in Prolog

The implementation of XGs in Prolog follows the same philosophy as the implementation of DCGs in Prolog: extra-arguments are added to terminal and non-terminal symbols in grammar rules. To translate XGs into Prolog, it is necessary to introduce four arguments, represented in a term:

```
x(context, type, symbol, xlist)
```

where:

- `context` is either gap if the symbol is preceded by a gap ('...') or nogap otherwise,
- `type` is either terminal or non-terminal,
- `symbol` represents the symbol itself and
- `xlist` is the current extraposition list at the level of this symbol.

For example, the second rule above:

```
np(subj), aux, ..., np(obj, I) --> np(+pro, obj, I), aux, np(subj).
```

is represented as follows in an extraposition list:

```
np(Subj, S0, S, X0,
    x(nogap, nonterminal, aux,
      x(gap, nonterminal, np(pro, obj, I)))) :-
        np(pro, obj, I, X0,X1),
        aux(X1, X2),
        np(subj, X2, X).
```

The translation is done automatically from the XG formalism, indeed it is unnecessary to define a normalized form, as it was the case for MGs. In XGs, when treating a rule with a gap. All the symbols in the left-hand part of the rule except the first one are inserted at the beginning of the extraposition list. These symbols are processed later by the parser. This procedure is more appropriate than the one used in MGs which consists of adding elements to the list of words to parse.

Let us examine the general case of the translation of gaps. The Prolog rule:

```
nt(V1, ..., Vn, S, S0, X) :- virtual(nt(V1, ..., Vn), X0, X).
```

where:

    virtual(C, X0, X)

defined below, reads as follows: C is the element which is between X0 and X in
the extraposition list. The variables V1 to Vn are the variables associated with
the symbol nt.

Finally, we have the following utilities:

```
virtual(NT, x(C, nonterminal, NT, X), X).


terminal(T, SO, S, X, X) :- gap(X), connect(SO, T, S).
terminal(T, S, S, x(C, terminal, T, X), X).


gap(x(gap, T, S, X)).
gap([ ]).


connect([T|S], T, S).
```

3. Restriction Grammars

Restriction grammars (RGs) (Hirshman and Puder 1986) are a logic-based
formalism which was designed to implement string grammars. They have been
extensively used in several systems, including the Pundit system.

3.1 Definitions

An RG rule is composed of a context-free grammatical skeleton and of
restrictions which express dependencies with respect to a context. The general
form of a restriction grammar rule is the following:

    A --> B1, B2, ..., Bn.

where:

    A is a non-terminal symbol and

    Bi $\in$ (V $\cup$ T $\cup$ Restr)* ,

Restr represents the Prolog calls encoding the restrictions. The symbols in V and
T do not have any argument.

Similarly to other logic-based grammars, restrictions are represented between
brackets to distinguish them from grammar symbols. The main difference

between RGs and the other logic-based grammars is that the context-dependent part of the system is treated not at the level of grammar symbols, but in separate procedures. This clearly makes the system more modular; it also permits the management of more global procedures in a simpler way (variables may be somewhat more global than in DCGs). Finally, there is a gain in linguistic expressiveness since, instead of using an indirect encoding of phenomena in grammar symbols (e.g. the precedence of symbols by means of difference lists), the phenomena are more directly encoded in the restrictions. This approach has been reconsidered and extended within the constraint logic programming framework, presented in Chapter 5.

Let us examine the characteristics of RGs more in depth. Like all other logic-based grammars, RGs are based on the notion that if it is possible to construct a tree representing the structure of a sentence that meets the requirements of the restrictions, then this sentence is well-formed with respect to the grammar. Restrictions can be viewed as well-formedness constraints on the syntactic tree produced by a grammatical context-free skeleton. Restrictions consult and often constrain *a posteriori* the syntactic tree being constructed, instead of using the passing of arguments, playing the role of parameters as in DCGs.

Restriction grammars are often paired with a set of meta-rules which permit the treatment of general linguistic phenomena such as coordination at a higher level (Hirshman 1986).

3.2 Restrictions

Restrictions introduce a very flexible way of dealing with linguistic phenomena such as: morphological agreements, subcategorization satisfaction and position constraints upon words or constructions in larger units (e.g. adjectives in NPs, adverbs in sentences). For example, the rule:

```
sentence ::= subject, finite_verb, {w_agreement}, object.
```

states that a sentence is constructed from a subject, followed by a finite verb, followed by the satisfaction of the restriction, and finally followed by an object. The restriction w_agreement checks the morphological agreements between the verb and its subject. It can be executed only when the subtrees corresponding to the subject and the verb have been fully constructed.

The following type of restriction implements a kind of look-ahead:

```
ntovo ::= {d_to_ahead}, np, [to], vo.
```

The restriction d_to_ahead checks for the presence of a literal *to* in the remainder of the string before constructing ntovo. vo represents a verb in the infinitive form.

Similarly, other restrictions like w_case will check that an np has an appropriate case assigned, as in:

    lpror ::= lpro, pro, {w_case}, rpro.

lpro stands for adjunct to the left of the relative pronoun and rpro for adjuncts to the right of the relative pronoun.

The restrictions in RGs are written by means of a limited number of operators, which limits their power *a priori*. This is not the case with all constraints written in Prolog.

Restrictions may essentially be of four types:

(1) *well-formedness restrictions* which check for the well-formedness of partial subtrees, as we have seen it in the first and third examples above,

(2) *disqualify restrictions*, which check for the allowability of a construction before it is effectively constructed (e.g. the d_to_ahead above),

(3) *pruning restrictions* whose goal is to prune grammatical options such as the subcategorization options for a verb,

(4) *selectional restrictions* which check for the validity of co-occurrence relations, for example within a noun phrase and within a clause (e.g. verb-argument relations).

3.3 Long-distance dependencies

The treatment of long-distance dependencies is realized by means of gap indicators or, in other terms, of indicators of traces. The following operators are used in RG rules:

    <<   creates a gap
    >>   realizes a gap
    <>   forbids a gap in the subtree dominated by this symbol
    ><   copy of the status of the gap (for conjunctions, for example).

The operator << creates the necessity of a gap which is solved by the realization of this gap, via the operator >> in the syntactic category marked by this symbol. For example, for a simple relative clause construction, we have the rule:

    relative ::– << pronoun, >> sentence.

which means that the pronoun triggers the existence of a gap and that this gap will be found within the symbol *sentence*. In sentence, an NP will be derived as an empty string. The nature of the phrase to be derived as an empty string is determined by a restriction added to the sentence, **w_sai**, which checks for the syntactic category and the case of the gap introduced by the pronoun. As can be noticed, the principles and the notations used here are very similar to those used in lexical functional grammars (Bresnan 1982) where meta-variables are introduced to percolate long-distance dependencies. The above example would be noted roughly as follows:

relative --> pronoun $\Downarrow_{NP}$, sentence $\Uparrow_{NP}$.

It is also remarkably equivalent to the *Slash* category system of GPSGs (Gazdar *et al.* 1986), where the above rule would then be written as:

relative --> pronoun, sentence/NP.

3.4 Implementation of RGs in Prolog

The translation of RG rules into Prolog is similar to the translation of DCGs concerning the adjunction of two arguments to treat the input and output lists of words. Besides the treatment of the input sentence, an additional argument is included in the symbols to allow for the construction of the syntactic tree. The propagation of information is only realized via the syntactic tree. Restrictions traverse the portion of the tree already constructed, locate the different constituents (e.g. head of a constituent, adjuncts, subject, ...) and check for the properties of words associated to the terminal symbols. Restrictions can only accept or reject a tree. They do not construct anything by themselves.

Restrictions must traverse a tree in an efficient way. Each restriction is attached to a precise node, namely the node in the left-hand side of the rule. Its execution is made on the basis of this attachment. RGs use several procedures for traversing a syntactic tree; to each of them is associated a recursive data-structure. We now present these data-structures.

The first data-structure represents the syntactic tree, and has the following arguments:

- name of the node,
- first daughter,
- next daughter,
- attached word, if any,
- associated intermediate representation:

tt(Name, First_daughter, Next_daughter, Word, Rept)

The second and third arguments are themselves trees. This structure allows for a tree inspection in a top-down way or for an inspection which goes to the right of the tree.

A second procedure allows for the inspection of the tree to the left or in a bottom-up way by means of two data-structures:

(1) the tree associated to the parent or to the left-daughter,

(2) the remainder of the tree going up in the tree.

These data-structures are linked to the data-structure t t by the following data-structure:

```
link(Current_node, Path_to_root)
```

with:

```
Path_to_root = top(Parent, Path_from_parent)
```

or:

```
Path_to_root = left(Left_daughter, Path_from_left_daughter)
```

The extraction of nodes adjacent to a given node is thus realized immediately without using complex operations involving, for example, the decomposition of terms, as would be the case with DCGs.

3.5 Meta-rules in RGs

The introduction of meta-rules in RGs allows for the expression of linguistic phenomena which operate on different structures at a more abstract and often linguistically more adequate level without explicitly mentioning these structures. Meta-rules are extensively used in various linguistic theories such as, for example, generalised phrase structure grammars (GPSGs) (Gazdar *et al.* 1986). Meta-rules permit, for instance, the expression of coordination by means of a single, general rule. A meta-rule is applied to a set of rules to produce a new set of rules. This application is often realized when the grammar is compiled and not at execution time, which would result in a substantial loss in efficiency.

Let us consider the meta-rule that treats coordination. It states that any rule of the form:

```
(npd ::= gn, Nvar, nd)
```

where gnd indicates that a general nominal structure with left and right adjuncts is rewritten into gn. The variables Nvar and nd, permit the creation of rules of the form:

```
(gnd ::= gn, Nvar, nd, [,] ; gn, Nvar, nd, conjunction, gnd)
```

The meta-rule is noted as:

```
(Npd ::= Gn, Nvar, Nd)  ==>
```

(Gnd ::= Gn, Nvar, Nd, [,] ; Nn, Nvar, Nd, conjunction, Gnd)

where we have capitalized the symbols representing variables.

Applied on a rule such as:

np ::= np, relative.

we obtain by the application of the meta-rule a new rule, which is incorporated into the grammar:

np ::= np, relative, [,], np, relative, conjunction, np.

4. Gapping Grammars

Gapping grammars (GGs) (Dahl and Abramson 1984) are a generalization of Extraposition Grammars. They allow for right as well as left extraposition and the treatment of gaps is much more flexible. Gaps can be moved to any position, duplicated or deleted. GGs have also sometimes been used as meta-rules rather than as rules because of their high degree of generality (their rule format is of type 0 in the Chomsky hierarchy) and because of the difficulty of giving them an efficient computational interpretation under the form of DCGs.

The general form of a GG rule is the following :

$$A_0, G_0, A_1, G_1, ..., G_{n-1}, A_n \; \mbox{-->} \; B_0, G'_0, B_1, ..., G'_{m-1}, B_m.$$

where :

- A_0 is a non-terminal symbol,

- $A_1, A_2, ..., A_n , B_0, B_1, ..., B_m$ are sequences of terminal and non-terminal symbols,

- G_i and G'_j represent finite sequences of gaps, G_i forming a set of gaps equal (in terms of ordered strings of words being skipped) to the set of gaps formed by G'_j.

For practical reasons, G will be noted as gap(G) in grammars, to avoid having variable functors in rules.

The use of this type of rule is delicate. However, it can be used elegantly in appropriate situations. The examples given in the remainder of this section illustrate the way the rules can be used and their expressive power.

4.1 Coordination

The following grammar treats coordination at sentence level and reconstructs the deleted/missing object NP. A semantic representation in the form of a three-branched quantifier tree (see Chapter 2) is constructed:

```
sentence(and(S1, S2)) --> sentence(S1),
                          [and],
                          sentence(S2).
sentence(S) -->   proper_noun(P),
                  verb(P, Y, P1),
                  object(Y, P1, S).


object(X, P2,P) --> det(X, P1, P2, P),
                    noun(X, P1).
object(X,P2,P), [and], gap(G), object(Y,P2,P) -->
                                [and], gap(G),
                                object(Y, P2,P).


     %   lexical entries (sample)
determiner(X,P1, P2, the(X,P1, P2)) --> [the].
noun(X, train(X)) --> [train].
```

The second rule for `object` omits an expected object in the first sentence and reconstructs its internal representation by unification in the left-hand part of the rule in order to get a complete representation for each sentence. As can be seen, unification allows the bounding of variables in an appropriate way. In particular, this is the case for the variable P2 in the second rule for object which, in the left-hand part of that rule, reconstructs a semantic representation for the object of the first sentence. This can be illustrated by the following sentence:

John cleans and Mary paints the wall.

where the semantic representation of *the wall* is introduced in the semantic representation of the incomplete sentence *John cleans* in order to have an explicit object NP for the verb *clean*.

4.2   Relative clause construction

The syntactic structure of relative clauses can also be represented in an appropriate way by means of GG rules. The principle is somewhat similar to the one used for XGs: a relative marker and a non-contiguous NP are derived into a relative pronoun and a trace.

The relevant portion of the grammar is the following:

```
sentence(P) -->   np(X, P1, P) ,
                  vp(X, P1).
np(X, P1, P) --> det(X, P2, P1, P),
                 noun(X, P3),
                 relative(X, P3, P2).
np(X, P, P) --> trace.
vp(X, P) -->        transitive_verb(X, Y, P1),
                    np(Y, P1, P).
relative(X, P1, and(P1, P2)) --> rel_marker,
                                 sentence(P2).
relative(_, P, P) --> [ ].
rel_marker, gap(G), trace --> relative_pronoun,
                              gap(G).
```

4.3 Application to formal languages

The language:

$$L(G) = \{\ a^n\ b^m\ c^n\ d^m \mid n, m \in N\ \}$$

can be described by the following GG grammar, using the technique presented in the XGs section:

```
s --> as, bs, cs, ds.
as --> [ ].
as, gap(G), xc --> [a], as, gap(G).
bs --> [ ].
bs, gap(G), xd --> [b], bs, gap(G).
cs --> [ ].
cs --> xc, [c], cs.
ds --> [ ].
ds --> xd, [d], ds.
```

This grammar makes use of markers xc and xd to memorize the right extraposed a's and b's. The use of extra symbols can be avoided elegantly with GGs by deriving in parallel the a's and the c's on the one hand and the b's and the d's on the other. We then have the following grammar :

```
s -->  as, bs, cs, ds.
as, gap(G), cs -->  [a], as, gap(G), [c], cs.
as, gap(G), cs -->  gap(G).
```

bs, gap(G), ds --> [b], bs, gap(G), [d], ds.

bs, gap(G), ds --> gap(G).

Similarly, the language :

L(G1) = { $a^n\ b^n\ c^n\ d^n$ }

can be recognized by a GG grammar with more than one gap per rule:

s --> as, bs, cs, ds.

as, gap(G1), bs, gap(G2), cs, gap(G3), ds -->

   [a], as, gap(G1), [b], bs, gap(G2), [c], cs, gap(G3), [d], ds.

as, gap(G1), bs, gap(G2), cs, gap(G3), ds --> [ ].

In this last rule, gaps are necessarily empty, which motivates their derivation into an empty string.

Besides the examples given here, GGs are also appropriate for describing free-word order languages.

4.4 Implementation of gapping grammars

The implementation of GG rules in Prolog generalizes the technique used for translating MG rules into Prolog. In a GG rule, a gap, noted as gap(X), can be viewed as a substring that is skipped unanalysed and appended elsewhere in the output string. The treatment of gap(X) can thus be viewed as a version of the concatenation operation. During the translation into Prolog, the arguments of the concatenation are made explicit and the gap(X) symbol becomes gap(X, X1, X0) which states that X1 is the appending of X to X0. The output string X1 is the only string which is known, it is thus decomposed non-deterministically into two substrings X and X0. The rule:

as, gap(G), xb --> [a], as, gap(G).

given in the examples above can be translated into Prolog as follows:

as([a| X0], X) -->

        as(X0, X1), gap(G, X1, X2), gap(G, X, X3), xb(X3, X2).

or, using the concatenation operation conc as:

as([a| X0], X) -->

       as(X0, X1), conc(G, X2, X1), conc(G, X3, X), xb(X3, X2).

Notice how the remainder of the rule's left-hand side becomes part of the body of the resulting Prolog clause. The left-hand side of the clause is also as unrestricted in its form as the right-hand side.

The above translation is clearly very inefficient; furthermore it cannot work backwards, i.e. to generate sentences from a semantic representation. Dahl and

Abramson (1984) give restrictions on the form of gapping grammars which permit more efficient parsing systems.

Here is a compiler (Dahl and Abramson 84) that translates GG rules into Prolog:

```
synal((A,B --> C), Clause) :- !,
  expand_term((c_non_term --> C), CClause),
  expand_term((b_non_term --> B), BClause),
  clauseparts(CClause, CHead, CBody),
  clauseparts(BClause, BHead, BBody),
  CHead =.. [c_nonterm, CTree, X, Z],
  BHead =.. [b_nonterm, BTree, Y, Z],
  A =.. [Pred| Args],
  form_node(CTree, BTree, Pred, ATree),
  conc(Args, [ATree, X, Y], NewArgs),
  NewA =.. [Pred | NewArgs],
  combine(CBody, BBody, Body),
  formclause(NewA, Body, Clause).


clauseparts((Head :- Body), Head, Body) :- !.
clauseparts(Head, Head, true).


formclause(Head, true, Head) :- !.
formclause(Head, Body, (Head :- Body)).


combine(true, B, B) :- !.
combine(A, true, A) :- !.
combine(A, B, (A,B)).


form_node(node(_, N1, Sem), node(_, N2,_), Pred,
          node(Pred, N, Sem)) :-  conc(N1,N2,N).


gap([ ]) --> [ ].
gap([Word| List]) --> [Word],
                    gap(List).
```

5. Discontinuous Grammars and Dislog

Discontinuous Grammars (Saint-Dizier 1987) emerged mainly from the need to specify a computational model for *government and binding theory* (noted hereafter as GB) (Chomsky 1982, 1986), in particular to model *movement theory* and *quantifier raising* with their related constraints and filters. A logic programming language emerged from these grammars: Dislog (Saint-Dizier 1990). The goal was not to model GB theory per se, but to transfer to natural language processing some of its principles which appeared to be promising and worth investigating. The GB description of linguistic phenomena turns out to be concise, modular and parametrized; more interestingly, it is a constraint-based linguistic description of language. All these reasons make GB attractive to logic programrs. Finally, preliminary experiences show that some GB principles, paired with other natural language processing devices dealing with lexical issues (e.g. lexical semantics), feature representation and logical form construction, can form an efficient and well-designed system.

Dislog is not only a tool appropriate for GB modelling, it permits the expression in a simple, modular and declarative way of relations or constraints between non-contiguous elements in a structure. The examples developed in this section show several application domains. Dislog has also been used in areas other than natural language processing such as compiler design and planning, where long-distance relations need to be expressed. The main features of a compiler for Dislog clauses in Prolog are presented at the end of this section.

5.1 Introducing Dislog

5.1.1 Dislog clauses

A Dislog clause is a finite, unordered set of Horn clauses or literals f_i of the form:

$$\{ f_1 , f_2 , \ldots\ldots , f_n \}.$$

The informal meaning of a Dislog clause is: *if a clause or a literal f_i in a Dislog clause is used to construct a given proof tree, then all the other f_j of that Dislog clause must be used to construct that proof tree, with the same substitutions applied to identical variables.* Moreover, there is *a priori* no hypothesis made on the location of these clauses or these literals in the proof (or parse) tree.

For example, the following Dislog clause composed of two Prolog facts:

```
{ arc(a,b),   arc(e,f) }.
```

means that, in a graph, the use of arc(a,b) to construct a proof is conditional upon the use of arc(e,f).

If one is looking for paths in a graph, this means that all paths going through the arc (a,b) will have to go through the arc (e,f) or conversely. The full program is the following:

```
{ arc(a,b),   arc(e,f) }.
arc(b,c).
arc(c,e).
arc(b,f).  etc...


path(A,B)  :-  arc(A,B).
path(A,B)  :-  arc(A,C),
                    path(C,B).
```

All clauses are treated in the same way. Only the first fact states a co-occurrence constraint.

A Dislog clause thus permits us to express the co-occurrence of clauses or of literals in a proof tree. The constraint stating that all identical variables in a Dislog clause must be substituted by the same term permits the transfer of feature values between non-contiguous elements in a declarative and very convenient way.

5.1.2   Constraining Dislog clauses

A Dislog clause can be subject to various types of restrictions. One type of restriction is to impose constraints on the order of the use of clauses or literals in a Dislog clause. Informally, a clause or a literal r_i has precedence over a clause or a literal r_j in a proof tree if either r_i appears in that proof tree to the left of r_j or if r_i dominates r_j. Notice that this definition of precedence is independent of the strategy used to build the proof tree.

To model this definition of precedence, we add to Dislog clauses the traditional notation for indicating linear precedence:

$$a < b$$

which means that the definite clause with head a (or the literal a) precedes the clause with head b (or the literal b).

This can be illustrated by the following Dislog clause:

{ arc(a,b),   arc(c,d),   arc(e,f) }   arc(a,b) < arc(e,f).

which imposes the restriction that the literal (or fact) arc(a,b) precedes arc(e,f) in a proof tree using an instance of that Dislog clause. Consequently, all valid paths going through (e,f) will have first to go through the arc (a,b).

When the order of clauses in a Dislog clause is complete, the more convenient following notation is used:

f1 / f2 / ... / fn .

which means that f1 precedes f2 which precedes f3, etc. The relation / can be viewed as an accessibility relation.

Another improvement to Dislog is the adjunction of modalities. We want, for example, to allow definite clauses or literals in a Dislog clause to be used several times. This permits us, for example, to deal with parasitic gaps and pronominal references. For that purpose, the modality m is introduced and applied to a clause or to a literal to show that it can be used any number of times in that Dislog clause. For example, in:

{ f1 , f2 , m(f3) }.

the clause f3 can be used any number of times, provided that f1 and f2 are used. Substitutions for identical variables remain the same as before.

Finally, let us introduce in Dislog the notion of bounding domain. In linguistics, roughly speaking, the different variants and forms of what is usually called *bounding theory* state constraints on the movement of constituents, or, in non-transformational terms, constraints on relations between non-contiguous elements in a sentence. The main type of constraint is expressed in terms of domains across which relations cannot be established. For example, if A is a bounding node, then the domain of A is the tree rooted in A, and no constituent X inside that domain can have relations with a constituent outside it (at least not directly).

This restriction can be perspicuously expressed in Dislog as follows : if an instance of a Dislog clause is activated within a bounding domain, then, the whole Dislog clause has to be used within that domain. For a given application, bounding nodes are specified as a small database of facts and are interpreted by the Dislog system.

5.1.3   General form of Dislog clauses

The general form of a Dislog clause is the following:

$\{\mu_1(r_1), \mu_2(r_2), \quad ...... \quad , \mu_n(r_n) \}$ constraints$(r_1, r_2, ... , r_n)$.
where:

- r_i are Horn clauses (or definite clause grammar rules, which are grammar rules encoded in Prolog). They can also be extensions to Horn clauses like modal Horn clauses, clauses of the constrained logic programming framework (see Chapter 5) or logical type construction rules (see Chapter 4).

- μ_i are modalities: m, m$^+$, the empty modality, etc....

- constraints$(r_1, r_2, ..., r_n)$ is a conjunction of constraints. These constraints are global to the Dislog clause and thus cannot be encoded in a particular r_i; they can be of very different types, for example linear precedence restrictions and bounding constraints.

5.1.4   Dislog definite programs

A dislog definite program clause is a finite, unordered set of program definite clauses of the form :

    { A --> A1, B --> B1, ..., N --> N1 }.

The informal semantics of a Dislog definite clause is:

for each assignment of values to all variables occurring in that definite clause, if A1, B1, ..., N1 are all true, then A, B, ..., N are true.

A Dislog definite program is a finite set of Dislog definite clauses.

The definition of a predicate p in a Dislog program is the set of all Dislog definite clauses which contain at least one definite clause with head predicate p.

A Dislog program can be viewed as a definite program with a finite set of clause co-occurrence constraints. The traditional definition of Herbrand Base and Universe can still be used, but their definition in the case of a Dislog program needs to take into account the variable substitution constraints among different clauses which must co-occur. This is defined in detail in Saint-Dizier (1990).

5.1.5 Procedural semantics of Dislog

We now introduce the procedural semantics of Dislog programs. The basic principle is similar to that of definite programs, except that an additional data-structure, noted S, and called the list of pending clauses (those rules which must be applied), is used. Each time a Dislog clause is used, S is updated: it contains the instances of clauses constructed from the current Dislog clause being considered which must be used in the proof tree. Each time a clause in S is used, it is withdrawn from S, unless it is marked with a modality such as the modality

m. At each stage i of the proof procedure, S has a particular instance S_i. A well-formedness condition states that at the beginning of the proof procedure S_0 is empty and at the end of that procedure it is also empty (except for the clauses marked with modality m). This means that all the pending rules have been used, as required.

Let us now give the procedural semantics of Dislog. Let G_i be the goal:

$$\leftarrow A_1, A_2, ..., A_m.$$

and D be the Dislog clause:

$$\{ B_1, B_2, ..., B_n \}.$$

Then, G_{i+1} is the goal derived from G_i and D using the most general unifier (mgu) θi if:

(1) A_1 is the selected atom (let us consider Prolog's computation rule),

(2) Let $B_i : \alpha_i :- \beta_{i,1} , ..., \beta_{i,p}$. be the selected clause from D,

(3) θi is the mgu of A_1 and all the B_i,

(4) Gi+1 is the following goal:

$$\leftarrow (\beta_{i,1} , ..., \beta_{i,p} , A_2, ..., A_n) \theta_i ,$$

(5) and we have the following possible cases for S_{i+1} :

$$- S_{i+1} = S_i \cup \{ B_1\theta_i, ..., B_{i-1}\theta_i , B_{i+1}\theta_i, B_n\theta_i \}$$

if D is a new instance of a Dislog clause,

$- S_{i+1} = S_i - \{ B_i \}$ if B_i was already in S_i,

$- S_{i+1} = S_i$ if B_i is not subject to any co-occurrence constraint, i.e. the Dislog clause D has only one element.

Notice that all the clauses in D are affected by the substitution. This permits the establishment of links between variables in the different clauses in D. The SLD-resolution applied to Dislog clauses is sound and complete.

5.2 Dislog for natural language processing

5.2.1 Parsing and generating sentences with Dislog

A Dislog clause can be a set of definite clause grammar rules. Compared to other approaches dealing with discontinuous constituency, Dislog has the following specific features:

- Dislog clauses are declarative, no procedural commitment (e.g. computation rule or parsing strategy) is made, moreover each clause is independent of the others.

- Discontinuous constituency is expressed in a modular way, apart from other grammatical aspects. These other aspects are dealt with by other rules of the grammar.

- Discontinuous constituency is expressed in a concise and simple way, with no complex apparatus or meta-level of abstraction.

- No additional argument is used to carry gap introduction and gap satisfaction information, unlike GPSGs (with slash categories or, more recently, with slash features) and LFGs (with meta-variables indexed by category values). Discontinuous constituency in Dislog is expressed solely by grammar symbols and co-occurrence constraint.

- No strong hypothesis is made on the nature of the elements in a Dislog clause. Dislog can thus be used in a number of different linguistic and computational linguistic approaches such *logic grammars*, *unification grammars* and *tree-adjoining grammars*. It is not committed to any particular linguistic theory.

Let us illustrate the above features by a simple example treating long-distance relations in a programming language. In a conventional programming language, there are several one-to-one or one-to-many relations between non-contiguous instructions. For example, there is a long-distance relation between a procedure declaration and its corresponding calls and there is another relation between a label declaration and its related branching instructions.

Let us consider the compiler given by Sterling and Shapiro (1986) that transforms a program written in a simplified version of Pascal into a set of basic instructions. This compiler can be augmented with two pairs in Dislog:

{ procedure declaration, procedure call(s) }

{ label statement, branching instruction(s) to this label }.

In Dislog, in order to allow for a procedure call to appear before the declaration of the corresponding procedure, we do not state any precedence constraint. Furthermore, procedure calls are marked with modality m since a given procedure is usually called several times in a program. We have the following program:

```
parse(Struct) -->    [program],
                identifier(X),
                [';'],
                statement(Struct).
statement(( S ; Ss)) --> [begin],
                statement(S),
                rest_statement(Ss).
```

```
statement(assign(X,V)) --> identifier(X),
                   [':='],
                   expression(V).
                                      % procedure declaration and calls
{ (statement(proc_decl(N,S)) --> [ procedure ],
                   identifier(N),
                   statement(S),
                   [ end ] ),
   m(statement(proc_call(N,S) --> identifier(N) )   }.
                                      % label statement and branching
{ (statement(label(N)) --> identifier(N),
                   [':']   ),
   m(statement(goto(N)) --> [goto],
                   identifier(N) )   }.
```

Notice how information is shared between the two clauses of each Dislog rule. In the procedure declaration and call, the body S of the procedure, represented by the variable N, is shared (more elaborate tools such as pointers could have been used instead); in the branching instruction and declaration, the two clauses are related by the identifier N.

Finally, bounding constraints can be stated to prevent, for example, a label declared inside a given procedure from being referred to outside that procedure. Then, the particular instance of the Dislog clause for label statement and branching will have to be active only within the domain defined by a procedure declaration. From that point of view, the node proc_decl is a bounding node.

5.2.2 Modelling movements

Dislog was first designed to model move-α, quantifier raising and bounding theory in GB (Chomsky 1982, 1986). Move-α needs to be somewhat instantiated to be computationally tractable; this instantiation however does not affect the generality of the rule.

Let us consider again the examples given in sections 2.1 and 2.2 of this chapter. The first example:

Edith seems to have written the story.

is treated as follows in Dislog:

```
{ ( pro(dummy) --> np(I) ),
     ( np(I) --> trace )   }.
```

This rule says that an NP, indexed with I, is substituted for a dummy pronoun (here, it) while an NP, which is also co-indexed by I, is derived into a trace.

Let us now consider the sentence:

What will Edith write ?

This sentence is handled by the following Dislog rule :

```
{ ( cp --> spec(pro, I), c' ),
   ( c --> aux(K), ip ),
    (i --> trace(K) ),
      (np --> trace(I) )  }.
```

This rule permits the correct establishing of the co-indexation links.

These two example are clearly very *ad hoc*. A more elaborate implementation of movement theory such as move-α in GB theory would simply consist of a constructive 'principle', expressing the definition of move-α:

Move any category α anywhere.

and restrictive principles will then limit the generative capabilities of this very general movement rule.

5.2.3   Free word order in Dislog

Dislog is well adapted for dealing with languages that exhibit a certain degree of free word or phrase order. Consider, as an example, the following grammar:

```
s --> np(subj),  vp.

vp --> v,  np(obj).
```

If we want to have a free np order in the language recognized by this grammar, then the grammar will have to be composed of six context-free rules. Instead, we can write the following Dislog rule. To avoid repetition of the axiom s, we introduce a 'working' node s1:

```
s --> s1.     s1 --> [ ].

{ (s1 --> np(subj), s1), ( s1 --> v, s1), (s1--> np(obj), s1) }.
```

If we want, at the same time, to reconstruct a 'normalized' parse tree corresponding to the above grammar, we can write the following grammar:

```
s --> s1, np(subj, I), vp.        s1 --> [ ].

vp --> v(J),  np(obj, I).

s1 --> np(Case, I), s1 / np(Case, I) --> [ ].

s1 --> v(J),  s1 / v(J) --> [ ].
```

Symbols beginning with a capital letter represent variables. The variables I and J are indexes; they permit the co-indexation of overt elements with their traces. The above grammar permits us to obtain a tree like the following:

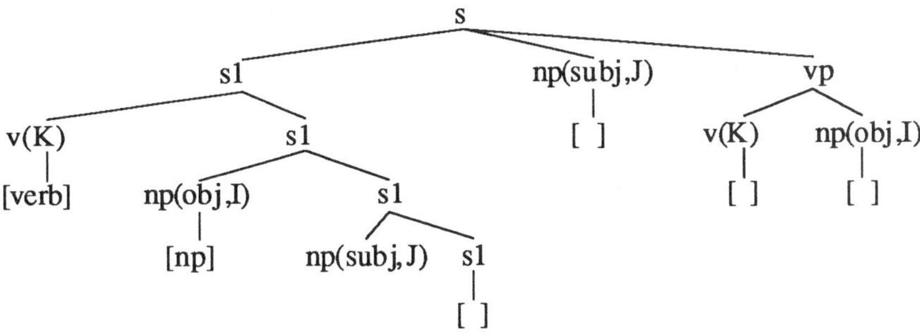

where the normalized form of the parse tree is constructed by means of co-indexation of variables in the right-hand side of the tree.

Notice that, at this level, Dislog clauses are not a re-interpretation of the ID/LP system at the linear precedence level since clauses in a Dislog clause need not appear at the same level in the parse tree (i.e. to be sisters), which is the case for symbols in ID/LP rules. If the structures are not completely free to occupy any position of the appropriate category, constraints can be formulated to ensure this.

5.3   An implementation of Dislog in Prolog

We now present the main features of an implementation of Dislog in Prolog. For the sake of clarity, we will present here a simple translation method and then a more elaborated meta-interpreter having the same functionalities as the compiler.

Dislog clauses are translated into Prolog using additional arguments. Two arguments are used to store the list of instances of rules in Dislog rules which have to be executed in the future for the proof or parse tree to be correct. These two arguments are called the input and the output list of pending rules. When a new instance of a Dislog clause is activated, the pending rules are added to the current list of pending rules. When a pending rule is being used to construct a proof, it is withdrawn from the list of pending rules. If it is marked with modality m, it is simply consulted (without instantiating its free variables in the list of pending rules) and it remains in the list. Let us consider here a simple example. A Dislog clause of the form:

    as--> a, as / bs --> b, bs.

is translated as follows into Prolog:

```
as(X,Y,LE,LS) :-
         append(LE,[d(bs,b,bs,I)],LE1),
         a(X,Z,LE1,LE2),
         as(Z,Y,LE2,LS).
bs(X,Y,LE,LS) :-
         check_withdraw(LE,d(bs,b,bs,I),LS1),
         b(X,Z,LS1,LS2),
         bs(Z,Y,LS2,LS).
```

The call check_withdraw(X,Y,Z) checks whether Y is in X and Z is X without Y. The structure d(_,_,_,I) permits the system to store pending rules in a convenient way. The variable I is used to carry the index. All variables shared by clauses or literals in Dislog clauses receive appropriate unifications because they are appended to the list of pending rules.

Let us now consider a more general schema. Here is a direct implementation of the procedural semantics of Dislog, as given in section 5.1. It is introduced by means of a meta-interpreter. For that purpose, the Prolog meta-interpretor presented by Sterling and Shapiro (1986) has been extended. Here is a simple Dislog meta-interpreter:

```
solve(L,L,true).
solve(L,L1,(A,B))  :-
          solve(L,L2,A),
          solve(L2,L1,B).
solve(L,L1,A)  :-
          clause(A,B),
          solve(L,L1,B).
solve(L,L1,A)  :-
          dislog_clause(C),            %call to a Dislog rule,
          find(A,C,L,L2,[ ], Body),    % strategy encoding,
          solve(L2,L1,Body).
```

The built-in predicate clause(A,B) is true if it finds a clause with head A and body B. A Prolog fact with an empty body has a body B equals to 'true'. The Dislog meta-interpreter itself manages the list of pending rules L in the two first arguments of the predicate solve.

Dislog clauses are stored in dislog_clause facts, together with precedence restrictions. The call to find permits us to encode a Dislog clause look up and choice strategy and the way a clause with head A and body Body is extracted from a list (in the second argument). The variable H is used to memorize the rules in the pending list which have been examined as possible candidates but have been rejected:

```
find(A,[(A:-Body) | Tail ], L, L2, H, Body) :-
        append(L, H, L3),
        append(L3, Tail, L2).
find(A, [H | Tail], L, L2, H1, Body) :-
        append(H1, [H], H2),
        find(A, Tail, L, L2, H2, Body).
```

Dislog can be used to build a parser as well as a generator for a natural language. Contrary to gapping grammars, Dislog has *a priori* no problems with the treatment of gaps in generation.

5.4 An interpretation of Dislog based on an admissibility constraint on proof trees

It is possible to characterize the well-formedness of a proof tree with respect to a program. Deransart and Maluszynski (1990) show that, besides their declarative and procedural readings, definite clauses also have a grammatical reading when they are considered as rewrite rules of a grammar. The concept of proof tree then becomes purely declarative. In Clark (1979), it is shown that a proof tree is the result of pasting together instances of clauses of a program R. The pasting operation is done following a given computation rule and a resolution strategy (Lloyd 87). The difference with respect to parse trees is that clauses in R usually include variables which may have an infinite number of instances defined by the Herbrand universe of R. Those instances can, however, be considered at the same level as terminal symbols of a grammar (Maluszynski 1984, Deransart *et al* 1988).

A definite clause grammar rule can be viewed as an attribute grammar rule without any terminal symbol, where the domain of each variable is *a priori* the Herbrand universe. Similarly to context-free grammar rules and to attribute grammar rules, a definite clause grammar rule introduces two distinct, local relations:

- a linear precedence relation,

- an immediate dominance relation.

For example, in the clause:

a --> b, c, d.,

- *a* immediately dominates *b*, *c* and *d*

- *b* linearly precedes *c* and *d*

- and *c* linearly precedes *d.*

The linear precedence relation is not inherent to definite clause programs and is added to definite clause grammar rules via the difference lists technique.

Let us now briefly consider the notion of proof tree admissibility. Let R be a set of definite clauses; then a proof tree t is admissible from R iff:

(1) t is terminated,

(2) every local subtree t is locally admissible from some $c \in$ R, modulo appropriate substitutions for variables.

A local subtree is composed of a root node and its immediate daughters. A local subtree such as:

r(d1, d2, ..., dn)

is locally admissible if there exists some $c \in$ R such that c is a definite clause of the form:

(r --> d1, d2, ..., dn).

Furthermore, r has to meet the variable substitution constraints expressed by the sequence of most general unifiers θ_i applied in the goal reduction procedure to build the proof tree. The idea, now commonly adopted, is that a proof tree can be decomposed into two elements: a context-free skeleton tree and a labelling mechanism which decorates the nodes of the tree with appropriate terms.

This approach can be extended to Dislog clauses. Let us consider a set of Dislog clauses D (forming a Dislog program) of the form:

$\{ C_1, C_2, ..., C_n \}$ LPC($C_1, C_2, ..., C_n$).

where LPC denotes linear precedence constraints on C_i. The notion of local admissibility can be extended and reformulated to meet the requirements of Dislog. The reformulation requires that co-occurrence constraints are met, together with the linear precedence constraints and the variable substitution requirements.

A local tree such as:

c1 -->d1, d2, ..., dn.

is locally admissible if there exists a Dislog clause $C \in$ D such that there is a clause C_i in C of the form:

c1 --> d1, d2, ..., dn.

which satisfies the variable substitution constraints. In addition, the other clauses:

$$C_1, ..., C_{i-1}, C_{i+1}, ..., C_n \in C$$

in the Dislog clause with appropriate substitutions must be satisfied, together with the linear precedence stated in the linear precedence restrictions LPC of C in the parse tree being elaborated on.

The interpretation formulated in terms of subtree admissibility from a Dislog program D, gives a complete declarative reading to Dislog clauses. This interpretation also gives a simple declarative semantics to D. Let us consider all the complete admissible types which can be constructed from D meeting co-occurrence and variable binding constraints of the Dislog clauses in D. This set is unique, up to variable renamings. It gives all the computed answer substitutions of D from the most general atomic goals.

6. Other Logic-Based Formalisms and Perspectives

In this chapter, we have presented the major logic-based grammar formalisms of theoretical and practical interest and which have been used to develop applications. Most of them are motivated by the desire to enhance the linguistic adequacy and transparency of formalisms in order to help grammar writers specify their syntactic knowledge. These formalisms now tend to be integrated into larger systems, particularly those involving constraints and feature-values. One of the main motivations of this integration is the increasing importance of lexical projection as an operation in language processing, logic-based grammars needing to be more flexible at the feature level. One of the very first system, incorporating feature structures was PatrII (Shieber *et al.* 1983). While keeping the declarative capabilities, the linguistic adequacy and the transparency of logic-based grammars, the introduction of more elaborate feature systems allows the definition of more perspicuous feature structures and the use of more adequate unification mechanisms. These feature structures will be presented in the next chapter.

Besides the logic-based grammars presented here, a number of other variants have been developed. For example, *definite clause translation grammars* (Abramson 1982) have been designed to facilitate the writing of grammars by automating the construction of semantic representation, and by making a clear separation between the syntactic aspects and the construction of a semantic representation. They allow, for example, several semantic computation rules to be associated with a single syntactic rule, the appropriate semantic rule being chosen on lexical and semantic grounds. *Modifier structure grammars* (Dahl and McCord 1983) permit a general treatment of coordination by meta-rules which are then compiled into extraposition grammar rules. Finally, *modular grammars* (McCord 1989) also feature a number of automatically added general capabilities, such as parse tree generation. This formalism has been used to build a rather impressive machine translation system.

Chapter 4

Feature Systems in Logic Programming

With the development of highly parameterized syntactic theories such as government and binding theory and head-driven phrase structure grammars, and with the development of theories in which rewriting and unification play a central role, such as categorial grammars and unification grammars, there is an increasing need for more appropriate and more efficient feature systems.

Feature systems must be designed to preserve the adequacy, expressiveness and explanatory power of a linguistic system that one wants to model. Real parsing as well as generation systems often require the manipulation of large sets of features; these systems must therefore offer great flexibility in the specification of features in grammar symbols and in lexical descriptions. They must also have a significant degree of modularity so that each linguistic aspect (morphological, categorial, etc.) can be dealt with independently. Features are often subject to various constraints. These constraints cannot always be evaluated at the level at which they are stated (e.g. a feature value is not yet known or only partially known) but have to be evaluated later and must remain in effect throughout the whole parsing or generation process.

The development of principle-based approaches to language processing also requires the definition of more abstract formal systems in order to handle these principles in an adequate way. Principles indeed often apply not at grammar rule level but they involve a larger part of a parse tree. They must be expressed by a constraint system which is global to the whole grammar and not local to a rule, and which is capable of handling partially instantiated representations. This latter point will be explored in more depth in Chapter 5.

The purpose of this chapter is to present different operational frameworks to deal with complex feature systems for language processing. One of the first computer models which introduced features structures are *unification grammars* (Kay 1983). In this chapter, we present first the basic formalism and properties of unification grammars, then a simple implementation which takes into account the new flexibility introduced by unification grammars. Next, a bottom-up parser is given. We then introduce a more advanced way of treating complex type feature systems (TFS) and present some aspects of Login (Aït-Kaçi and Nasr 1986), in particular the notion of types, type construction and hierarchy of types. To illustrate this framework, we propose a parser and a generator using the same grammar bi-directionally. Finally, we present a parametrized inheritance system for feature values.

1. Introduction to Unification Grammars

1.1 Motivations

This short introduction to unification grammars is based on Shieber (1986) which gives a good and simple overview of this important approach to representing linguistic knowledge. Unification grammars permit the encoding of a very large spectrum of linguistic systems in a relatively simple and adequate way, such as: functional unification grammars, lexical functional grammars, generalized phrase structure grammars and head-driven phrase structure grammars (Sells 1987 provides the reader with a general overview of several of these approaches). It is important to note that unification grammar systems must be considered as a computationally tractable representational framework but not as a linguistic theory. In this chapter, we will focus mainly on the treatment of feature structures from a logic programming perspective, independently of any particular linguistic approach.

One of the main motivations of unification grammars was to provide grammar writers with more flexible systems for encoding linguistic knowledge. The grammar formalisms presented in Chapters 2 and 3 have shown that standard Prolog terms are very rigid: each argument has a precise informational content whose meaning is implicit. All the arguments of a term must be present at each level of the grammar with the same implicit meaning and in the order they have been specified, for the system to be able to work. Unification grammars offer at this level a much greater flexibility: at each level of a linguistic description, grammar writers only write the relevant information, which may be specified in any order.

Unification grammars also allow for the specification of complex feature structures in a way that is much more elegant and easy to read than structured Prolog terms. Unification grammars also permit re-entrancy of structures and, consequently, recursive descriptions. From that point of view, they offer a slightly greater expressivity and descriptive adequacy than usual Prolog terms, while remaining declarative.

Complex feature structures can be trees or graphs, defined over a finite set of atomic values and arc labels. They also permit the specification of sets of values and of disjunctions of structures. We now present the main concepts of unification grammars that will be used throughout this chapter.

1.2 Basic concepts of unification grammars

1.2.1 Feature structures

The basic notion used in unification grammars is that of an atomic feature structure. It is represented as a feature-name / feature value pair. In the following example, the category is labelled by the identifier (or feature name) *cat* and has the atomic feature value NP:

$$[\ cat\ :\ \mathrm{NP}\ ]$$

This structure represents an element of syntactic category *np*. From a set theoretic perspective, the denotation of that feature structure is the set of all strings which form an np for a given grammar and lexicon.

From this basic notion, we can define a complex feature structure, involving different types of information. In the example below, besides the *cat* feature-value pair, we have a structured feature description encoding agreement information:

$$
\begin{bmatrix}
[\,\text{cat: NP}\,] \\[2ex]
[\,\text{agreement} : [\,\text{number: singular}\,]\,]
\end{bmatrix}
$$

In terms of informational content, the second example above is more specific than the first since it includes information about agreement. We then say that the first structure subsumes the second one, since the denotation of the first structure is any np, whereas the denotation of the second np is limited to nps in the singular. Similarly, this second example is more general and thus subsumes the following feature structure (in which some obvious square brackets have been removed to facilitate reading):

$$
\begin{bmatrix}
\text{cat : NP} \\[1ex]
\text{agreement:} \begin{bmatrix} \text{number: plural} \\ \text{person: third} \end{bmatrix}
\end{bmatrix}
$$

In this example, a field person has been added under the feature label agreement. It introduces more restrictions. The value of the feature agreement is non-atomic: it is called a *complex feature structure*. Notice that this feature structure can equivalently be represented by a tree where leaves denote feature values:

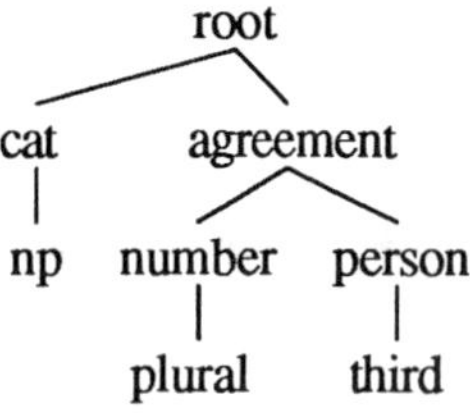

Unification grammars also permit the description of shared structures in an economical and convenient way by means of indexes. In the example below, the value of agreement is imposed to be the same as the value of the subject feature. To avoid repetition on the one hand and, more importantly, to preserve this constraint, an index, noted here as (1), is used and will be kept throughout all unifications :

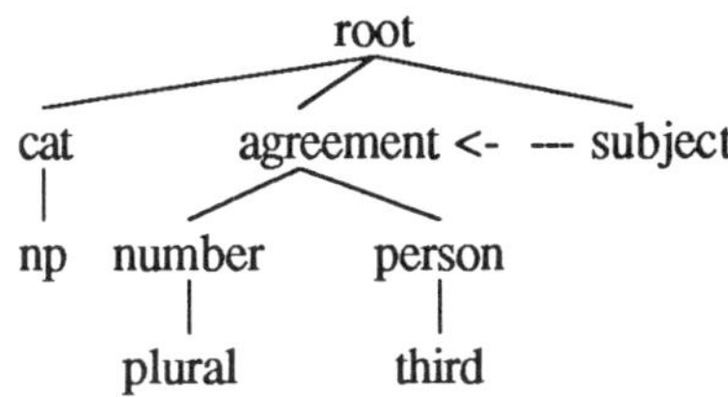

This structure is then represented by a graph:

```
                              root
        ______________________/\________________
       /                     /                   \
     cat              agreement <- --- subject
      |                   /\
     np     number          person
              |                |
            plural          third
```

Let us now consider the unification of two complex feature structures. The
following two feature structures :

$$\begin{bmatrix} \text{cat}: \text{NP} \\ \text{agreement}: \begin{bmatrix} \text{number}: \text{plural} \end{bmatrix} \end{bmatrix}$$

and :

$$\begin{bmatrix} \text{cat}: \text{NP} \\ \text{agreement}: \begin{bmatrix} \text{person}: \text{third} \end{bmatrix} \end{bmatrix}$$

unify to give the union of the two structures:

$$\begin{bmatrix} \text{cat}: \text{NP} \\ \text{agreement}: \begin{bmatrix} \text{person}: \text{third} \\ \text{number}: \text{plural} \end{bmatrix} \end{bmatrix}$$

Unification proceeds roughly as follows. In the case of complex features, each
branch of the feature system is recursively explored and treated until terminal
elements are reached:

- a copy of identical feature-value pairs in the two feature structures appears in
the resulting structure.
- features that appear only in one structure are added to the resulting structure.

Unification fails when values, either atomic or complex, for a given feature in the two feature structures are different.

The resulting structure is subsumed by the two original structures. Thus unification:

- adds information,

- is idempotent,

- permits the unification of an empty structure with any other structure to yield the latter structure.

Non-elementary feature labels introduce the notion of path (or address). In the above example, we have several feature paths such as:

  agreement : person

and

  agreement : number.

Unification also takes reference links into account. For example, the following feature structure :

$$\begin{bmatrix} \text{agreement: } (1)\,[\text{number: plural}] \\ \text{subject: } [\text{ agreement : } (1)\,] \end{bmatrix}$$

unified with:

$$\begin{bmatrix} \text{subject: } [\text{ agreement : } [\text{person: third}]\,] \end{bmatrix}$$

results in:

$$\begin{bmatrix} \text{agreement : } (1) \begin{bmatrix} \text{number: plural} \\ \text{person: third} \end{bmatrix} \\ \text{subject: } [\text{agreement : } (1)\,] \end{bmatrix}$$

This example illustrates r-eentrancy in unification, which is a very useful constraint. However, re-entrancy introduces a major change in the feature structure: instead of having trees we have graphs to represent feature structures. These graphs introduce an additional level of formal and computational complexity which should be used with care and only when necessary. Moreover, re-entrancy can be sometimes 'simplified' as trees at some stage of a parsing process. In Chapter 5, we propose a constraint logic programming approach to re-entrancy which eliminates the problems raised here.

1.2.2 Unification grammars

In unification grammars, grammar rules are often expressed by means of combinatory rules. This type of rule expresses two main aspects:

- a grammatical construction, including the handling of strings of words, and
- a set of relations between feature structures associated with the grammar symbol.

Let us consider the following grammar rule:

$$X_0 \;\to\; X_1 \;,\; X_2.$$
$$<X_0 \;\; cat> = s$$
$$<X_1 \;\; cat> = np$$
$$<X_2 \;\; cat> = vp$$
$$<X_0 \;\; head> = <X_2 \;\; head>$$
$$<X_0 \;\; head \;\; subject> = <X_1 \;\; head>$$

In this grammar rule, the equations read as follows:

$$<X \;\; feature1> \;=\; <Y \;\; feature2>$$

This means that the substructure rooted by feature1 in the feature structure X unifies with the substructure rooted by feature2 in the feature structure Y.

Let us assume that X1 has the following feature structure :

$$\left[\, head : \begin{array}{l} cat:\ np \\ \left[\begin{array}{l} number:\ plural \\ person:\ third \end{array}\right] \end{array}\, \right]$$

and that X2 has the following feature structure:

$$\left[\, head : \left[\begin{array}{l} cat:\ vp \\ form:\ finite \\ subject: \left[\, agreement: \left[\begin{array}{l} number:\ plural \\ person:\ third \end{array}\right]\,\right] \end{array}\right]\,\right]$$

The resulting feature structure for X0, taking into account the equations given in the above rule, is the following:

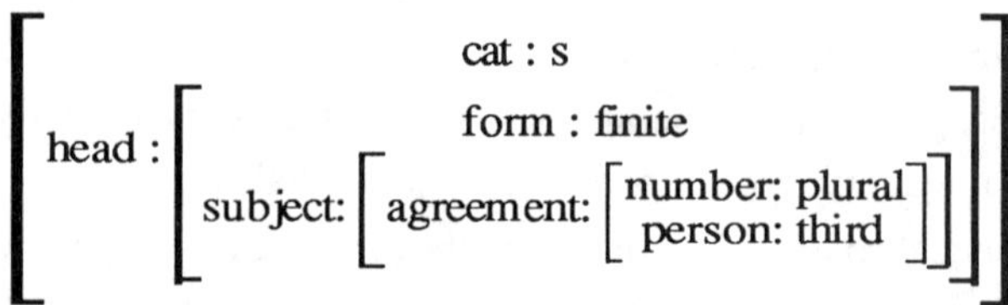

Subcategorization is treated in a similar way. In the following example, the vp1 (the verb phrase of the main clause) controls either the object or the subject np of an embedded sentence with an explicit verb phrase noted vp2:

John persuaded Mary to come.

The same phenomenon is illustrated in:

John promised Mary to be on time.

In the first example, the 'virtual' subject associated with the infinitival proposition is Mary, whereas in the second sentence, the virtual subject is the subject of the main clause. In more linguistic terms, we can say that the PRO (roughly, a pronoun with an empty realization) in the subordinate cause is co-indexed with the object NP of the main clause in the first example and with the subject NP of the main clause in the latter example. For this example, we have the following equational system (in which the sentence has been reduced to the explicit verb phrase):

```
vp1  -->  v,  np,  vp2.
<vp1 head> = <v head>
<vp2 head form>  =  infinitival
<vp2 subject pred>  =  <vp1 subject pred>
<v subcat>  =  npinf.
```

In this set of equations the equality symbol = represents unification. The feature structure of the verb *persuade* is the following:

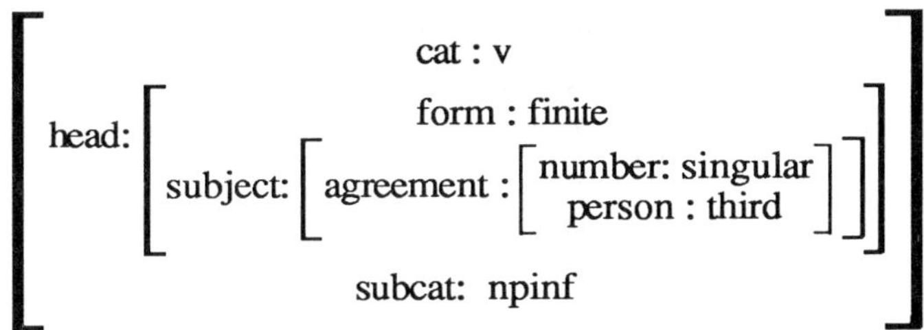

The logical form of the first example above can also be represented by a feature structure in which the different arguments and predicates are labelled by identifiers with semantic meaning.

Mary comes is represented by the following structure:

$$\begin{bmatrix} \text{pred: com e} \\ \text{arg1: mary} \end{bmatrix}$$

The verb *persuade* has three arguments; the representation of the above sentence becomes:

$$\begin{bmatrix} \text{pred: persuade} \\ \text{arg1: john} \\ \text{arg2: (1) mary} \\ \text{arg3:} \begin{bmatrix} \text{pred: come} \\ \text{arg1 : (1)} \end{bmatrix} \end{bmatrix}$$

Notice how re-entrancy in this representation permits us to express in a very elegant way the co-indexation of the object NP with the empty subject position of the non-finite clause.

1.2.3 Disjunction and negation in feature structures

To avoid redundancy or duplication of feature structures, it is sometimes useful to be able to specify that the value associated with a certain feature label may be one of the values of a given set of values. For that purpose, the notion of *disjunction* of feature value is introduced. For example, in French the word *un* may be either a indefinite determiner (and would be translated by *a* in English) or a numeral (and would be translated by *one* in English). Since all the other characteristics (e.g. morphology) remain the same, it would be inappropriate to define two different feature structures. Instead, it is possible to introduce a feature, e.g. cat, with two possible values:

    un :   [cat : or([indef_det, numeral])].

    This structure unifies with :

    [cat : indef_det]

or with:

    [cat : numeral]

It also unifies with itself. Disjunction can also operate on complex feature structures. For example, the determiner *Die* in German may be, for example, either singular feminine, plural masculine or plural feminine for the case nominative. We can thus have a feature structure of the following form with a disjunction embedded into another:

$$
\begin{bmatrix}
string : Die \\
cat : det \\
case : nominative \\
agreement : or\left(\begin{bmatrix} number :singular \\ gender : fem \end{bmatrix}, \begin{bmatrix} number : plural \\ gender : or(masc, fem) \end{bmatrix}\right)
\end{bmatrix}
$$

In terms of unification, two disjunctions of feature values unify if they have an non-empty intersection. The result of the unification is then that intersection. For example, the result of unifying:

    or([masc, neutral]

with

    or([fem, neutral]

is the intersection of the two sets:

    or([neutral] = neutral.

For similar reasons, it may be useful in some cases to indicate that a feature value may take any value except one or more given values. This statement is more delicate to treat. The usual approach is to use *negation* specified over a set of values, as in, for example:

    gender : not([fem])

while this statement gives the values that this feature must not be bound to, it does not say anything about the values it may be bound to. However, we can consider that all feature labels are implicitly typed and that the extension of their type is *a priori* the set of values they are bound to in the grammatical and lexical descriptions considered. For that reason, only negation over atomic values can be considered. Negation on complex features is more problematic since it is not always straightforward to construct the complement of a negation. With this pseudo-typing in mind, we can then infer from the above example that gender can be bound in this example to any value in the set:

{ masc, neutral }

if we consider a German grammar. In French, we would only have:

{ masc }

since neutral is not a value for gender.

If we now consider the problem of unification, two feature structures, one of which has a value that is a negation of a set of values, unifies if the intersection of the values is empty. The result is the feature structure which does not contain any negation. For example:

gender : not([fem])

unifies with:

gender : masc.

The result of unification is that latter feature-value pair.

Two feature structures with negated values unify if the complement of their union is non-empty. The result of the unification is the union of the negated values. For example, if we have the two following feature structures:

gender : not([masc])

gender : not([fem])

they unify in German because the complement of their union is:

{neutral}

which is non-empty, whereas they do not unify in French, since that complement is empty (French has only two genders). The result of unification in German is:

gender : not([masc, fem]).

The basic formalism we have presented here for unification grammars allows us to express in a simple and declarative way most of the basic linguistic phenomena one finds in any grammatical system: agreement, subcategorization, control and semantic representation construction.

1.3 Feature logics

Two types of feature descriptions have been investigated in the literature. The first approach uses boolean combinations of equations built from features, constants and variables; the second approach uses set-denoting expressions, also called feature-based terms (Smolka 1989). The first approach has been illustrated in section 1.2; it was developed in lexical functional grammars (Kaplan and Bresnan 1982), in PatrII (Shieber *et al*. 1983) and within attribute-value logic (Johnson 87). The second approach was developed within functional unification grammars (Kay 79, 85), Login (Aït-Kaçi and Nasr 86) and by Kasper and Rounds (1990). This latter approach is presented in detail in section 3 of this chapter.

In Smolka (1989), it is shown that these two types of descriptions can be captured as sub-languages of first-order predicate logic with equality. This result simplifies and clarifies the concepts underlying the two approaches.

This section presents a more elaborate treatment of features in unification grammars from a logical point of view, as presented by Shieber (1986) and Smolka (1989). This logical treatment will be considered again in Chapter 5, where we develop a constraint logic programming approach to feature descriptions and processing.

Let us consider the following grammar:

S --> NP, VP

        <S subj> = <NP>

        <S> = <VP>.

NP --> Det, N

        <NP> = <Det> = <N>.

VP --> V, NP.

        <VP> = <V>

        <VP obj> = <NP>.

The equations associated with these rules define constraints on every phrase structure tree licensed by these rules. Features can be viewed as partial functions, the variables ranging over abstract objects representing the different aspects of concrete phrases. Any phrase structure tree must satisfy the following set of constraints (definitions and notations are the same as in the above grammars):

∃ NP, VP, V, NP1, Det, N,

<S subj> = <NP> ∧ <S> = <VP> ∧ <NP> = <Det> = <N> ∧

    <VP> = <V> ∧ <VP obj> = <NP1> ∧

    <NP1> = <Det1> = <N1>.

The variable NP1 has been introduced to represent in a simple way the object NP. In a real grammar, this index should be clearly represented by the contents of that NP, which are different from the content of the subject NP.

Let us now consider lexical entries. These can also be represented by a set of constraints:

```
Det --> [the]
  <Det number> = sing.
N --> [car]
  <N number> = sing
  <N pred> = car(X).
```

The noun phrase *the car* is associated with the following satisfiable set of constraints :

$$<NP> = <Det> = <N> \wedge <Det\ number> = sing \wedge <N\ number> = sing \wedge$$
$$<N\ pred> = car(X).$$

If the noun car had been in the plural, yielding:

$$<N\ number> = plu$$

then the formula would not have been satisfiable because the two numbers have to be identical as required by the first equation in the formula:

$$<NP> = <Det> = <N>.$$

The same procedure can be applied to the treatment of VPs and sentences.

A finite sequence of words is licensed by a grammar with constraints if it is possible to construct at least one phrase structure tree whose leaves are these words in the correct order and whose associated set of constraints is satisfiable. This satisfiable set can be considered as being the logical representation of the different readings of the sentence.

Constraints associated with a phrase structure tree are usually constructed incrementally. If one is not directly interested in the parse tree, partial sets of constraints can then be simplified during the construction of the phrase structure tree. This can be easily done since the set of constraints is built from feature equations using only conjunction and existential quantification. The resolution method can then be reduced to the treatment of conjunctions of constraints in normal form.

From these specifications, it turns out that there are many similarities between logic programming and grammar formalisms based on feature unification.

2. A Basic Feature System in Prolog

We now present a simple feature structure description formalism in logic programming and a set of operations which manipulate these features. The grammar and the lexicon given here can easily be extended to construct a more refined system with a greater linguistic coverage, following the same principles and techniques. The basic tools presented here can be used for a number of linguistic operations.

2.1 Tools and formalisms

Let us consider a small subset of natural language, as given in Chapter 2. Let us first consider the lexicon. The general form of a lexical entry is the following:

    category(syntactic_tree, feature_structure, difference_lists)

The syntactic_tree argument is, as described in Chapter 2, the contribution of this grammatical level to the construction of a syntactic tree. The difference lists are also a well-known structure, explained in chapter 2. The feature_structure argument is a list of feature-value pairs, each with the following form:

    feature_label   :   associated_value

If the value is a set of disjunctive possibilities, then it is represented by a list. The features considered here are some of the basic features of English. Other features such as gender for Romance languages can be treated identically. The feature labels and their associated values are the following:

number: with values sing (singular) or plu (plural),

tense: with tense values such as pres (present), etc.

sem: proper semantic feature of the entity considered, its associated value is a set of values such as hum (human), nhum, vehicle, etc.

sems: semantics of acceptable subjects for verbs, which is a list,

semo: semantics of acceptable objects for transitive verbs, which is also a list.

Features can be given in any order. A variable standing for a feature value means that it can have any value; the presence of the feature label indicates that this feature is relevant at this level. Features which are of no interest for the given lexical entry are simply omitted. In this formalism, the difference between a feature which is of no interest (but is not inappropriate) and a feature which is irrelevant (i.e. which must not appear) at a given level remains ambiguous.

The lexicon of our toy-grammar is the following:

```
det(det(the), [number: sing], [the|L],L).
det(det(a), [number: sing], [a|L],L).
n(n(car), [number: sing, sem : [vehicle]], [car|L],L).
n(n(worker), [number: sing, sem : [hum]], [worker|L],L).
```

```
v(v(sing), [number: sing, tense : pres, sems : [hum], semo : [nhum],
           scat : [np]], [sings|L],L).
v(v(drink), [number: sing, tense : pres, scat: [np],
           sems : [hum], semo : [liquid]], [drinks|L], L).
v(v(drive), [number: sing, tense : pres, scat: [np],
           sems : [hum], semo : [vehicle]], [drives|L], L).
n(n(coffee), [number: sing, sem: [liquid]], [coffee|L],L).
a(a(warm), [number: sing, sem: [liquid]], [warm|L],L).
```

Some feature values are represented as lists even if they contain only a single element. The reason of this notation is that they may potentially be sets of values.

Let us now consider the grammar. The general form of a grammar symbol is similar to the form of a lexical entry:

```
symbol(syntactic_tree, feature_structure, difference_lists)
```

Grammar rules include different predefined calls to control procedures. We have the following procedures:

```
extract(T, Label, Value)
```

extracts in the feature structure T the Value associated to the feature label Label, If Label does not exists in T, then extract is evaluated to false.

mb(X,Y) is true is X is a member of the list Y.

unify(T1, T2, T3) is evaluated to true if T1 and T2 unify and yield as result T3.

The grammar is as follows; controls realized here are identical to those given in Chapter 2. Equality of feature values is expressed by the use of identical variables.

```
:- op(600,xfx,':').            % operator declaration


% s --> np, vp.
s(s(NP,VP))      -->
    np(NP,T1),
    {extract(T1,number,V1),    extract(T1, sem,S)},
    vp(VP,T2),
    {extract(T2,number,V1),    extract(T2,sems,S)}.
```

```
% np --> det, n.
np(np(Det,N), T)    -->
    det(Det,  T1),
    n(N,  T2),
    {unify(T1,T2,T)}.


 % np --> det, ap, n.
 np(np(Det,A,  N), T)  -->
    det(Det,  T1),
    ap(A,  T3),
    n(N,  T2),
    {unify(T1,T2,T),    unify(T3,  T2,  _)}.


% vp --> v, np.
vp(vp(V,NP), T1)   -->
    v(V,T1),  {extract(T1,scat,Scat),    mb(np,Scat)},
    np(NP,  T2).


% ap --> a.
ap(ap(A),T1)    -->
    a(A,T1).
```

The procedures that make up the different controls are defined by the following programs (some of these definitions are given by Gal *et al.* (1990)):

```
% unification procedure
% identical sets
unify( Featureset, Featureset, Featureset):-   !.
unify(Anything,[ ],Anything):-    !.
unify([ ],Anything,Anything):-    !.


% same feature same value
unify([Feature1:Value1|Rest1], [Feature1:Value1|Rest2],
      [Feature1:Value1|Result]):-   !,
         unify(Rest1,Rest2,Result).
```

```
% same feature different value
unify([Feature1:Value1|Rest1], [Feature1:Value2|Rest2],Result):-
      !,  fail.


% different features
unify([Feature1:Value1|Rest1], [Feature2:Value2|Rest2],Result):-
      unify([Feature1:Value1],Rest2,NewRest2),
      unify(Rest1,[Feature2:Value2|NewRest2],Result),   !.


% features can be complex and set-valued
% same feature setvalue
unify([Feature1:SetValue1|Rest1], [Feature1:SetValue2|Rest2],
      [Feature1:Result1|Result]):-
                not(atom(SetValue1)),
                not(atom(SetValue2)),
                unify(SetValue1,SetValue2,Result1),
                unify(Rest1,Rest2,Result),!.


%   extraction of features
extract(T1,Nom,Val)  :-  mb(Nom:Val, T1),  !.
extract(T1,N,Val).


mb(X,[X|_]).
mb(X,[_|Y])  :-   mb(X,Y).


A call to this program is the following :
?-  s(Synt,  [the,worker,drinks,a,warm,coffee],[ ]  ).
    Synt  =  s(np(det(the),n(worker)),
          vp(v(drink),np(det(a),ap(a(warm)),n(coffee)))))
```

2.2 A bottom-up parser for unification grammars

For reasons advocated in Chapter 2, section 5, it can be interesting to have a
bottom-up parser rather than a top-down parser for processing such grammars.
The control tools given above remain the same; the formats of the grammar and
the lexicon have to be slightly modified for practical reasons, but these changes

remain superficial.

The grammar given above is represented as follows (to show the flexibility of notations, we introduce here a slightly different notation than in Chapter 2, section 5):

```
% s --> np, vp.
  s(s(NP,VP))  --->
    [ np(NP,T1),    extract(T1,number,V1),    extract(T1,sem,S),
      vp(VP,T2),    extract(T2,number,V1),    extract(T2,sems,S)].


% np --> det, n.
np(np(Det,N),  T) --->
    [ det(Det,  T1),
      n(N,  T2),    unify(T1,T2,T)].


% np --> det, ap, n.
np(np(Det,A,N),  T) --->
    [ det(Det,  T1),
      ap(A,T3),
      n(N,  T2),
      unify(T1,T2,T),   unify(T3, T2, _) ].


% vp --> v, np.
vp(vp(V,NP),T1)  --->
    [ v(V,T1),
      extract(T1, scat, Scat),   mb(np, Scat),
      np(NP,T2)].


% ap --> a.
  ap(ap(A),T1)  --->   [a(A,T1)].


/*   LEXICON   */


det(det(the), [number: sing]) ---> [the|L].
det(det(a), [number: sing]) ---> [a|L].
n(n(car), [number: sing, sem :[vehicle]]) ---> [car|L].
n(n(worker), [number: sing, sem: [hum]]) ---> [worker|L].
```

```
v(v(sing), [number: sing,tense : pres, sems : [hum],
           semo : [nhum],scat : [np]]) ---> [sings|L].
v(v(drink), [number: sing,tense : pres, scat: [np],
           sems : [hum], semo : [liquid]]) ---> [drinks|L].
v(v(drive), [number: sing, tense : pres, scat: [np],
           sems : [hum], semo : [vehicle]]) ---> [drives|L].
n(n(coffee), [number: sing, sem: [liquid]]) ---> [coffee|L].
a(a(warm), [number: sing, sem: [liquid]]) ---> [warm|L].
```

The meta-interpreter that handles the bottom-up parsing procedure uses the
same technique as the one presented in Chapter 2: the left-corner technique. It is
adapted here to the treatment of feature structures but has many similarities with
the bottom-up parser given in Chapter 2:

```
parse(Phrase,X,X)  :-
    call1(Phrase), !.          % treatment of non-grammatical symbols
parse(Phrase,X,Y)  :-
    leaf(Sp,X,Z),              % left-most leaf
    leftcorner(Sp,Phrase,Z,Y).


leaf(Phrase,[X|Y],Y) :-   (Phrase ---> [X|Y]).


    % treatment of non-grammatical elements in the grammar
call1(extract(A,B,C))  :-   extract(A,B,C).
call1(unify(A,B,C))  :-   unify(A,B,C).
call1(mb(A,B))  :-   mb(A,B).


leftcorner(P,P,X,X).
leftcorner(Sp,SuperP,X,Y)  :-
    (Phrase ---> [Sp] ),
    leftcorner(Phrase,SuperP,X,Y).
leftcorner(Sp,SuperP,X,Y)  :-
    (Phrase ---> [Sp|Rest] ),
    parse_next(Rest,X,Z),
    leftcorner(Phrase,SuperP,Z,Y).
```

```
parse_next([ ],X,X).
parse_next([P|PP],X,Y)  :-
    parse(P,X,Z),
    parse_next(PP,Z,Y).
```

3. Feature Structures as Types

Feature systems can be defined in a more formal and organized way. In particular, it is of much interest to be able to define in a more explicit way hierarchical relations between features and the set of values a given feature value may be bound to. Feature values can be represented as types (Carpenter 1992). A type can be 'basic' (e.g. integer, boolean, string, list of predefined constants), or it can be complex if it corresponds to a complex feature structure. The definition of types permits the introduction of hierarchies of types, defined according to the subsumption (or subtype) relation. As a result, it is possible to organize the different characteristics of a linguistic domain by means of partial lattices of types. Unification is then extended to take into account the hierarchical relations between types. Two feature structures unify if they have a common greater lower bound according to the type lattice. From a terminological point of view, feature systems based on typed structures are often called *typed feature structures* (TFS).

In this section, we first introduce the foundations and the linguistic motivations for using TFS, then we introduce Login (Aït-Kaçi and Nasr 1986) (and elements of LIFE, an extension of Login with equality and functions) which is probably one of the most elaborate and well-defined systems, from a formal point of view, and embedded within the logic programming framework. Finally, we show how aspects of Login can be used for natural language processing.

3.1 Structuring linguistic knowledge by means of hierarchies

Hierarchies can be used as a means to better organize and to better capture generalizations and regularities about linguistic knowledge. Hierarchies may be based on different kinds of relations (e.g. the *part-of* relation). We are essentially concerned here with the subtype relation, also known as the hyperonymy relation in lexical semantics. The subtype relation introduces a partial ordering on types. It allows for inheritance of properties from mother nodes to daughter nodes.

Hierarchies are constructed from feature definitions. A TFS is a structured set of features, organized as types, describing a certain set of linguistic data in an homogeneous and coherent way.

As we have seen above, feature structures are usually composed of a structure identifier and of a set of associated properties represented as feature-value pairs. For example:

```
xp(cat : n).
```

is a feature structure which can be interpreted as a type, denoting a phrasal level (xp) of syntactic category cat with value n. Basic feature types are just atomic values (e.g. masc, fem).

Most of the different linguistic aspects involved in language processing can be represented in an appropriate way by a more or less complex and general hierarchical description. For example, here is a portion of a classification of spatial prepositions for French:

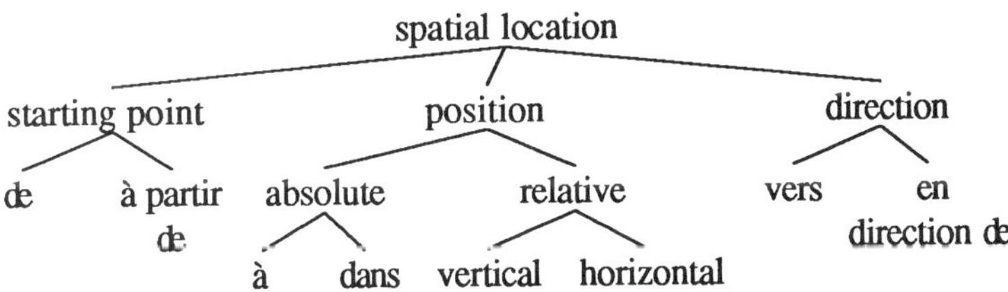

where vertical has the following subtypes: devant, derrière (respectively in front of and in the back of), and horizontal has the following ones: sur, sous, dessus, dessous (respectively on, under). The other prepositions translate roughly as follows: de and à partir de: from; à and dans: in; vers and en direction de: towards. Similarly, we can define a portion of a hierarchy of types of physical locations:

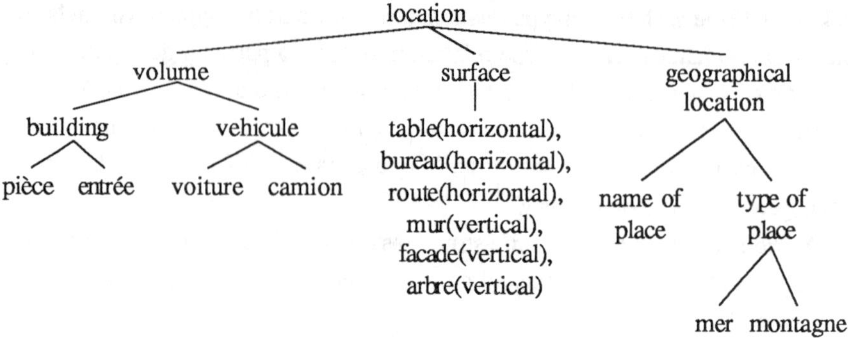

The French terms translate roughly as follows: pièce: room; entrée: entrance; voiture: car; camion: truck; table: table; bureau: desk; route: road; mur: wall; façade: front (of a building); arbre: tree; mer: sea; montagne: mountain. Notice that we have represented here the concepts of verticality and horizontality by means of a property, whereas we have introduced two subtypes for prepositions. Both notations are equivalent. It is particularly easy to switch from one notation to the other when the properties involved have boolean values.

Our structured representations involve trees. Some authors have developed graphs to represent linguistic and domain knowledge. We, however, think that graphs should be avoided whenever possible for practical and representational reasons. In particular, most of the literature in lexical semantics tends to avoid graph representations and to propose alternative solutions, which seems to be more satisfactory (Cruse 1986).

It is possible to define independent hierarchies corresponding to different aspects of lexical, syntactic or semantic knowledge. The description of a concept, of a word or of any constituent is the union of its partial descriptions found in different type hierarchies. These elements are subject to what is usually called multiple inheritance. This notion is further developed in section 4 of this chapter.

3.2 An introduction to Login

The TFS approach presented in section 3.1 has been formally defined in Login (Aït Kaçi and Nasr 1986) within the logic programming framework. Type hierarchies are based on a pre-order relation called subsumption. The feature-based terms considered are called ψ-terms. The set of all ψ-terms that can be defined from a given vocabulary (feature labels and feature values) forms a pre-lattice, provided the sort symbols are ordered as a lattice. Unification of two ψ-terms is defined as the computation of the greater lower bound of each symbol of those ψ-terms, with respect to the pre-lattice of ψ-terms.

3.2.1 Basic structures: ψ-terms

Feature terms can be used to describe feature-based types. For example, using Login syntax, the feature term:

```
car( color => blue, make => 'Renault')
```

denotes all the elements of type car (in the world considered) whose features color and make have respectively the values blue and 'Renault'. In Login, the symbol => stands for the separator ':' in the examples we have developed so far.

We now informally present the syntax of Login. A structured term is a ψ-term. It consists of:

(1) A *root symbol*, which is a type constructor and denotes a class of entities.

(2) *Attribute labels*, which are record field symbols. Each attribute denotes a function; that function is defined in extension, from the root to the attribute value. The attribute value can itself be a reference to a type.

(3) *Co-reference constraints,* which indicate that the corresponding attributes denote the same structure. They are indicated by variables.

Here is a representation of the concept of *person*:

```
person( id => name(first => string,
                    last => X: string),
        born => date(day => integer,
                     month => monthname,
                     year => integer),
        father => person( id => name(last => X ))).
```


In this example, the root symbol is *person*; *id, born* and *father* are three sub-ψ-terms which have either constants or types as values. X indicates a co-reference. All different type structures are tagged by different symbols. Notice also that in the latter field only relevant information about *person* is mentioned. Infinite structures can also be specified by co-reference links. Variables are in capital letters, constants in small letters. The empty type is noted as $\perp$ and read bottom; it denotes a contradiction. The maximal (or universal) type is noted as $\top$ (read top) and subsumes all the other types.

To establish a link between unification-based systems also refered to as feature-based types and type constructors, Smolka and Aït-Kaçi (1989) have shown that they are dual concepts. Type constructors are indeed primarily defined by giving their constructor (the root of the structure) while feature-based types are only defined by their selectors: the feature-value specifications.

3.2.2 Sorts, lattices of sorts and inheritance

Sorts denote sets and are partially ordered with a subsort ordering which denotes set inclusion. Sorts may share common subsorts, allowing thus a form of multiple inheritance. There is no conceptual difference in Login between sorts and values. A value is a sort with a single element. To state that A is a subsort of B we use the following notation:

    A <| B.

For example, we can define a type nbr, for the feature *number*, whose subtypes are the values sing (singular) and plu (plural):

    sing <| nbr.

    plu <| nbr.

Similarly, we can define a hierarchy for semantic restrictions as follows, where ψ-terms have attributes:

    alive(alive => 1) <| entities.
    inert(alive => 0) <| entities.
    animate(prop => moves) <| alive.
    inanimate(prop => fixed) <| alive.
    human(concious => 1) <| animate.
    etc...

Notice that only ψ-terms on the left of the isa hierarchy relation symbol have attributes.

The type human inherits of the properties of all its parents. For example, in a term of the form:

    x0(string => [john], type => human).

human is implicitly equivalent to:

    human(alive =>1, prop => moves, concious => 1).

There must not be any incoherence in the specification of the properties of the elements in a hierarchy, otherwise inheritance fails and subtypes are not accessible.

Besides subtyping, it is also possible to attach attributes to any sort by means of the operator : :, as in the following example where we add two properties to the root type entities:

```
:: entities( basic => distinguishable, name => string).
```

Login also allows for multiple inheritance, as long as there is no conflict in the values attached to properties. For example, consider the following hierarchy:

```
mammal(hairs => 1, pups => external) <| animal.
human(limb => [leg, arm]) <| mammal.
horse(limb =>leg)  <| mammal.
```

The type human is also defined in this hierarchy. The complete definition of human is the union of its various (partial) descriptions, if there is no conflict. Redundancies are eliminated. In this example, the union of the properties becomes:

```
human(alive =>1, prop => moves, concious => 1,
          hairs => 1, pups => external, limb => [leg, arm]).
```

Logic allows for the representation of disjunctive structures. It is represented as follows:

```
<feature label> => { <type> ; <type> ; ... ; <type> }.
```

The symbol ; reads *or*. For example, to state that the colour of a coat can be either blue, black of grey, we can write:

```
color => { blue ; grey ; black}.
```

The elements in the disjunction form a subset of the type of the values associated with the feature label color.

Let us now consider the operator := which is not a primitive operator - it can be expressed in terms of the two operators : : and ◁. It is, however, a useful shorthand for defining complex sorts. The left-side operand of this operator is indeed a symbol that represents the sort specified to the right. The notation:

```
t := u
```

where t is a symbol, declares that t is a subsort of u. However, when we write:

```
t := { u; v; w}
```

t is then a supersort of u, v and w. As a consequence,

```
t := u
```

is not equivalent to:

```
t := {u}
```

since in the first case we have:

```
t <| u
```

while in the latter we have:

u <| t.

Nevertheless, this operator is a really convenient shorthand to manipulate complex sorts.

3.2.3 Computing greatest lower bounds

The greatest lower bound (GLB) of two sorts is their intersection. It is defined as their largest common subsort if it exists. If the intersection is the empty sort, then the two sorts do not have any GLB. Two sorts may also have more than one GLB. In that case, the result is the set of all the maximal common subsorts, represented by a disjunction of sorts:

$\{ glb_1 ; glb_2 ; \dots ; glb_n \}$

Let us now consider the following hierarchy of sorts (given in Life user's manual):

    bike <| two_wheels.
    bike <| vehicle.
    truck <| vehicle.
    truck <| four_wheels.
    RV <| four_wheels.
    car <| four_wheels.
    car <| vehicle.
    renault <| car.

This hierarchy can be represented by the following graph:

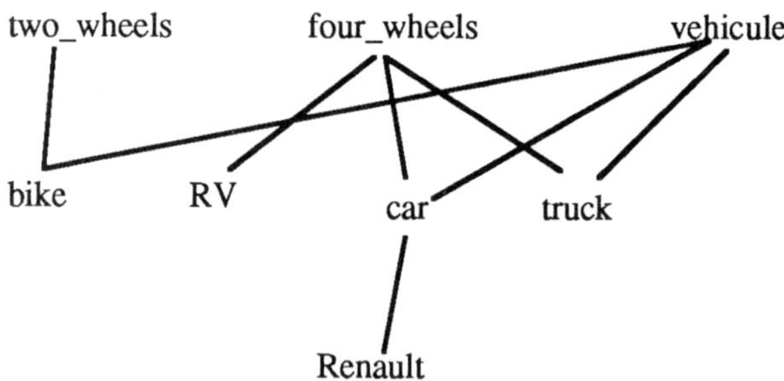

We can then define the following GLBs:

    GLB(two_wheels, vehicle) = {bike}
    GLB(four_wheels, vehicle) = {truck; car} (disjunctive set)
    GLB(four_wheels, two_wheels) = ⊥ (failure)
    GLB(car, @) = car (the symbol @ represents the universal sort).

Let us now examine how GLBs are computed for ψ-terms with attributes. Every type constructor and value is concerned by the search of GLBs. If a GLB between two sorts cannot be found then the two ψ-terms do not have any common GLB. For example, if car and vehicle are defined with the following attributes:

    four_wheels(color => red, wheels => 4)
    vehicle(make => string, wheels => integer).
then the GLB of these two ψ-terms is:
    { car(color => red, wheels => 4, make => string);
      truck(color => red, wheels => 4, make => string) }
since:
    - the GLB of four_wheels and vehicle is car or truck,
    - the GLB is the union of the properties of vehicle and four_wheels, if they do not conflict,
    - for the feature wheels, the GLB of 4 and integer is 4.
This process is applied recursively if values associated to feature labels are types.

Let us now consider the problem of evaluation. In that case, the operation of *matching* is considered. This operation resembles the notion of *subsumption*, except that it includes in its operational definition a notion of *residuation*.

A ψ-term U matches a ψ-term V iff U <| V. This means that the denotation of U is smaller than the denotation of V; in other words, V subsumes U, and the different ψ-terms associated with labels of U match the corresponding ψ-terms in V. The two cases where U and V do not match are:
    - GLB(U, V) = $\perp$
    - U is not included in V.

When one of the two terms U or V is not sufficiently instantiated to determine non-ambiguously whether U matches V, the evaluation is suspended (residuation) and evaluation resumes as soon as sufficient information is available. This facility is of much interest for the implementation of constraint resolution, as shall be seen in Chapter 5.

3.2.4 Constrained sorts

Sorts may be subject to various constraints that must always hold. Constraints usually deal with atomic values and express characteristics which cannot easily be represented by sorts. The introduction of constraints is noted as follows:
    :: sort(attributes) | constraints.

where constraints has the form of a definite clause body. The operator | reads 'such that'.

If sort1 differs from sort2 only in the constraints attached to sort1 as expressed in:

    sort1 <| sort2.

    :: sort2(Attributes).

    sort1 | constraints.

then a more convenient formulation is the following:

    sort1 := sort2(Attributes) | constraints.

Constraints associated to a given sort are inherited by its subsorts.

For example, we can constrain a quantifying expression to be composed of less than five words:

    quant_expr(string => L: list_of_strings,
                    cat => syntactic_category) |
                            length(L, N), N<5.

    length(L,N) :- card(L,N).   % N is the cardinal of the set L.

and if we have the subsorts:

    det <| quant_expr.

    temporal_exp <| quant_expr.

then the subsorts det and temporal_exp inherit the constraint of being less than five words long. If det and temporal_exp had their own constraints, then the constraints coming from their ancestor(s) would have been merged with their own constraints. Login does not check for the consistency of any set of constraints. However, Login tries to be clever in developing a dynamic constraint checking that remembers which constraints have been triggered.

3.3 Representing linguistic constructions by means of ψ-terms

Let us now consider how lexical entries and grammar rules can be written in Login. In the following examples, we only have two main type constructors:

   - x0 corresponding to lexical entries,

   - xp corresponding to phrase structures.

Let us consider the hierarchies developed in section 3.1. They are described as follows in Login:

```
% preposition hierarchy
starting_point <| spatial_location.
position <| spatial_location.
direction <| spatial_location.
absolute <| position.
relative <| position.
vertical <| relative.
horizontal <| relative.

   % spatial location hierarchy
volume <| location.
surface <| location.
vert_surf(orientation => vertical) <| surface.
horiz_surf(orientation => horizontal) <| surface.
geographical_place <| location.
building <| volume.
vehicule <| volume.
name_of_place <| geographical_location.
type_of_place <| geographical_location.

   % hierarchy of lexical syntactic categories
a <| syn_categ.
v <| syn_categ.
det <| syn_categ.
prep <| syn_categ.
n <| syn_categ.
adv <| syn_categ.
proper_n <| n.
common_n <| n.
aux <| v.
transitive_dir <| v.    % transitive verb with a direct object
transitive_prep <| v.  % same with a propositional object
```

Let us now define the lexical entries of our system. The main type is lex. It has features which indicate that a lexical entry is represented by a word of type string_of_car. Furthermore, a constraint states that the word is non-empty.

Then, each lexical element has a syntactic part and a semantic part. Notice how types are used for type constructors and for feature values.

```
      % lexical entries of prepositions
  :: lex( syntax => syn_categ( string => S : string_of_char ))
         | not(S = []).
  x0(syntax => prep(string => [de]), sem_prep => starting_point)
     <| lex.
  x0(syntax =>  prep(string  => [a,partir,de]),
     sem_prep => starting_point)  <| lex.
  x0(syntax => prep(string => [a]), sem_prep => absolute)  <| lex.
  x0(syntax => prep(string => [dans]), sem_prep => absolute)  <| lex.
  x0(syntax => prep(string => [sur]), sem_prep => horizontal)  <| lex.
  x0(syntax => prep(string => [sous]), sem_prep => horizontal)  <| lex.
  x0(syntax => prep(string => [devant]), sem_prep => vertical)  <| lex.
  x0(syntax => prep(string => [derriere]), sem_prep => vertical)
     <| lex.
  x0(syntax => prep(string => [a,cote,de]), sem_prep => relative)
     <| lex.
  x0(syntax => prep(string => [vers]), sem_prep => direction)  <| lex.
  x0(syntax => prep(string => [en, direction, de]),
     sem_prep => direction)  <| lex.


      % lexical entries of location nouns
  x0(syntax => common_n(string => [maison]), sem => volume)  <| lex.
  x0(syntax => common_n(string => [voiture]), sem => volume)  <| lex.
  x0(syntax => common_n(string => [table]), sem => horiz_surf)
     <| lex.
  x0(syntax => common_n(string => [bureau]), sem => horiz_surf)
     <| lex.
  x0(syntax => common_n(string => [route]), sem => horiz_surf)
     <| lex.
  x0(syntax => common_n(string => [mur]), sem => vert_surf)  <| lex.
  x0(syntax => common_n(string => [facade]), sem => vert_surf)
     <| lex.
  x0(syntax => common_n(string =>[arbre]), sem => vert_surf) <| lex.
```

```
x0(syntax => proper_n(string => [paris]), sem => name_of_place)
   <| lex.
x0(syntax => common_n(string => [mer]), sem => type_of_place)
    <| lex.
x0(syntax => common_n(string => [montagne]),
    sem => type_of_place)  <| lex.
```

Let us now describe lexical entries of a few verbs which express spatial location or motion and let us concentrate on the type of preposition and of nominal complement they require. The features c_1 and c_2 represent the elements in the subcategorization frame of the verb. Verbs can be defined as follows:

```
% to enter (a room, a building)
x0(syntax => transitive_prep(string => [entrer]),
   scat => pp(c1 => x0(syntax => prep(string => [dans])),
             c2 => xp(syntax => common_n, sem => volume)))
 <| lex.
```

```
% to arrive (at a place)
x0(syntax => transitive_prep(string => [arriver]),
   scat => {pp(c1 => x0(syntax => prep(string => [dans])),
             c2 => xp(syntax => common_n, sem => volume)))  ;
            pp(c1 => x0( syntax => prep(string => [a])),
  c2 => xp(syntax => common_n, sem => geographical_location)))})
   <| lex.
```

```
% to run (towards a point)
x0(syntax => transitive_prep(string => [courir]),
   scat => pp(c1 => prep(sem_prep => direction),
             c2 => xp(syntax => common_n,
                     sem => {type_of_place ; name_of_place }))
 <| lex.
```

Let us now consider the grammar of a few VP constructions. The same features, c_1 and c_2 are used to represent the different constituents in the NP or PP subcategorized by the verb and present in the VP construction. We first define a general type `xp` for structures with two elements. The string manipulations are expressed at this level. The call to `conc(S1, S2, S)` implicitly indicates that the structure associated with `c1` precedes the structure associated with `c2`. Notice the use made here of re-entrancy to project the verb subcategorization into the type describing the VP. Such a projection has already been exemplified for DCGs. The grammar is the following:

```
% grammatical types


% general type xp
:: xp( syntax => syn_categ(string => S : string_of_char),
     c1 => { x0( syntax => syn_categ(string => S1: string_of_char) ;
                 xp( syntax => syn_categ(string => S1: string_of_char) },
     c2 => { x0( syntax => syn_categ(string => S2: string_of_char) ;
                 xp( syntax => syn_categ(string => S2: string_of_char) })
     | conc(S1,S2,S).


vp(syntax => v,
     c1 => x0(syntax => transitive_prep,
              scat => X : xp)
     c2 => xp(syntax => pp, scat => X) )  <| xp.


pp(syntax => p,
     scat => xp(c1 => X : x0(syntax => prep), c2 => Y: np),
     c1 => X,
     c2 => Y) <| xp.


np(syntax => n,
     c1 => x0 syntax => det),
     c2 => x0(syntax => n) )  <| xp.
```

To parse a VP, a call is of the form:

```
?- vp(syntax => syn_categ(string => [string,to,parse])).
```

3.4 Parsing with ψ-terms

To parse a sentence is to construct a well-formed feature-based type describing the sentence structure. The type constructor approach of Login introduces a new way of defining a parsing process, in terms of type construction. In this section we present an abstract machine which describes how types are constructed. This machine is based on the procedural semantics of Prolog but it resembles a pushdown tree automaton whose stack is updated each time a subtype is modified.

There are two kinds of type constructors: those corresponding to non-terminal structures (such as xp in our examples above) and those corresponding to terminal structures (e.g. x0). We now present a step in the construction of a feature-based type. The proof construction process is based on Prolog's procedural semantics (see Chapter 1). It can be decomposed into three stages:

(1) Current state σ_i:

$$c_0(a_1 => t_1, \ a_2 => t_2, \ ..., \ a_n => t_n) ,$$
where the t_i are any type different from the empty type.

(2) Selection of a type construction specification TC in the current program P such that:

$$glb(t1, TC) = c_1(b_1 => t'_1, \ ..., \ b_m => t'_m)$$
such that t_1 subsumes it modulo the mgu θ_i.

(3) New state σ_{i+1} : t_1 is replaced by :
$$c_1(b_1 => t'_1, \ ..., \ b_m => t'_m),$$
resulting in the following type:

$$c_0(a_1 => c_1(b_1 => t'_1, \ ..., \ b_m => t'_m) , \ a_2 => t_2, \ ..., \ a_n => t_n) \ \theta_i$$

The process goes on and treats t'_1. The type construction strategy is here similar to Prolog's strategy and computation rule: depth-first and from left to right. The main difference at this level with SLD-resolution is that only types corresponding to non-terminal structures are expanded. Informally, when a type t_j corresponds to a terminal structure, an attempt is made to find a terminal type description t'_j in the program which is subsumed by t_j. If it is found, a replacement occurs. t'_j is said to be in a *final state*. If t'_j does not exist, backtracking occurs. The next type description immediately to the right of t'_j is then treated in the same manner. The type construction process successfully ends when all subtypes corresponding to terminal symbols are in a final state, and it fails if a terminal type description t_p cannot reach a final state.

The above abstract machine can be implemented straightforwardly in Prolog by means of a meta-interpreter. Here is its Prolog implementation:

```prolog
parse(R,R) :-
    atom(R), !.        % An atom, a list or an integer are
                       % basic and are leaves of
                       % the process; they are represented by themselves.


parse(R,R) :-
    list(R), !.                % list is true if R is a list.
parse(R,R) :- integer(R), !.


parse(G,R) :-
    G =.. [A|B],  %Decomposition of the type to be expanded in its head A
              % and in the list of its feature-value pairs B
    symbol_terminal(A),  !,
              % A is a terminal symbol, given in the program
              % as parameters, e.g. :  x0 and morph
          % Cond: conditional part, equals empty if there is no constraint
          % treats, for example, the input/output sequences of words.
          % the symbol if is used instead of | to avoid confusion
    R1 if  Cond,           % Search for a type in the grammar
    glb(G, R1, R),             % which is subsumed by the current type G.
       Cond.        % If R is acceptable, then execution of Cond.


parse(G,R) :- G1 if  Cond,   % General case, G is not a terminal type
    glb(G, G1, G2),              % procedure is similar for subsumption
    Cond,
    G2  =.. [C|T],
          % All the subtypes of G1 are then processed till terminal types
              % are reached for each subtype.
    parse2(T,T1),         % This is realized by the call to parse2.
    R =.. [C|T1].


          % Finally, the result R is reconstructed by term composition.

parse2([ ],[ ]).
```

```
parse2([(A => B) | C ], [(A => B1)|D1] ) :-
      parse(B,B1),
        % separates label from value and call for processing of value
      parse2(C,D1).
        % recursive processing of the list of feature-value pairs
        % computation rule is similar as in Prolog, from left to right.
```

3.5 Generating sentences with ψ-terms

From the above grammar and lexicon, an abstract machine for language generation can also be defined. At the level of type construction, generation proceeds by monotone-increasing restrictions: a phrase structure is described by a type constructor linking a set of subtypes. Such a procedure is monotone-increasing restrictive because the linking operation introduces restrictions on the possible left and right contexts that each of the subtypes could potentially have if they were independent from each other. The degree of generality of the selected type constructor linking those subtypes can be subject to various interpretations. For example, the most general or the most specific type constructor can be chosen.

Finally, generation is guided by the semantic representation of the sentence to be generated. As we shall see below, the semantic representation will determine the computation rule and the subgoal selection procedure. It is thus much more deterministic than its parsing counterpart.

Let us now briefly consider the abstract machine for language generation. The general technique, already presented in Chapter 2, consists of:

(1) writing a formal grammar of the semantic representation from which the generation process starts,

(2) identifying the phrasal units and the lexical units (and intermediate units if necessary) which can be associated with the symbols of that formal grammar,

(3) associating generation points to these symbols (terminal and non-terminal) which will generate natural language fragments based on a consultation of the grammatical and the lexical resources.

Our semantic representation is relatively straightforward, thus it is quite simple to define exactly where to introduce generation points and what their role would be.

It should be noticed that the location of generation points in the grammar rules induces the generation strategy. In the examples presented here, calls to generation points occur after the parsing of the corresponding semantic structure is completed. This means that calls to generation points are stacked (by Prolog) and then unstacked in the reverse order: the strategy is *bottom-up and right to left* or *left to right* depending on generated structures.

Generation points determine, by means of calls to the grammatical system, the resulting syntactic category and the way the partial strings of words are assembled. The way types are constructed by generation points is modelled by the following abstract machine.

The abstract machine for language generation can be described by its initial state and a step in the construction procedure. Similarly to the abstract machine for parsing, it has the general form of a finite state tree automaton. The initial state is σ_0, it is the type :

    x0(cat => C).

Let us now consider a step σ_i .

(1) Two cases arise: it is either

    (a) a set of subtypes from which a more general type can be constructed:

σ_i = (a) $(C_1, C_2, ..., C_n)$ where the C_j form an unordered sequence of subtypes;

    or

    (b) a single type: $\sigma_i = C_1$

(2) Type constructor selection:

Let DC be such that DC has exactly k attributes c_j (the c_i represent constituents as in the examples above),

   $k \leq n$, and DC is of the form:

$DC := xp(..., c_1 => C'_1, ..., c_k => C'_k)$

  and:

    $\forall j \in [1,k], \exists j' \in [1,n], (j_1 \neq j_2 \Rightarrow j'_1 \neq j'_2)$ and $glb(C'_j, C_j, C''_j)$
(notice that the type constructor DC may contain the subtypes together with other information like category and morphology, this is represented here by the dots ...).

After computation of the GLB, if it exists, we have:

$DC' = xp(..., c_1 => C''_1, ..., c_k => C''_k)$

(3) σ_{i+1} = (a) $(DC , C_{k+1}, ..., C_n)$

or
$$(\mathbf{b})\ (C_1, DC).$$

It should be noticed that the constructor DC' is determined according to the existence of a common GLB with t1, which is a process more general and more expressive than standard unification. It corresponds better to the process of incremental generation of phrases. The process ends when a type with category *sentence* is reached. This is a terminal state in the automaton; more precisely it is the root of the tree automaton, since our generation system proceeds in a bottom-up fashion.

Let us now consider step 2 above devoted to the selection of a type constructor. This selection is mainly guided by the generation points given in the formal grammar of the semantic representation. They indeed directly characterize which of the C_i are included in the type construction at the current stage. A Prolog meta-interpreter can be written in the same manner as the parser given above.

4. Inheritance in Feature-Based Systems

In this section we present an extension to Login which allows us to deal with inheritance with conflicting values. We present a meta-interpreted system in which inheritance is parametrized by means of default options. It also illustrates how some internal procedures to Login can be implemented. For the sake of clarity, we concentrate here on inheritance capabilities and we do not consider unification based on a type lattice, which introduces a different kind of inheritance. The inheritance schema we propose in this section can in fact work on top of Login, to improve its inheritance capabilities.

Inheritance may be multiple, i.e. a node may have several mother nodes. Inheritance may also be non-monotonic, i.e. it may involve the inheritance of conflicting feature values. Some aspects of non-monotonicity can be solved in a quite simple way by means of inheritance rules which specify for each feature what is the preferred inheritance in the case of a conflict.

In this section, we present a general purpose program that handles a variety of inheritance situations in feature-based systems, parametrized by inheritance rules.

We present the architecture of this system step by step.

Let us first consider a small knowledge base about verb subcategorization. We have, for example, the following descriptions, with feature-value pairs given *a priori*, without adhering to any precise syntactic theory. The operator isa is introduced to avoid any confusion and conflict in the meta-interpreter, with the subtype operator ◁ of Login.

```
:-  op(600,xfy,isa).
v := x0( syntax => syn( cat => v, bar => 0),
         scat => distribution( subject =>
             xp( syntax => syn( bar => 2,
                 obligatory => 1,
                 case => nominative)))).


v_with_a_direct_cpt := x0( scat => distribution( cpt1 =>
                xp( syntax => syn( bar => 2,
                    obligatory => 1,
                     prep => empty))))     isa    v.


v_with_a_prep_cpt := x0(scat => distribution( cpt1 =>
                  xp( syntax => syn( bar => 2,
                      obligatory => 1,
                      prep => prep))))          isa    v.


v_with_2_cpts      isa    v.


v_with_a_direct_nom_cpt := x0(scat =>
                   distribution(cpt1 =>xp( syntax => syn( cat => n))))
        isa         v_with_a_direct_cpt.


v_with_a_direct_cpt_inf := x0(scat =>
             distribution(cpt1 =>
                 xp( syntax => syn( cat => n, infl => infinitive))))
        isa         v_with_a_direct_cpt.
```

The general call to the inheritance system is:

prop_word_mult(Word, Prop).
which is true if Prop is the structured set of all the properties of the word Word,
for all possible inheritance paths. For example, a call to the subtype
v_with_a_direct_nom_cpt involves the inheritance of the features of v and
the features associated with v_with_a_direct_cpt; it entails the production of
the following value for Prop:

```
?-  prop_word(v_with_a_direct_nom_cpt,  P).


P = x0(syntax => syn(cat => v,bar => 0),
        scat =>
        distribution(subject =>
               xp(syntax =>  syn( bar => 2, obligatory => 1,
                    case => nominative)),
                  cpt1 =>
               xp(syntax =>
                  syn (bar => 2, obligatory => 1,
                     prep => empty, cat => n))))
```

The general call is written as follows :

```
prop_word_mult(Mot,Prop) :-        % call for multiple inheritance paths
   setof(P,prop_word(Word,P),S),
   construct(S,Prop).  % merging by construction of the partial results


   prop_word(Word,Prop) :-          % call for one inheritance path
      set_prop(Word,Set),
      construct(Set,Prop).
   set_prop(Word,Set)  :-
     Word := Y isa Word1,
      set_prop(Word1,Set1),
      conc([Y],Set1,Set).
   set_prop(Word,[Set]) :-          % reaching the root
      Word := Set,
      not(Set = A isa B).
```

The procedure that merges partial type descriptions is construct. The first
argument of construct is a list of feature-value pairs. Feature labels may be of
any complexity, they can in particular be partial subtrees, which are assembled

by this call. The second argument is the result, constructed recursively. This main call is associated with an integration procedure with two subprocedures, integration1 and integration2, whose goal is to treat the different levels of ψ-terms: the type constructor level and the feature label level. Finally, the definition val_term treats terminal values which can be either atoms, integers, variables, conjunctions or disjunctions. These two latter structures are represented by the following terms:

```
and( [ list of elements ] )
or( [ list of elements ] ).
```

The program is the following (the code could have been slightly optimized, but would have obscured readability):

```
construct([S1,[ ]],S1)  :- !.
construct([S1,[ ] |S2],R) :- !,
   construct(S2,R1),
   integration(S1,R1,R).
construct([A],A)  :- !.
construct([S1|S2],  R)  :-
   construct(S2,R1),
   integration(S1,R1,R).


integration([ ],R1,R1).                    % integration operation
integration(S1,R1,R) :-
   S1 =.. [ =>, S2 |S3],
   R1 =.. [=>, S2 |R3], !,
   integration1(S3,R3,R4),
   compose(=>,[S2|R4],R).
integration(S1,R1,R)  :-
   not_liste(S1),                          % S1 is not a list
   not(S1=.. [=>|_]),
   S1 =.. [S2|S3],
   R1 =.. [S2|R3], !,
   integration1(S3,R3,R4),
   compose(S2,R4,R).


integration1([S1|S2],R1,R)  :-
   S1 =.. [=>,S3,S4],
```

```prolog
      atom(S3), val_term(S4),
      inheritance(S1,R1,A,Herit),      % inheritance label A of S1 in R1
      withdraw(A,R1,R2),                  % withdraws the element from R1
                                          % associated to S1, stored in S2

      integration1(S2,R2,R4),
      conc(Herit,R4,R).                % added to what is coming
  integration1([S1|S2],R1,R)  :-
    integration2(S1,R1,R2),
    integration1(S2,R2,R).
  integration1([],R,R).


  integration2(S1,[R1|R2],R)  :-
    integration(S1,R1,R3),  !,
    concat([R3],R2,R).
  integration2(S1,[R1|R2],R)  :-
    integration2(S1,R2,R3),
    concat([R1],R3,R).
  integration2(S,[],S).


  val_term(X)  :-  atom(X).
  val_term(X)  :-  integer(X).
  val_term(X)  :-  var(X).
  val_term(and(X)).
  val_term(or(X)).
  val_term(X)  :-  not(var(X)), X =  A : B.
```

The utilities are the following :

```prolog
  withdraw([],Y,Y).       % withdraws an element from the 2nd arg
                          %  to yield the 3rd arg
  withdraw(X,[X|Y],Y)  :-     !.
  withdraw(X,[H|Y],Z)  :-
    withdraw(X,Y,T),
    conc([H],T,Z).


  compose(and,[S|T],and(T1))  :- !,    % composition of lists
    conc_no_doubles(S,T,T1).            % withdrawal of copies
```

```prolog
compose(or,[S|T],or(T1))  :-  !,
   conc_no_doubles(S,T,T1).
compose(:,[A,B],A)  :-  var(A),  var(B),  !.
compose(S2,L,R)  :-
   R =.. [S2|L].


conc_no_doubles([],Y,Y).              % append without copies
conc_no_doubles([X|Y],Z,[X|T])  :-  not(mb(X,Z)),
        !,          conc_no_doubles(Y,Z,T).
conc_no_doubles([X|Y],Z,T)  :-  conc_no_doubles(Y,Z,T).
```

Finally, here is the treatment of inheritance. Inheritance is called at the level of integration1, to handle conflicting values. It also processes lists of elements in conjunctions and in disjunctions. For that purpose, it uses a specification of incoherent values encoded by means of the predicate :

   incoherent(feature_label, value1, value2)

meaning that for the feature label considered, value1 and value2 are incompatible. For example, for a verb, its aspectual feature aspect cannot be both telic and atelic:

   incoherent(aspect, telic, atelic).

The basic strategy is to give the lower feature value priority over the most global one in the inheritance tree. Different types of rules can be specified. In the examples below, we show how to implement them. Examples such as the treatment of conjunction of features and detection of incoherence have been emphasized. Some choices can be revised and adapted to different theoretical frameworks. The program is as follows:

```prolog
inheritance(X,Y,[],[])  :-  mb(X,Y).         % same elements
inheritance(X,Y,Z,[H])  :-
    mb1(X,Y,Z),                              % same label, different values
    merging(X,Z,H).                          % integration operation


mb1((A=>B),[(A=>C)|_],(A=>C))  :-  !.
mb1(X,[_|Y],Z)  :-
            mb1(X,Y,Z).
```

```prolog
/*    Rules for inheritance    */


        % same label with 2 conjunctions, coherence test
merging((A=>and(B)),(A=>and(C)),(A=>and(D)))  :-
  test_coherence(A,B,C,D),  !.      % D contains what is coherent


merging((A  =>  prep),(A=>X),(A=>X))  :- !.


merging((A=>B),(A=>C),(A=>C))  :-
  C =.. [B|_], !.      % C is of the same type than B, but more precise


merging((A=>B),(A=>and(C)),(A=>and(D)))  :-
  test_coherence(A,[B],C,D),  not(B =.. [and|_]),  !.


merging((A  =>and(B)),(A=>C),A=>and(D))  :-
  test_coherence(A,B,[C],D),  not(C =.. [and|_]),  !.


        % same label, with 2 coherent values
merging((A=>B),(A=>C),(A=>and([B,C])))  :-
  not(incoherent1(A,B,C)),
  not(subsume(B,C)),  !.      % without B subsuming A


% same as above with subsumption
merging((A=>B),(A=>C),(A=>B))  :-
  not(incoherent1(A,B,C)),
  subsume(B,C),  !.


        % same label with two incoherent values
merging((A=>B),(A=>C),(A=>B))  :-
                        % the value of the lower node is kept
  incoherent1(A,B,C),    !.


test_coherence(Add,A,[],A).      % coherence of 2nd list wrt the 1st
test_coherence(Add,A,[B1|B2],[B1|Resul1])  :-
  test_coh1(Add,A,B1),  !,
  test_coherence(Add,A,B2,Resul1).
```

```
test_coherence(Add,A,[_|B2],Resul1)  :-
  test_coherence(Add,A,B2,Resul1).


test_coh1(Add,[],B).
test_coh1(Add,[A1|A2],B)  :-  diff(A1,B),
  ttest_coh(Add,A1,B),
  test_coh1(Add,A2,B).


ttest_coh(Add,A1,B)  :-
  not(incoherent1(Add,A1,B)),  !.


      % test of coherence of a list of features
test_coh_liste(_,[]).
test_coh_liste(Add,[L1|L2])  :-
  test_coh1(Add,L2,L1),
  test_coh_liste(Add,L2).


incoherent1(A,B,C)  :-  incoherent(A,B,C).
incoherent1(A,B,C)  :-  incoherent(A,C,B).


subsume(X,Y)  :-
  (X := T isa Y), !.
subsume(X,Y) :-  (X := T isa Z),  subsume(Z,Y).
```

5. Conclusion

In this chapter, we have shown how feature-based systems can be modelled and implemented in logic programming. For that purpose, we have first presented a simple system that handles feature descriptions and an associated bottom-up parser. Next, we have shown how several elements from Login can be used fruitfully to represent linguistic knowledge and we have presented a parser and a generator which uses a grammar and a lexicon bi-directionally. Finally, we have presented a simple and parametrized way of dealing with inheritance, including inheritance of conjunctions of feature values. These latter examples are relatively simple, but sufficient in many cases. They can easily be extended following the same method.

The type-based approach clearly offers practical advantages for the grammar writer over DCGs and standard logic grammars. It introduces a greater flexibility in the description of feature-value pairs: in a grammatical description or in a lexical description, only the relevant features are mentioned and in any order. The necessity of labelling features also introduces a greater readability. Feature values are typed, which helps grammar writers to ensure that correct values are assigned to each feature. The format of feature-based grammars also enforces declarativity: no procedural attachment or similar mechanisms is present in the formalism. This formalism offers a great degree of transparency to the grammar writer.

At a more abstract level, the logical semantics behind most feature-based systems make the manipulation of feature values more clear. The notion of type constructor presented here is also a major feature that introduces a more refined and principled way of structuring linguistic knowledge and of describing grammatical constructions. These grammatical constructions are no longer real rewriting rules as they were in logic-based grammars (Chapter 3); their semantics is more restricted, and better adapted to the needs of linguistic descriptions.

Several operational systems have been designed using the TFS approach. We have already mentioned some of these in the above sections. There are also several major and large-size EEC projects within Esprit (e.g. the project Acquilex), Eurotra and Eureka (e.g. Genelex and Graal).

From an operational point of view, feature-based systems often suffer from some degree of inefficiency because of the overhead introduced by the type notation. Some projects or studies aim at defining appropriate compilers for these formalisms, for example transforming the feature-based system into DCGs.

Feature-based systems have some similarities and common properties with object-oriented programming languages. Object-oriented programming has been much studied within logic programming and has been shown to be of much interest. This approach is developed in Chapter 7, where comparisons with TFS are made.

Some feature values can be treated as active constraints, enhancing the expressive power of the system, without changing the basic philosophy underlying feature-based systems. This is explored in depth in Chapter 5. Also, some aspects of feature-based systems can be better formulated using a higher-order specification. From that point of view, the use of languages such as λ-

Prolog (see Chapter 8) is of much interest, for example to compute semantic representations. Finally, in Chapter 6, devoted to parallel logic programming, we show how independent feature systems in a TFS can be processed in parallel.

Chapter 5

Constraint Logic Programming for Language Processing

Constraint logic programming (hereafter noted as CLP) emerged from the logic programming paradigm in the past decade and is now playing a major role in a number of various classes of problems and applications. It arose from informal ideas implemented in Prolog II, and was treated in a more comprehensive, systematic and rigorous way in Prolog III (Colmerauer 1990), Chip (Dincbas *et al.* 1988) and CLP(R) (Jaffar and Lassez 1986), to mention the most prominent CLP languages.

Standard logic programming is based on the notion of SLD resolution and on the notion of equality, defined by Clark's equality theory and implemented within Robinson's unification algorithm. Equality has a special status in logic programming: it is directly interpreted and not treated in a symbolic way as is the case for program predicates. Constraint logic programming can be considered as a generalization of this point of view: besides standard predicates which are interpreted in a symbolic way, CLP specifies a set of interpreted predicates called constraints. These predicates operate on specific domains which are not necessarily composed of first-order terms such as booleans, arithmetic numbers, strings of characters, finite domains of various kinds, etc. A constraint of a certain type is resolved by a specific constraint solver which implements its interpretation and reflects its associated properties.

CLP allows us to type variables and to have specific interpretation mechanisms for each type of constraint on a given domain. This approach has several advantages over classical logic programming, which we shall develop in this chapter. As shall be seen, CLP is of much interest to language processing: it introduces a greater expressive power which permits the description of linguistic knowledge at a higher level of abstraction, linguistic adequacy and modularity.

In this chapter, we look at the notion of constraint logic program and explain its basic theoretical foundations. Next, we present and illustrate different classes of constraints which can play a central role in language processing. We focus in particular on the substantial enhancement CLP offers with respect to unification and resolution, and illustrate it with two families of constraints which are probably the most interesting ones for natural language processing: boolean constraints and constraints on finite domains.

To finish this introductory section, let us note that the term *constraint* has a number of interpretations which vary greatly from one linguistic or computational system to another. For example, the right-hand side of a Prolog clause can be viewed as a set of constraints which must be true for the consequent (the left-hand side) to be true. In linguistic systems, the equality or the inclusion of a feature value into another one can also be viewed as a linguistic constraint. Another way to classify constraints can be based on the type of resolution system that can handle them.

The procedural interpretation of Prolog is an interpretation, in which constraints are evaluated locally. If a constraint cannot be resolved at the clause level, then it is often evaluated as false. For example in a statement such as:

    X is Y + 3.

if Y is not instantiated at the moment of the evaluation of this statement, then it is evaluated as false. It would be more appropriate to postpone the evaluation of this statement till Y is bound to a value. The CLP interpretation offers a more global view of the evaluation of a constraint: it postpones the evaluation of that constraint till enough information is available. Constraints are thus evaluated at the level of the global resolution process. This is the reason why these constraints are called *active constraints* to distinguish them from the more classical ones.

Finally, the procedural interpretation of constraints can be based on the notion of generate and test, which is the strategy used in conventional logic programming languages. Constraint resolution can also be based on the notion of an *a priori* pruning of the search space associated with the variables involved in a constraint, when information about the domains of variables subject to constraints is known.

1. Constraint Logic Programming for Natural Language Processing

In this section, we first focus on the basic limitations imposed by conventional logic programming languages such as Prolog, besides their obvious advantages, and then give a brief introduction to CLP.

1.1 Limitations of standard logic programming for natural language processing

Before introducing CLP, let us study in more detail the limitations of Prolog, as briefly described above. One of the first limitations is the *lack of naturalness and of linguistic adequacy* with which linguistic information is encoded in Prolog terms. To illustrate this problem let us consider the well-known problem of linear precedence in grammar rules. A standard grammar rule can be of the following form (with simple arguments):

```
sentence --> np(Number,Person), vp(Number,Person).
```

This rule means that a sentence is composed of an np followed by a vp. Its direct translation into Prolog is not straightforward from a conceptual point of view. Indeed, the comma symbol in the rewrite rule means the linear precedence, whereas in Prolog it means the logical AND. To overcome this difficulty, the difference list technique has been defined (see Chapter 2). The above rule is then translated as follows into Prolog:

```
sentence(X,Y)  :-
        np(Number,  Person,X,X1),
        vp(Number,  Person,X1,Y).
```

Practically speaking, this clause is perfectly adequate. However, from a conceptual point of view, the arguments of the predicates np and vp are of very different natures: some of them represent linguistic information while others are related to the treatment of the structure to be parsed, represented as a list of words. It would be more appropriate to separate these two levels and to have a linear precedence constraint specified at the end of the rule:

```
sentence  :-
        np(Number,  Person),
        vp(Number,  Person),
        np < vp.              % constraint : np precedes vp.
```

During resolution, unification cannot be used to adequately treat precedence; precedence requires a specific treatment, with its own resolution mechanism, which has to be interpreted in some way.

Finally, it should also be noticed that the difference list technique does not directly reflect one of the main properties of linear precedence: transitivity, whereas it is certainly possible and desirable to incorporate this property into the resolution mechanism associated with the precedence constraint.

A second limitation of Prolog is related to the *lack of typing of arguments*. Let us first consider the status of arguments. In a logic program, the domain of any variable is the Herbrand Universe defined by that program. This domain can be defined by a non-ambiguous context-free grammar. A grammar rule (for example, of the form of a W-grammar, a form of grammar which is the closest to definite clauses) is composed of symbols whose arguments range over specific domains, also definable by a context-free grammar. These arguments bear as a consequence a more specific typing than arguments in definite clauses.

In a definite clause, variables being untyped may be bound to any kind of value: an integer, a boolean, a tree, a string, etc. As a result, a unique, very general operation can be used on these variables: unification. Although the use of Prolog terms associated with unification allows an adequate description of a large number of phenomena, it fails to account in an adequate way for a few others. As an example of this limitation, symbols in terms, such as the arithmetic symbols, are uninterpreted and the unification of:

2 + 4   with   4 + 2,

which would be natural, is blocked.

In a number of circumstances, it is thus more adaptable to have the means for typing arguments and to have specific, dedicated operations. More generally, the encoding of a linguistic phenomenon into a term hides some of the natural properties of that phenomenon which are integral parts of that phenomenon and which often turn out to be useful for guiding and, consequently, for improving the efficiency of the resolution process. Furthermore, using Prolog terms often prevents the encoding of the phenomenon at the appropriate level of abstraction: the level of abstraction that would have allowed for the production of more general and more abstract results. For example, it is relatively easy to express long-distance dependencies by means of a specific argument that encodes, for example, a slash category in GPSG, but it almost impossible to encode in an argument the notion of bounding node or the subjacency (or similar) principle. This restrictive principle, that blocks the percolation of long-distance dependencies beyond a certain domain, must be meta-interpreted at the highest level of the parsing or generation procedure.

Another limitation is the *lack of an adequate level of modularity* of Prolog for natural language processing systems. The only real level of modularity is the clause, or the definition (the set of clauses with the same head identifier). This level is often felt to be too low. Such a level of modularity does not indeed permit a full encoding of a linguistic treatment usually represented as a linguistic module. Furthermore, as we have shown above with the difference list technique, all the linguistic and computational aspects are represented in a clause and in a term at the same level. It would certainly be preferable to have these elements represented in different components. This can be better realized, for example, within object-oriented logic programming (see Chapter 7).

In Prolog and, more generally, in standard logic programming languages, a response to a query is a set of substitutions for variables. It would be preferable in a number of situations to have a more 'intensional' formulation of the result, in which relations between variables are expressed. Such an intensional response would directly incorporate in itself the notion of multiple solutions. This can be exemplified by the linear precedence phenomenon presented above in a generation phase. Instead of generating one after the other, via backtracking, all the possible sentences associated with a given internal representation, where the difference between these sentences amounts to permutations of words or phrases, it would be preferable to produce a set of linear precedence equations whose solution space is that former set of sentences.

Finally, Prolog clauses are evaluated at the time they are considered. When information is missing because, for example, it has not yet been evaluated, this may cause a failure where the clause would have otherwise succeeded. Prohibiting postponing the evaluation of a predicate in a clause can be a serious inconvenience when modelling a linguistic treatment for which some elements cannot necessarily be available immediately. Notice that having a procedure that postpones evaluation of a predicate in a clause does not affect *a priori* the declarative semantics of that clause; it simply slightly improves the completeness of the programming language.

1.2 Introduction to constraint logic programming

Let us first introduce the abstract machine which is at the basis of a CLP resolution system. The general form of a CLP clause is the following:

    Head :- Body, { Constraints }.

It thus has the form of a Prolog clause with a special section for encoding constraints. The constraint resolution abstract machine, as presented in Prolog III is the following:

(1) Let us consider a certain stage i in the proof construction procedure, which can be represented by the following triple:

    { W , t1 t2 t3 ...... tn , S }

where :

- W is the set of variables in the original query,
- t1...tn is the current goal to prove and
- S is a set of satisfiable constraints.

(2) To proceed to the next stage i+1, and to produce a new resolvant, there is a selection of a CLP clause in the current program, for example:

    p :- q1 q2 ... qm, { R }.

where R is a set of active constraints. That selection can be made according to various strategies, as can be done within any logic programming language.

(3) If we adopt Prolog's computation rule, then, at stage i+1 a rewriting operation of t1 into the body of the selected clause takes place and constraints are merged, yielding the following triple :

    { W ,   q1 q2 ... qm t2 t3 ...... tn , S∪R∪(p = t1) }

provided that: $S \cup R \cup (p = t1)$ is coherent.

Constraint resolutions and simplifications are performed on this set of constraints. It should be noticed that the notion of the most general unifier has been replaced by the constraint $p = t1$. This equality has a different semantics depending on the type of the terms p and t1. It can also be noticed that, besides constraints, standard terms are treated as in Prolog. We can say that CLP has a global rule-based framework that permits an easy handling of constraints. CLP thus associates unification, resolution and constraint solving. CLP programs aim at being fully declarative and they are soundly based within a unified framework of formal semantics.

CLP rules and resolution procedures will be exemplified in section 2, where we will mainly focus on the gain in expressivity. Let us summarize here the main advantages of such an approach with respect to conventional logic programming languages. These advantages will become more clear in the next section. CLP allows the improvement of:

(a) *efficiency*: whereas Prolog uses the 'generate and test' schema, CLP systems proceed by reducing *a priori* the search space associated with a given variable by taking into account the constraints stated on this variable, i.e. before the generation of the values. The CLP approach usually proposes a single (or a small number of) response(s) to a query; this response being a set of constraints, it potentially contains the different possible solutions to a query, thus avoiding duplication of solutions. It should also be noticed that the resolution method associated with a given constraint is probably more efficient *a priori* than unification since it is specifically dedicated to solve it.

(b) *expressivity:*   since active constraints have a different, more general semantics. CLP introduces new computation domains (i.e. boolean domain, arithmetic domain, finite domains, etc.) besides the usual Herbrand Universe. One can thus directly describe the objects and their properties in the discourse domain.

(c) *genericity and reusability:* since constraints developed for language processing treat very basic aspects. They can therefore be used for different areas of language processing and purposes.

Here are now the major characteristics of the constraints introduced by the constraint logic programming framework (Jaffar and Lassez 1987; Dincbas *et al.* 1988; Colmerauer 1990):

- their *coherence* is checked at each step of the proof construction,

- they are *maintained active* throughout the whole proof construction process until they can be adequately resolved,

- they are *resolved as soon as there is sufficient knowledge available* about their variables,

- they introduce a *greater modularity* since each constraint system is dealt with independently,

- the *result of a query is a set of constraints* on variables from which it is straightforward to define domains of values for variables, furthermore, constraints cannot only be viewed as coming down to defining domains for variables, they also express complex relations between variables,

- *fully declarative* and easy to use since they are directly stated,

- and thus, they are *independent of the way they are used* (e.g. for parsing or for generating sentences, with a bottom-up or a top-down strategy, etc.).

To compare the CLP approach with the well-known 'parsing as deduction' approach, one can say that using a certain lexical entry, translating a certain construction into another one, etc., can be viewed as a general *constraint satisfaction problem.*

2. Boolean Constraints

Boolean constraints may be used for the representation of feature structures and for unifying feature structures with disjunctive and/or negative statements, for instance in the manner proposed by Günthner (1988), as shown in the examples below. One may define boolean constraints as constraints upon terms with boolean arguments, following the method used in CHIP (Dincbas *et al.* 1988). A boolean constraint solver suitable for this approach may be designed starting from the variable elimination based algorithm proposed by Büttner and Simonis (1987). In Prolog III (Colmerauer 1990), the terms that may occur in boolean expressions may be either Prolog terms or constraints.

2.1 A boolean interpretation of feature values:

We now illustrate the treatment of feature structures by means of boolean constraints. Our aim is to show (1) that disjunctive and negated feature structures can be expressed by means of a set of constraints on boolean terms in a simpler way than in DCGs and (2) that unification on feature structures which include disjunction and negation can be replaced in an efficient way by a boolean constraint resolution mechanism that checks for the satisfiability of a set of boolean constraints and that performs simplifications on this set whenever possible.

Let us first illustrate the representation of feature structures with disjunction by means of boolean constraints. Let us consider the string *read*. In terms of morphological features, this string may be associated with the following sets of feature-value pairs, represented here as a logical formula:

read : ((nbr = sing $\wedge$ ((person = 1) $\vee$ (person = 2))) $\vee$

       (nbr = plu $\wedge$ ((person = 1) $\vee$ (person = 2) $\vee$ (person = 3)))))

       $\wedge$ cat = v.

The feature-value pairs nbr, person and cat can be represented as boolean terms, for example as follows:

cat :   s : 111   (represented on three boolean positions)

          np : 100

          vp : 101

          det : 000

          n : 001

          v : 010

          pronoun : 011

nbr :   sing : 0

          plu : 1.

person :   first : 00

          second : 01

          third : 10.

We can then define the two following boolean predicates (or vectors) for handling the above booleans variables:

pers(P1,P2) (e.g. *second* is encoded as pers(0, 1)),

cat(C1,C2,C3) (e.g. *np* is encoded as cat(1,0,0)).

Number remains a single variable, Nb.

Let us now consider a DCG representation of the feature structure of *write*. For that purpose, let us use the SICSTUS Prolog boolean constraint solver syntax (Sics 91). Boolean expressions are composed of the following operands:

(1) the constants 0 and 1, respectively for false and true,

(2) logical variables,

(3) symbolic constants,

(4) logical connectives, defined as follows, where P and Q are boolean expressions and X a logical variable:

~ P is true if P is false (negation),

P * Q is true if P and Q are both true (logical AND),

P + Q is true if at least one of P and Q is true (non-exclusive OR),

P # Q is true if exactly one of P or Q is true (exclusive OR)

X ^ P is true if there exist an X such that P is true.

P =:= Q is equal to ~ P # Q,

P =\= Q is equal to P # Q,

P =< Q is equal to ~ P + Q,

P >= Q is equal to P + ~ Q,

P < Q is equal to ~ P * Q,

P > Q is equal to P * ~ Q and

card(I,E) is true if the number of true expressions in E is a member of the set denoted by I.

Sicstus Prolog also has two built-in predicates:

```
bool:sat(<expression>)
```

which checks for the consistency of the expression with respect to the accumulated constraints, and:

```
bool:labeling(<list of variables>)
```

which instantiates variables according to the accumulated constraints and prints them.

The representation of the feature structure of *read* is then the following in Sicstus Prolog:

```
lex(Nb, pers(P1,P2), cat(0,1,0)) --> [read],
                    {bool:sat( ( ~Nb * ~P1 ) # Nb ) }.
```

The constraints say that if Nb is false (= singular) then P1 must be false (= 0), thus *person* is either first or second, or if Nb is plural then *person* can have any value. This constraint allows us to directly express a relation between two different feature values: if number is singular then person is either first or second and if number is plural, then person can be bound to any value. If at the time this clause is called the variables Nb, P1 or P2 are not instantiated, then the evaluation of the constraint is postponed till they all get instantiated.

Writing directly such a relation in a DCG rule is not possible. The following clause:

```
lex(Nb, Pers, verb) --> [read],
                    {(Nb = sing, Pers < 3 ) ; Nb = plural) }.
```

is not equivalent to the boolean constraint since Nb and Pers may not be instantiated when that lexical entry is called, for example in bottom-up parsing. As a consequence, either any value for Nb and Pers will make the call true or the call Pers < 3 will fail because Pers is a free variable (Pers < 3 can also be written here as (Pers = 1; Pers = 2) , but this does not alter our arguments).

The reader can evaluate the simplicity of the above boolean expression. Underspecified variables are left unbound. Writing this lexical entry in DCG form can be done in two ways:

- by defining as many entries as there are cases which cannot be factored out. For our above example we would have to write three lexical entries, one for the plural with an uninstantiated variable for person and two for the singular,
- by incorporating a notation for the disjunction (and also for negation) into the DCG formalism, which would then have to be either compiled (into 3 clauses as above) or interpreted, involving costly overhead processing.

The same type of entry can be defined for the string *screw*, which exhibits a higher degree of ambiguity since it can be either a noun or a verb:

```
lex(Nb, pers(P1,P2), cat(0,C2,C3)) --> [screw],
      {bool:sat( ((( ~Nb * ~P1) # Nb)  *        % verb definition
                 ( C2 * ~C3)) #
                 ( ~Nb * (P1 * ~P2) *
                 ( ~C2 * C3))) }.              % noun definition
```

Within boolean CLP, unification of two feature structures is replaced by the (partial) resolution of a set of boolean constraints. Let us consider two feature structures F1 and F2. As we have seen it, these feature structures can be rewritten into a set of boolean equations, B1 for F1 and B2 for F2. F1 and F2 unify iff the set {B1, B2} is satisfiable. The result of the unification is that set. To make it as simple as possible, the boolean constraint solver simplifies this set as early as possible.

Let us consider again the string *read*. Let us consider the tense feature: *read* can be either in the present or in the past. If we note the tense feature as follows:

Tense: present = 1, past = 0,

then we have the following representation:

```
lex(Nb, pers(P1,P2), cat(0,1,0), Tense) --> [read],
          {bool:sat( ( Tense * (( ~Nb * ~P1 ) # Nb) ) #   ~Tense)}.
```

Let us now consider the two following pronouns:

```
lex(Nb,  pers(P1,P2),  cat(0,1,1)) --> [he],
                       {bool:sat(~Nb * (P1 * ~P2))}.
lex(Nb,  pers(P1,P2),  cat(0,1,1)) --> [we],
                       {bool:sat(Nb * (~P1 * ~P2))}.
```

Let us finally consider the two sentences *he read* and *we read*. Both require an agreement in number and in person. Since in our examples we only treat these features, we just have to merge the sets of constraints associated with *he* and *read* on the one hand and with *we* and *read* on the other hand:

he read:

```
{( ( Tense * (( ~Nb * ~P1 ) # Nb) ) #   ~Tense), (~Nb * (P1 * ~P2))}
```

which results in, after simplification:

```
{ ~Tense * (~Nb * (P1 * ~P2))}
```

which means that read is necessarily in the past tense.

we read:

```
{(( Tense * (( ~Nb * ~P1 ) # Nb) ) #   ~Tense), (Nb * (~P1 * ~P2))}
```

which results in:

```
{ Nb * (~P1 * ~P2) }
```

and the variable Tense is left unspecified.

2.2 Abstracting over grammar rules: representing X-bar syntax by means of boolean expressions

Boolean constraints also allow us to factor out grammar rules into a single rule. Let us consider a version of X-bar syntax that we can summarize as follows:

X2 --> specifier, X1.

X1 --> X0, complement.

with the following possible distribution:

X = C, specifier = empty, complement = Infl2,

X = Infl, specifier = N2, complement = V2,

X = V, specifier = aux , complement = N2,

X = N, specifier = Det2, complement = P2,

X = P, specifier = Adv, complement = N2.

If we just consider the features for category and bar level, we can write the second rule of the X-bar system as follows:

category notation:

C : 111

I : 110

V : 101

N : 100

P : 011

Adv : 010

Det : 001

```
xp (cat(C1, C2, C3), bar(0,1)) --> xp(cat(C1, C2, C3), bar(0,0)),
                                xp(cat(Cs1, Cs2, Cs3), bar(1,0)),
{bool:sat(((((C3*~Cs3)*((C2=:=Cs2)*(C1=:=Cs1)))  #
        ((~C3*C2*~Cs2*Cs3)*(C1=:=Cs1))  #
        (~C3*~C2*C1*~Cs1*Cs2*Cs3)))  }.
```

The boolean expression states that, in the boolean notation we have defined for the syntactic categories, the complement of a certain category X is represented by the value of X minus 1. The notation X=:=Y in Sicstus Prolog indicates that X and Y are equal. This approach permits us to express by means of a boolean expression a set of rewrite rules that would have required five DCG rules.

Notice that we cannot write an expression such as:

```
xp(Cat, 1) --> xp(Cat, 0), {Cat1 is Cat -1}, xp(Cat1, 2).
```

with the same notation as above because it is not equivalent to the above formulation: for certain parsing strategies (e.g. right to left) the value of Cat may not be known at the time (Cat -1) is evaluated and would thus provoke a failure of the parse.

Other examples of use of boolean features are given by Blache (1992) where the feature system of GPSGs is transformed into a set of boolean expressions, providing the grammatical system with a simpler and more uniform axiomatization.

2.3 Towards more advanced uses of boolean constraints

As can be noted from the previous examples, the use of boolean expressions alters the readability of programs. Boolean expressions must in fact be used only when they allow for a simpler and a more direct formulation of a phenomenon. This is the case, for example, when describing the combination of feature structures with several embedded disjunction or negations. Boolean expressions are appropriate for representing feature values when the domain of values that a given feature may have is relatively small (e.g. less than 16); otherwise, the boolean vector that represents the domain of values is too large (i.e. it would then have more than four binary positions) to be easily usable in a grammatical system.

Besides representing feature-value systems, boolean vectors and boolean expressions can be used to represent linguistic constructions such as trees, operations on trees and basic linguistic principles such as subcategorization and the thematic role assignment criterion (known as the θ-criterion). We illustrate these points below.

2.3.1 Representing trees

The different nodes that form a tree can be numbered in a non-ambiguous way. Let us consider here binary trees, i.e. trees where nodes have at most two daughters. The notation proposed here can be easily extended, however ,to trees of any kind. Let us assign the boolean 1 to the root of a tree. Then, let us adopt the following strategy: the left daughter keeps the number of its mother node and inserts the boolean 0 to the right of that number. For example, the left daughter of the root is noted 01. The right daughter also keeps the number of its mother nodes and it adds the boolean 1 to the right of it. Thus, the right daughter of the root is noted 11. This strategy applies to any node in the tree. If we had nodes with more than two daughters, then vectors would be necessary to represent these nodes.

As an example, consider the following tree:

```
                    n1
                 /      \
               n2        n3
              / \        / \
            n4  n5     n6   n7
                              / \
                            n8  n9
```

It can be numbered as follows:

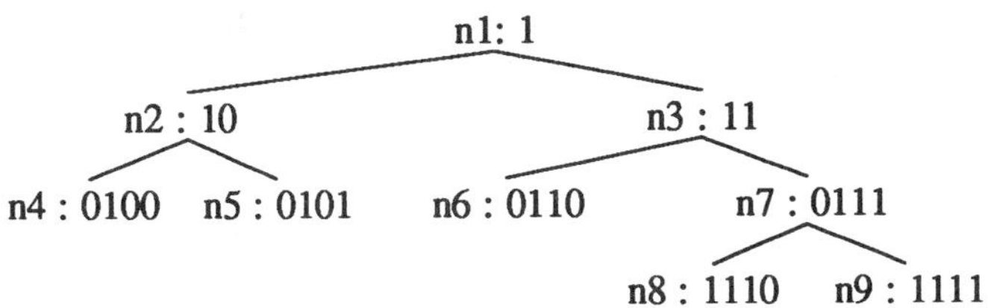

This tree can be represented as a set of vectors of arity 4, to which we also add the name of the node to facilitate the reading. If we call the tree t1, we can have, for example, the following notation:

```
tree(t1,
    [[n1,0,0,0,1],[n2,0,0,1,0],[n3,0,0,1,1],
     [n4,0,1,0,0],[n5,0,1,0,1],[n6,0,1,1,0],
     [n7,0,1,1,1],[n8,1,1,1,0],[n9,1,1,1,1]]).
```

In this representation, notice that, in order to have uniform vectors, we have added as many 0s as necessary before the relevant boolean numbers. In this representation, we have used a single fact to represent the tree, but we could have equivalently used separate facts for each node, as it is illustrated below.

We can now define simple operations on trees, using the properties of that representation instead of inspecting up in the tree, which is usually costly in Prolog. Here is the predicate that defines the notion of immediate dominance, where, in:

```
imm_dominates(A,B)
```

A immediately dominates B. The definition is the following:

```
imm_dominates([N,_,N2,N3,N4],[M,N2,N3,N4,_]).
```

We can extend this definition and write the predicate dominate(Node1, Node2), where Node1 dominates Node2:

```
dominate([A,B,C,D,E], [F, G,H,I,J])  :-
  imm_dominates([A,B,C,D,E], [A1, B1,C1,D1,E1]),
  dominate([[A1, B1,C1,D1,E1], [F, G,H,I,J]).
dominate([A,B,C,D,E], [F, G,H,I,J])  :-
  imm_dominates([A,B,C,D,E], [F, G,H,I,J]).
```

Similarly, we can define a predicate that determines positions of daughters. This predicate is true if in:

```
left_daughter(A,B)
```

A is the left daughter of B. The definition is the following:

```
left_daughter([N,N1,N2,N3,0],[M,N1,N2,N3,1]).
```

2.3.2 Representing subcategorization

Let us now consider again boolean constraints. Let us consider the specification of subcategorization frames which often involves the description of a number of various possibilities. The facilities offered by the disjunction in boolean constraints is of much interest here.

Let us consider again the verb *write*, as defined in section 2.1 above, and let us add its subcategorization frame. For that purpose, we define a two-place vector:

```
subcat(<first object>, <second object>)
```

each category being defined by a three-place vector:

```
subcat1(C1, C2, C3)
```

where the notation given in section 2.1 for syntactic categories is used. These two vectors represent two possible subcategorized phrases. We then have the following lexical entry for the verb *write*, assuming that it can have the following subcategorizations:

(1) object np alone,

(2) two objects: an np and a pp, or

(3) two object nps.

```
lex1(Nb,  pers(P1,P2),  cat(0,1,0),
            subcat(subcat1(Sc11,Sc12,Sc13),
            subcat2(Sc21,Sc22,Sc23)))
                          --> [write],
      {bool:sat( (( ~Nb * ((~P1 * P2) # (P1 * ~P2))) #
            ( Nb * ((~P1 * P2) # (P1 * ~P2) # ( P1 * P2)))) *
            ( (Sc11 * ~Sc12 * ~Sc13) #      % np alone
                                     % np, pp
            (Sc11 * ~Sc12 * ~Sc13 * Sc21 * Sc22 * ~Sc23) #
                                     % np, np
            (Sc11 * ~Sc12 * ~Sc13 * Sc21 * ~Sc22 * ~Sc23))))}.
```

The use of that subcategorization frame in the derivation of a vp can then be defined as follows:

```
xp(cat(1,0,1),          % vp
  subcat(subcat1(Sc11,Sc12,Sc13),subcat2(Sc21,Sc22,Sc23)))
    -->
  lex1(Nb, Pers, cat(0,1,0),     % v
      subcat(subcat1(Sc11,Sc12,Sc13),subcat2(Sc21,Sc22,Sc23))),
  xp(cat(Sc11,Sc12,Sc13)),            % 1st subcat
  xp(cat(Sc21,Sc22,Sc23)).            % 2nd subcat
```

When an `xp` has an unbound category vector, then it is not realized. This implements the optionality of a constituent. The expression of subcategorization by means of boolean constraints can be felt to be a little bit too heavy and too hard to read and to maintain. However, this approach is really well adapted to constituents such as verbs which accept a large number of subcategorization frames. Furthermore, in that case, the parser does not proceed by a generate and test method, which would be really costly, but it simply reduces the search space (i.e. the acceptable subcategorizations) step by step when it treats the different elements in the right-hand side of the derivation.

2.3.3 Modelling the theta criterion

The θ-criterion (Chomsky 1986; Haegeman 1991) can be modelled in a simple way by means of boolean constraints. This criterion roughly says:

(1) that one and only one thematic role must be assigned to each nominal phrase in a proposition and

(2) that each such phrase must be assigned a different thematic role.

Let us consider only four different thematic roles, that we note as follows in boolean terms, using the two-place vector:

```
tr(Tr1, Tr2) :
```

agent : 00

patient : 01

instrument : 10

theme : 11.

Notice that the boolean notation also allows us to directly encode the hierarchy which exists among thematic roles (Dowty 1991; Grimshaw 1991).

The thematic role assignment is often presented as a process independent of (and probably more global than) the derivation rules. Thus, let us simply encode in a derivation rule that the θ-criterion has to be met at the end of the parsing process. If thematic role assignments are done after the derivation, then the evaluation of the constraint will simply be postponed till boolean variables are instantiated. The definition of the θ-criterion in a VP derivation can then be implemented as follows:

```
xp(cat(1,0,1),        % vp
  subcat(subcat1(Sc11,Sc12,Sc13),subcat2(Sc21,Sc22,Sc23)))
          -->
  lex(Nb, Pers, cat(0,1,0),                    % v
      subcat(subcat1(Sc11,Sc12,Sc13),subcat2(Sc21,Sc22,Sc23))),
  xp(cat(Sc11,Sc12,Sc13),tr(Tr11,Tr12)),        % 1st subcat
  xp(cat(Sc21,Sc22,Sc23),tr(Tr21,Tr22)),        % 2nd subcat
                % thematic   roles must be different
{bool:sat((Tr11 # Tr21) + (Tr12 # Tr22))}.
```

In the last line of this program, notice the combined use of the non-exclusive and the exclusive logical OR, represented respectively by the symbols + and # . At the end of the parsing process, if a thematic role has not been assigned to a nominal phrase then evaluation of the constraint is not fulfilled and it rejects the derivation, the θ-criterion will not be met and the parse will fail. The implementation presented here is thus more powerful than unification.

3. Constraints on Finite Domains

Constraints on finite domains can be viewed as an attempt to embed consistency techniques into logic programming (Jaffar and Lassez 1986; Höfeld and Smolka 1988; Van Hentenrick 1989; Cohen 1990; Colmerauer 1990). They form another family of constraints that allow a more powerful and a more flexible treatment of feature values. The basic idea is that most of the set of values which can be assigned to a given feature label forms a finite domain of constants. The introduction of types permits us to avoid the assignment *a priori* of values to variables and to reduce the space of the denotations of these variables when constraints are applied to them. This approach is based on the notion of set intersection rather than on the notion of unification and backtracking.

Constraints on finite domains and *constraint satisfaction problems* are usually solved by means of domain specific consistency techniques. Consistency techniques roughly consist of associating every relevant variable with its domain of values (postulated to be finite), and every constraint defined on these variables with the relation that describes its solution space.

In this section we first examine the use of finite domain constraints in a number of relevant cases, and then introduce and illustrate finite domains and the notion of constraint satisfaction.

3.1 Introduction to constraints on finite domains

In the relation between a head and its complement(s) or modifier(s), there are many phenomena which cannot be reduced in a simple way to a unification problem. This is the case, for example, for controls on subcategorization and on selectional restrictions. The reader can compare the methods used here for the treatment of subcategorization with the use of boolean constraints presented in section 2.3.2.

Example 1: set inclusion in a many-to-one relation

To a verb may be attached different subcategorization frames corresponding, for example, to a transitive or to a di-transitive use of that verb. This subcategorization frame is usually represented as a disjunction of frames, represented here by the set Subcat_frames:

```
vp --> verb(Subcat_frames), np.
```

The well-formedness of the derivation is guaranteed by the adjunction of a control, expressed in terms of inclusion of an element (a subcategorization) into a set:

```
vp --> verb(Subcat_frames),
           { included_into([np],Subcat_frame) },   np.
```

This subcategorization problem can be more complex. Consider the following example, from Martin (1992)[1]:

John knows$_{[-Wh, +Wh]}$ [that whales are mammals]$_{-Wh}$ and
[whether they have lungs or not]$_{+Wh}$.

---

[1] Some native English speakers tend to think that this sentence is agrammatical. In that case, we can consider its French translation, which is perfectly correct:
Jean sait que les baleines sont des mammifères et si elles ont des poumons ou pas.

The verb *knows* has a variable that represents the subcategorization relation it has with its sentential complement. This variable may bear either the value +Wh or -Wh. In that sentence, it must bear both, which is not possible within a unification framework. One may argue that that variable may then be bound to a disjunction: (+Wh $\vee$ -Wh), but this representation is not adequate for two reasons:

  - the disjunction says that one or the other value is appropriate for a given construction, not both.

  - the disjunction fails to capture the 'deep' relation that holds between the subcategorization of the verb *knows* and its complements : an inclusion relation of one set (e.g. [+Wh]) into the other (namely [+Wh, -Wh]). The discussion of representing this disjunction as a type (e.g. ±Wh) is discussed in section 3.2.

A way to model this phenomena in terms of CSP for that precise example, would be as follows:

```
VP --> V(WhSubcat),  S(Wh),
    {domain(X, WhSubcat), domain(Y, Wh), included_into(Y, X)}


S(Wh) --> S(Wh1), [and], S(Wh2),
         { domain(X, Wh), domain(Y, Wh1), domain(Z, Wh2),
             included_into(Y, X), included_into(Z,X)   }.
```

where domain(X,Y) assigns the domain denoted by Y to the variable X; if Y contains disjunctions, then this predicate constructs all the necessary extensions. Thus X may be a set of sets. The predicate included_into permits us to manipulate domains of values and to check for the inclusion of one set into another. These two rules illustrate the way domains are specified and the way they can be reduced. The predicate included_into expresses a constraint between two sets. It cannot be expressed directly in Prolog (and thus the two above rules cannot be directly interpreted as DCGs) since, for example in the second rule above, the variable Wh is free and the determination of its domain would thus be impossible. Wh is not the conjunction of Wh1 and Wh2. Binding Wh to WhSubcat in the first rule above, in order to have an instantiated argument for S in the second rule, would also be linguistically incorrect. The only solution for an appropriate treatement of subcategorization is to have a constraint based on the notion of set inclusion and to check for the satisfiability of that constraint whenever a new inclusion constraint is encountered in the parsing process.

This approach may clearly be used for any phenomena in which a variable may be bound to more than one value in a given construction. This can be the case, for example, with thematic roles, where a given NP may be assigned several different roles, some of them possibly being more prominent than others (e.g. as in buy or sell, (Dowty 1991; Jackendoff 1991), within *secondary predication* (Marrafa and Saint-Dizier 1991) or when a constituent is assigned more than one case.

Example 2: set intersection

Similarly, in a VP, selectional restrictions imposed by the verb on its object must be coherent with the semantic type of the object NP. A constraint must state that the object NP's selectional restrictions must be included into those required by the verb for its object. A basic formulation of this constraint can be the following (leaving aside hierarchies of semantic types):

```
VP --> Verb(Object_NP_selectional_restr), NP(Semantic_type),
        {included_into(Object_NP_selectional_restr, Semantic_type)}.
```

This constraint is simple and can be treated by a DCG. However, in a sentence which includes a cataphor, as in:

When I met her, Mary looked ill.

The control on the object in the subordinate clause cannot be realized at the time the clause is evaluated. It can only be realized when the cataphor is solved, i.e. when the main clause has been parsed. This construction can be treated in a simpler way if included_into is interpreted as a CLP constraint. The control on the object of *met* would then be done in a transparent way as soon as the cataphor is resolved. The above rule is then expressed by the following CLP clause:

```
VP --> Verb(Object_NP_selectional_restr), NP(Semantic_type),
        { domain(X,Object_NP_selectional_restr),
        domain(Y, Semantic_type),
        included_into(X,Y) }.
```

Example 3: trees as finite domains

This example illustrates the way finite domains are handled in a parsing environment. In grammatical systems such as *tree adjoining grammars* (TAGs) (Joshi 1985), the well-formedness of a sentence is based on the existence of a tree, whose root is the axiom (sentence, for example) and whose leaves enumerate, in the correct precedence order, the different words of that sentence. This tree is usually constructed from a predefined set of partial trees, expressing different constructions, by means of two basic operations:

- substitution, where a node at the bottom of the tree being built is replaced by a subtree whose root is that node (including substitutions on the arguments of that node, if any),
- adjunction, where a tree is adjoined either to the right or to the left of a node in the tree.

These operations can be illustrated as follows:

(1) *substitution*: in the following sentence construction:

the symbol np can be substituted by the following tree:

producing the following result:

(2) *adjunction*: the following tree:

can be adjoined, for example to the right of the node vp in the above tree, producing the following new tree:

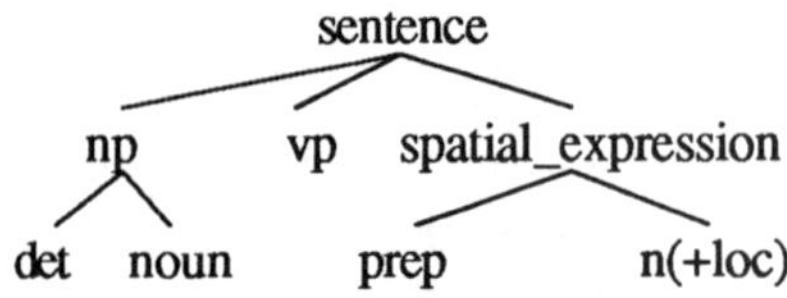

The predefined trees used to construct syntactic trees of sentences form a finite domain. This domain can be subdivided into several smaller finite domains according to their roots. For example, we can define the finite domain of trees having np as root. Thus, to each syntactic category, we can associate a finite domain of trees, modelled for example by a set of rules, whose right-hand sides contain the definition of the domain:

```
np --> {domain(np,
          [<set of trees in parenthetical form with root np>]) }.
vp --> {domain(vp,
          [<set of trees in parenthetical form with root vp>]) }.
```

The same can be defined for terminal symbols, where trees are of the form:

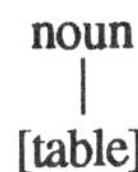

We then have the following definition for the finite domain associated with nouns:

```
noun --> {domain(noun,
          [<set of trees in parenthetical form with root noun>]) }.
```

Constructing a tree in a top-down fashion can then be viewed as a constraint satisfaction problem. Let us examine the construction process, which is a kind of breadth-first search. Starting from the axiom, the symbol sentence, its associated finite domain is selected, domain(sentence,S). Next, the nodes at the bottom of each tree in domain(sentence,S) are associated with the different finite domains they are connected to. For example, if we take the tree above, of which sentence is the root, the finite domains corresponding to np and vp will be associated respectively with the np and the vp nodes. At this stage, these domains can be restricted if np and vp have arguments (not given here) which state constraints on the form of these phrases. The process goes on till terminal elements are reached. At each stage of the process, nodes to which empty domains are connected correspond to failures: the syntactic trees under construction they were associated with are withdrawn from the solution space, and similarly for all the ancestors these trees have originated from in their respective finite domains.

This algorithm, which is still very rough, permits the elimination of solutions that lead to failures sooner than the classical breadth-first search strategy because of the complete elimination of all the ancestors of a tree to which no non-empty domain can be connected as soon as such a node is encountered. As a consequence, unproductive solutions are not considered and efficiency is improved. CSP consistency techniques are based on this principle. This algorithm can in fact be viewed as specifying a form of intelligent backtracking.

3.2 Foundations of constraint satisfaction problems (CSP)

Consistency techniques are developed to solve a class of problems which can be described as a set of constraints placed on variables ranging over finite domains. Let us concentrate on boolean CSPs, which consist of finding the variable bindings which satisfy the CSP constraints (Mackworth 1987).

A Boolean CSP is characterized by the following structures:

- A finite set $V = \{v_1, \dots, v_n\}$ of variables.
- A set $D = \{d_1, \dots, d_n\}$ of finite sets.

The element d_i of D $(1 \leq i \leq n)$ is the domain of the variable v_i of V.

- A finite set $C = \{c_1, \dots, c_m\}$ of subsets of V (i.e., $C \subseteq 2^V$). The members of C are called constraints.

A constraint c_j $(v_{j1}, \dots, v_{jk})$ is said to constrain the variables $v_{j1}, \dots, v_{jk}$.

- A set of relations $R = \{r_1, \dots, r_m\}$ such that:

For all j, $1 \leq j \leq m$, r_j is associated with the constraint c_j in the sense that if $c_j(v_{j1}, \dots, v_{jk})$, then r_j is a subset of $d_{j1} \times \dots \times d_{jk}$.

The relation r_j specifies which values of $v_{j1}, \dots, v_{jk}$ are compatible with each other.

This definition can be illustrated by means of the following well-known example. Given the map:

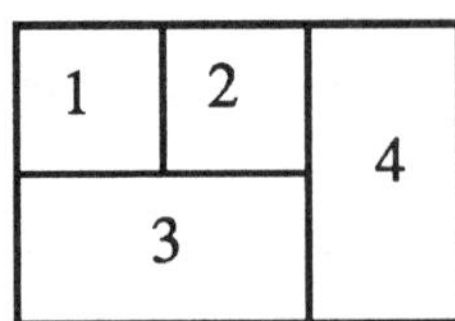

the problem is to colour it with three colors, red, blue and green in such a way that two regions which share a common edge (i.e. which are adjacent) have different colors. This problem corresponds to the following CSP:

- $V = \{v_1, v_2, v_3, v_4\}$
  where v_i ($1 \le i \le 4$) represents the color of region i,
- $D = \{d_1, d_2, d_3, d_4\}$

  where $d_1 = d_2 = d_3 = d_4 = \{r, g, b\}$,
- $C = \{c_{1,2}, c_{1,3}, c_{2,3}, c_{2,4}, c_{3,4}\}$
  where $c_{1,2}(v_1, v_2), c_{1,3}(v_1, v_3), c_{2,3}(v_2, v_3), c_{2,4}(v_2, v_4)$
  and $c_{3,4}(v_3, v_4)$,
- $R = \{r_{1,2}, r_{1,3}, r_{2,3}, r_{2,4}, r_{3,4}\}$
  where $r_{1,2} = r_{1,3} = r_{2,3} = r_{2,4} = r_{3,4} =$
  $$\{<r, g>, <r, b>, <g, r>, <g, b>, <b, r>, <b, g>\}.$$

The notion of a solution of a CSP is an assignment to each variable v_i ($1 \le i \le n$) of an element a_i of d_i such that the constraints $c_1, ..., c_m$ are all satisfied, or, in other words, such that:

$$\forall j, 1 \le j \le m, <a_{j1}, ..., a_{jk}> \in r_j.$$

For instance, a solution of the above map-colouring problem is:

$$v_1 = r, v_2 = g, v_3 = b, v_4 = r.$$

A solution of a CSP is a member of the intersection of the relations of R, or, more precisely, a member of the intersection of the relations $r'_1, ..., r'_m$ resulting from the extension of $r_1, ..., r_m$ to all variables of V.

The CSP resolution techniques are usually based on node consistency techniques (Mackworth 1977; Freuder 1978). They are based on the principle of an *a priori* pruning of the search space, represented by the different domains associated with each variable. In this chapter we shall not go into further detail about these algorithms which are too technical for our purpose. Informal ideas about the way they proceed are given in the example sections.

3.3 CSP and typed feature structures

Besides the CSP approach, there exist other tools and formalisms to treat phenomena such as those presented above in section 3.1 in a successful way. One of these formalisms is type-based unification over a lattice of typed descriptions such as those presented by Aït-Kaçi and Nasr (1986) and Aït-Kaçi and Podelsky

(1990) (see also Chapter 4 of this volume where typed feature structures are introduced). For instance, in example 1, the set [+Wh, -Wh] can be represented by a typed variable, whose denotation (or subtypes) is that set. The notion of inclusion is then replaced by the notion of subtype. Example 2 cannot fit into this type-based framework in a straightforward way since it requires the notion of set intersection rather than the notion of subtype.

More generally, type-based approaches impose restrictions on the nature and on the structure of the objects they manipulate (basically atomic identifiers) whereas CSP does not. Furthermore, types are always structured and thus are processed (e.g. for computing GLBs) according to lattices, whereas any kind of relation r can be associated with a finite domain constraint.

3.4 Set intersection as a CSP

Let us first illustrate the foundations of CSP presented in section 3.2 above by the example 2 given above in the introductory section 3.1. This example, besides the assignment of domains to variables, contains a single type of constraint: the notion of intersection of two sets:

```
vp --> verb(Object_NP_selectional_restr), np(Semantic_types),
          { domain(X,Object_NP_selectional_restr),
            domain(Y, Semantic_types),
            included_into(X,Y) }.
```

The boolean CSP that corresponds to this case of set intersection can be defined as follows:

- V : set of variables: {Object_NP_selectional_restr, Semantic_types}

- D : domains of values: let SL be the set of semantic types which can be used as selectional restrictions, then:

$domain(Object\_NP\_selectional\_restr) = 2^{SL}$

$domain(Semantic\_types) = SL$ (or possibly 2^{SL}, if several semantic types are associated with a nominal phrase).

- C : set of constraints: we have here only one constraint:

  c(Object_NP_selectional_restr, Semantic_types) and c = included_into(X,Y).

- R : set of tuples characterizing the solution of the constraint c: it is the set of tuples such that:

$\forall\ S1 \in domain(Object\_NP\_selectional\_restr)$

$\forall\ S2 \in domain(Semantic\_types)$

$$S2 \supset S1 \ \ or \ \ S1 = S2.$$

3.5 A more elaborate illustration: treating type coercion as a CSP

Type coercion, as defined by Pustejovsky (1989, 1991) is an operation which is rather complex from a computational point of view. It is an operation which is relatively difficult to implement by means of a generate and test method with a depth-first search strategy, as it could be implemented in Prolog. Coercion is more complex than the three motivational examples presented above; it shows in more depth the use of finite domain constraints, how they go beyond the limits imposed by unification and how they contribute to the capturing in a more adequate way the linguistic behaviour of that phenomenon.

3.5.1 Introduction to the Generative Lexicon

Let us first introduce type coercion and function application with coercion as defined by Pustejovsky (1989, 1991, 1993). Type coercion is a semantic operation that converts an argument to the type which is expected by a function, where it would otherwise result in a type error. Type coercion involves a shifting operation that converts a linguistic type into another. Let us assume that any expression E has available a set of shifting operators S(E) which operate over an expression, changing its type, so that E and that expression can be appropriately combined. Function application with coercion (FAC) is defined as follows:

If E1 is of type <b,a> and E2 is of type c, then:

- if the types b and c are identical then E1(E2) is of type a,

- if there is s $\in$ S(E2) such that s(E2) results in an expression of type b, then E1(s(E2)) is of type a,

- otherwise there is a type error.

Let us now illustrate type coercion as it is presented in Pustejovsky's work. In the *generative lexicon* approach, a specific structure is attached to each lexical entry, the Qualia structure, which contains information describing some of the facets of the lexical entry. For that purpose, the Qualia structure is divided into four fields called roles:

- the *formal* role, which describes the elements that allow us to distinguish the object represented by the lexical entry from the other objects in its environment. Among other things, this role includes the description of hyponyms of the lexical entry being considered,

- the *telic* role, which describes the telic aspects of the lexical entry,

- the *constitutive* role which, roughly speaking, describes the various components of the object denoted by the lexical entry,
- the *agentive* role, which describes the agentive aspects associated with that lexical entry.

For example, if we consider the lexical entry for *novel*, we can have the following Qualia structure:

```
word : novel
category : noun
predicate: noun(Y)
qualia:
  formal : book(Y)
  telic : read(X,Y), classify(X,Y)
  constitutive : cover(Z,Y), paper(Z1,Y), ...
  agentive : write(X,Y).
```

To illustrate type coercion very informally between a verb and its object. Let us consider the following sentence:

John begins a novel.

This sentence is ambiguous: it may mean that John starts reading or starts writing a novel. Basically, *begin* requires its object to be of type event. A novel is clearly not of type event, but rather of type object. Type coercion can be applied and two interpretations with type event can be derived respectively from the telic and from the agentive roles in the Qualia structure of novel: *writing a book* and *reading a book* are of type event..

Let us consider coercion from the perspective of syntactic and semantic analysis. Coercion occurs between a governor (E1) and a governed constituent (E2), which usually has the form of an argument. Let us assume for the sake of simplicity that in E1's Qualia structure, the formal role contains the description of the semantic types of the elements E1 may potentially govern. These semantic types are described by means of unary predicates (considered as types):

```
E1 : Formal : [p1, p2, ..., pn]
```

If E1 governs several elements, then the formal role is partitioned according to the restrictions on each of these elements. In a simple situation, where coercion is not used, one of the p_k in the formal role of E1 would directly unify with (or subsume) the semantic type(s) associated with E2. If this turns out not to be the case, then type coercion can be applied.

In the case of an application of type coercion, the formal, telic, agentive and constitutive roles of the Qualia of the governed element E2 contain types, one of which at least must match one of the types in the formal role of E1:

        E2 : Formal : [p'1, ..., p'm]
                Telic : [p'm, ..., p'i]
                Agentive : [p'i+1, ..., p'j]
                Constitutive : [p'j+1, ..., p'n].

Let us assume that the p_i and the p'_j are not clusters of predicates but single n-ary predicates. If the type of one of these elements matches with the type expected by E1, i.e.:

$\exists\ p_k \in$ formal(E1),

$\exists\ p'_t \in$ telic(E2) $\cup$ formal(E2) $\cup$ constitutive(E2) $\cup$ agentive(E2),

such that p_k and p'_t are of the same type,

(or p'_t is subsumed by p_k, if we have a predefined lattice of types)

then type coercion can be applied successfully.

The type of an element p'_t is defined in the lexical entry corresponding to that predicate, e.g. write(X,Y) is associated with the verb *to write* which is defined to be of type event.

The set of shifting operations S applied on E2 (i.e. S(E2)) is the set of all possible type coercions that can be applied on E2, using the different predicates in each roles of E2's Qualia structure. This set can be extended to take into account several successive applications of type coercion. For example, if we represent a type shifting by the role(s) involved, we may have:

$S = \{\ Q_T, Q_A, Q_F - Q_A, Q_T - Q_C, \text{etc.}\}$

where Q_T denotes a type coercion realized using an element in the telic role of E2, $Q_F - Q_A$ represents a two step coercion realized first from an element in the formal role of E2, yielding a new type E'2 (corresponding to a lexical entry L2 of semantic type E'2) and a coercion on that latter type based on the agentive role of L2's Qualia. The following equality must be verified:

$Q_A(\ Q_F(E2)) = Q_A(E'2) = e1$, and $e1 \in$ formal(E1)

The denotation of S is equivalent to the notion of type-path defined by Pustejovsky (1993).

To illustrate a two step coercion, let us consider the two step type coercion $Q_F - Q_C$:

The bank rejected the loan request.

The verb *reject* requires a subject of type human. To fulfil this requirement, the type of *bank* must be coerced to the type human. The type of bank is first coerced to a more general type: organization, via the reference to its formal role (i.e. Q_F) in which it is indicated that a bank is an organization; next, in the constitutive role of organization (i.e. Q_C), we have the information that an organisation is composed of humans, then we can have a second type shifting which allows *the bank* to be an acceptable subject for *reject..*

3.5.2 A declarative semantics for type coercion based on a fix-point semantics

We now give the declarative semantics of coercion. The above presentation of shifting operations allows us to define step by step the set of all the coercion paths for any given pair governor E1, governed element E2.

Let us consider a logic program P comprising a lexicon L and a set of clauses C implementing the coercion operation in logic programming. Let us assume that in L we only consider the Qualia structure and the argument structure. L is then a set of ground instances of lexical entries. The program C is defined roughly as follows:

```
coerce(A,B,[A,B])  :-
          agree(A,B).
coerce(A,B,[A,C|D])  :-
          agree(A,C),
          coerce(C,B,D).
```
    etc.

where A is a type, B a Qualia structure and the third argument of coerce represents a coercion path (or a type-path).

Then we can define S0 as being the set of all ground instances of unit clauses of L and C. S0 contains L in full, since L is a set of ground instances, and those predicates in C which are ground. If unit clauses contained variables, then they are replaced by the appropriate elements of the Herbrand Universe associated with the program P. Let us now consider the clauses of P and among these clauses the ground instances of those clauses where all the literals in the right-hand side are elements of S0. Let T(S0) be the set of heads of these ground clauses. T(S0) is the set of all ground terms constructed in a single step from the clauses of P. In our case, T(S0) characterizes all the coercion paths of length 1, i.e. the direct agreements. We have the result that S0 is included into T(S0). Similarly, T(T(S0)) characterizes the coercion paths of length 2, i.e. with reference to one intermediate constituent.

Let us now define $T^n(S0)$ as the result of n applications of T to S0. Since at each step of application of T, new ground instances may be produced, we have the following result:

$T^{n-1}(S0) \subseteq T^n(S0)$.

Let now, at a certain stage w, lfp be the least fix-point of T:

$T^{w-1}(S0) = Tw(S0)$.

$T^w(S0)$ is the smallest set such that this equality is true and it results in the application of T till no more ground instance is produced (Lloyd 1987). It characterizes the set of all possible coercion paths from any constituent to any other one.

From the definition of the fixed point follows an important result (Van Emden and Kowalski 1976):

coerce(X,Y,Z) is a logical consequence of P iff coerce(X,Y,Z) is an element of $T^w(S0)$.

Similarly, it is possible to define the finite failure set of P from which we are able to say if not(coerce(X,Y,Z)) is a logical consequence of P. These two problems are decidable in a finite amount of time since coercion path are finite (following from the finiteness of L, and the fact that, by construction, there are no cycles in coercion).

3.5.3 Type coercion in CSP

The reader may infer from the previous examples that the set S of shifting operations defined from a given entry may be relatively large. The determination of the correct type coercion or sequence of type coercion to apply is not straightforward and can hardly be directed by heuristics. There may also not exist a single solution because sequences of type coercion define a directed graph where nodes represent the different derived types. Psychological considerations allow us to think that the number of type coercions which can be successively applied on a given construction is strongly limited, i.e. a maximum of three to four applications. Consequently, since the size of any Qualia structure is finite (and probably also quite limited) the set of sequences of type coercions which may be constructed from a given lexical entry forms a finite domain. The derived types also form a finite domain of types.

Let us now show how coercion can be modeled in terms of a CSP. We have the following modeling:

(1) V : is composed of two variables P and T that respectively represent

      (i) predicates of lexical entries

      (ii) the types involved in the domain.

(2) D : is the set of domains associated with each of these variables: the set of predicates and the set of types. The definition of these domains depends on the grammar and the lexicon which have been defined.

(3) C : is the set of constraints. These constraints are the set of all shifting operations from any type to any other type. For example, it may be defined as follows:

$$S = C = \{\ Q_T,\ Q_A,\ Q_F - Q_A,\ Q_T - Q_C,\ \text{etc.}\}$$

where:

$$Q_T,\ Q_A,\ Q_F - Q_A,\ Q_T - Q_C,\ \text{etc.}$$

is as defined above. We can thus define *a language of constraints* which includes the different kinds of type coercions.

(4) R : gives the solution space for each constraint in C. This solution space is defined on P x T x T and it is given in terms of tuples of the form:

(predicate of word involved, original type, shifted type).

There is *a priori* no formal constraints on the definition of these tuples. For example, for the word novel as defined above, we have in R the constraint Q_T and the following tuple:

```
(novel(Y), object, event).
```

For practical reasons, to form a comprehensive set, R includes the empty coercion, where the original and the coerced types are identical. Original and shifted types, from a linguistic point of view, must be precise enough to avoid any ill-formed type coercion.

Type coercion can then be defined in terms of a CSP :

If E1 is of type <b,a> and E2 of type c, then :

- if c = b then E1(E2) is of type a,

- if there is an element s $\in$ C whose solution space r_i contains a tuple (predicate(E2), c,b) then E1(E2) is well-formed and is of type a,

- otherwise a type error is produced.

As can be seen from this definition, the CSP interpretation of type coercion is very close to the original formulation. It does not affect the notion of coercion, but it simply establishes a different mode of determination of the derived type. It also provides type coercion with a simple and declarative, computationally tractable interpretation which leaves a great freedom in the definition of what are the possible acceptable coercions for a given type (some coercions, technically possible, may turn out to be linguistically incorrect). This interpretation becomes more interesting and more efficient when the constituents of a phrase or a sentence are subject to various, non-independent forms of coercions. There may indeed exist, as in the map-colouring example above, constraints between several variables denoting linguistic constituents.

Let us now summarize the advantages to using a CSP approach to deal with type coercion. The determination of the set of tuples in R can be seen as a partial evaluation: to each lexical entry it is possible to attach a set of appropriate tuples r_i. Then, DCGs can perfectly be used. However, instead of using the generate and test strategy, the CSP approach associates with every variable a domain which is restricted each time a constraint on that variable is found. From that point of view, CSP offers two advantages:

- it is more efficient since there is no backtracking,

- it is more expressive since when several type coercions can be legitimately applied to validate a construction, it gives all the solutions at the same time.

Next, from a control point of view, the inclusion in R of the empty coercion (i.e. the case where coercion is not necessary) implicitly resolves the problem of determining when to apply coercion (e.g. when all the 'regular' attempts have been performed). In a DCG approach we would most probably examine all possible parses without coercion first and then would apply coercion in case of failure.

Finally, let us consider the case of co-composition (Pustejovsky 1991), where two constituents mutually influence each other, as in:

bake a cake

where *bake* is basically of type process and where *a cake* is an object which comes to being when it is combined with the verb *bake*. It is then of type transition. As a consequence, the type of *bake* must be coerced to become a transition. Let R1 be the set of tuples describing the possible coercions of *bake* and R2 the set of tuples associated with *cake*. Then the VP is well-formed if and only if the intersection of R1 and R2 is not empty. The resulting type is then that intersection. The notion of intersection directly captures the idea of co-composition.

4. Other Types of Constraints for Language Processing

To end this chapter, let us briefly consider two other types of constraints which may be useful for natural language processing: the linear precedence constraint and an interpretation of Dislog (see Chapter 3, section 5) in terms of active constraints.

4.1 Constraints based on the precedence relation

The linear precedence constraint we present here and two variants may be used to enhance logic grammars expressiveness and declarativeness. They can be associated with systems such as type feature systems (TFS). Linear precedence relations describe relations between symbols that belong to a single grammar rule; precedence relations are global, however, since they constrain the whole syntactic structure.

4.1.1 The precedence constraint

The most general and basic constraint is the linear precedence constraint (Saint-Dizier 1991). It has the following form:

precedes(A, B).

This constraint states that the syntactic structure derived from *A* must linearly precede the syntactic structure *B*.

Grammars can be written in which precedence relations are specified whenever necessary. Precedence constraints can also be stated within lexical entries (considered as terminal elements of the grammar).

This constraint is particularly useful for writing grammars for free phrase order languages in a very elegant and economic way. Besides, it is interesting from a computational point of view since it has the good properties (solution-compactness and satisfaction-completness) described by Jaffar and Lassez (1987a) which ensure the possibility of designing a consistent and sound constraint solver.

We propose below a comprehensive algorithm, which is simple to understand, even if it may not be the most efficient one. It clearly shows the gain in efficiency that we get, in particular when we have a certain degree of free constituent ordering.

In addition to the precedence constraint, we can add to these grammars two more specialized constraints, namely an immediate precedence constraint and a connectedness constraint. They are briefly presented below.

4.1.2 The immediate precedence constraint

The immediate precedence constraint (Hathout and Saint-Dizier 1992) has the following form: *immediately_precedes(A, B)* and states that the part of the syntactic structure derived from *A* must precede the one derived from *B* and that these two structures must be adjacent. We can describe this constraint by means of the precedence constraint in the following manner:

$$\text{immediately\_precedes(A, B)} \Leftrightarrow$$

$$(\text{precedes(A, B)} \wedge (\neg(\exists C, \text{precedes(A, C)} \wedge \text{precedes(C, B)})))$$

The immediate precedence constraint constitutes a tool for writing grammars which is finer than the precedence constraint and thus is, in many cases, more adequate than the latter. Besides, it is also more restrictive than the latter and thus increases the efficiency of the NL systems.

4.1.3 The connectedness constraint

The second constraint is a connectedness constraint (Hathout 1992). It has the following form *connected(X)*, where X is either a symbol of a grammar rule or an unordered list of symbols occurring in the right-hand side of a grammar rule. This constraint states that the part of the syntactic structure derived from X must be connected, i.e. a symbol not dominated by X cannot occur between symbols (according to the linear precedence relation) dominated by X. This can be reformulated by using the precedence and the domination relations in the following way:

$$\text{connected(X)} \Leftrightarrow (\forall C, \text{dominates(X, C)} \vee \text{precedes(C, X)} \vee \text{precedes(X, C)})$$

where the definition of the precedence constraint is extended in a natural way, i.e.:

$$\text{precedes(A, [B1, ..., Bn])}$$

is equivalent to the conjunction:

$$\text{precedes(A, B1)} \wedge ... \wedge \text{precedes(A, Bn)}.$$

However, the connectedness constraint is not a macro with respect to the precedence one. We need to design some specific resolution algorithms to cope with it. On the other hand, the immediate precedence constraint can be regarded as a kind of macro since:

$$\text{immediately\_precedes(A, B)} \Leftrightarrow (\text{precedes(A, B)} \wedge \text{connected([A, B])})$$

The connectedness constraint can be used, for example, to state that a phrase must be connected. This can be described by associating the constraint *connected(XP)* with the rules which describe the phrasal elements.

We can thus see that the precedence constraint is a very basic one, and that several others may be defined on top of it. Moreover, these constraints form a tool which makes the grammars more expressive and also more declarative since precedence, adjacence, and connectedness relations are explicitly stated.

4.2 A CLP interpretation of the precedence constraint

Precedence constraints can be treated as active constraints. The main advantages of this approach are the following:

(1) A string of words, potentially candidate for a sentence being generated, is discarded as soon as an incoherence among precedence constraints is detected.

(2) The way precedence constraints are treated, as shall be seen below, does not provoke bactracking, but, simply, a potential solution is no longer considered.

(3) Instead of producing, via backtracking, a set of sentences, the result of the parsing or generation process is a set of sets of precedence constraints. This gives an intensional specification in terms of constituent precedence of the well-formed sentences constructed from the grammar and the input form (a logical form, for example).

(4) Precedence constraint resolution mechanisms can be used for parsing as well as for generating sentences. It is of much interest for generation since all solutions can be produced at once. These constraints can also be used at a discursive level.

4.2.1 General treatment of the precedence constraint

Let us now examine the main features of the precedence constraint resolution mechanism. As explained in the preceding sections, each time a new step in the sentence processing is performed, constraints are added to the current set of active constraints and their consistency is checked. At the beginning σ_0 of the processing, the set of active constraints is either:

(1) equal to the set of constraints derived from the position of the words in the sentence, if we are in a parsing process. This set of constraints defines a complete order, or

(2) empty if we are in a generation process.

The general process can then be summarized as follows:

(1) Step σ_i: satisfiable set of active precedence constraints { S }.

(2) Selection of a rule describing a phrase structure with a set R of precedence constraints R.

(3) Step σ_{i+1} : set of active precedence constraints:
  { S ∪ R ∪ R' }
if the set of precedence constraints is consistent and R' is an additional set of precedence constraints, which is a consequence, as shall be seen below, of the merging of S and R.

We now define R' in more detail. One of the major motivations of R' is that the treatment of sentences will be done on the basis of precedence constraints on terminal elements. This is the reason why each time a phrase structure construction A --> B, C is used, the constraints on A must also be applied to B and C by transitivity, whenever appropriate. To derive these new constraints, let us introduce the notion of left and right corner of a derivation and then give a formal specification of the new precedence constraints that apply to these two corners. This fully defines R'.

When a phrase-structure construction rule does not have a complete order on its right-hand side symbols, then left and right corners are not unique. R' is then a disjunction of sets of constraints, each element of the disjunction correponding to a choice of left and right corner. When an element of the disjunction is not coherent with S ∪ R, then it is eliminated.

4.2.2 Left and right corners

Let a phrase structure type be of the form (we use the rule notation to facilitate understanding, but this is equivalent to the type notation previously introduced) :
  A --> B, { P }.
where B is a set of symbols and P is a set of precedence constraints. The set of possible left corners CG for B given P is defined as follows:
  CG = B - { E ∈ B | ∃ X ∈ B, p(X,E) ∈ P }.
E is thus a symbol which must be preceded by another symbol in B; it cannot therefore be a left corner.

Similarly, we define the set of possible right corners CD for B given P:
  CD = B - { E ∈ B | ∃ Y ∈ B, p(E,Y) ∈ P }.

In this case a symbol E which must precede another symbol cannot be a right corner.

From the CG and CD, we can define the set CGCD of all possible pairs of left and right corners for B given P; it is the cartesian product of the two sets without pairs comprising identical elements, since a symbol cannot be a left and a right corner at the same time:

CGCD = CG X CD - { (X,Y) | X = Y }.

At this stage, we must say a few words about the case where B has only a single element. Then, since this rule cannot have any precedence constraints, the single element is both a left and a right corner.

To conclude this section, let us consider a simple example. Consider the rule:

a --> b, c, d, e, f, p(b,c), p(d,e).

We then have:

CG = { b, d, f },
CD = { c, e, f },

and, finally:

CGCD = { (b,c), (b,e), (b,f), (d,c), (d,e), (d,f), (f,c), (f,e) }.

4.2.3 Precedence constraints associated with each pair in CGCD

Besides precedence constraints coming from the rule itself (i.e. R), there are additional constraints (R') which have to be added to the set of active constraints. Let us consider again the general rule format given above; we then have the following constraints in R':

(1) The first constraint follows from the choice of a given pair in CGCD. If p(W,Z) is selected, then we have the precedence constraints p(W,Z). From this choice will follow additional constraints. Each pair in CGCD originates a different set of precedence constraints. As a result, we have a disjunction of sets of precedence constraints.

(2) From a pair in CGCD, we deduce that all symbols preceding the left-hand side symbol A of the rule also precede the left corners of that rule and that all symbols preceded by A are also preceded by all their respective right corners. More formally, for each left corner cg in CG we have the following additional constraints:

{ p(X, cg) | ∃ p(X,A) ∈ S } (S is the current set of active constraints).

Similarly, we have for each right corner cd in CD:

{ p(cd, Y) | ∃ Y, p(A,Y) ∈ S }.

To summarize, from the set of pairs (cg,cd) in CGCD, we get a set R' of constraints of the form:

$$R' = \{ R'_1, R'_2, \ldots, R'_n \}$$

where:

$n = card(CGCD)$,

R'_i, to which corresponds the pair $(cg_i, cd_i) \in CGCD$ such that:

$$R'_i = p(cg_i, cd_i) \cup$$
$$\{ p(X, cg_i) \mid \exists \, p(X,A) \in S \} \cup$$
$$\{ p(cd_i, Y) \mid \exists \, Y, p(A,Y) \in S \}.$$

Finally, $S \cup R$ is merged with R', the R'_i which are inconsistent are withdrawn. Possible simplification, to avoid redundancy, is also performed at this level. The result is a disjunction of sets of constraints. If the disjunction is empty, then there are no solutions to the sentence being processed (i.e. it is ill-formed or it cannot be generated).

As an illustration, if we consider the above example and have:

$$S = \{ \, p(f,a), \, p(g,a) \, \},$$

we then have, for the pair in CGCD (b,c), the following set R'_j:

$$R'_j = \{ \, p(f,b), \, p(c,g) \, \}$$

and for the pair (d,c), we get:

$$R'_k = \{ \, p(f,d), \, p(c,g) \, \}.$$

Suppose (for short) that we only have the two above pairs in CGCD, we then get the following new set S of active constraints composed of a disjunction of two sets:

$$S = \{ \, \{ \, p(f,a), p(a,g), p(b,c), p(d,e), p(f,b), p(c,g) \, \},$$
$$\{ \, p(f,a), p(a,g), p(b,c), p(d,e), p(d,c), p(f,d), p(d,c) \, \} \, \}.$$

Notice that in the first set an occurrence of p(b,c) has been eliminated to avoid redundancy.

4.3 A CLP interpretation of Dislog

Another class of constraints of much interest for syntactic processing but also for many other types of processing is the expression of long-distance relations between constituents in a syntactic or semantic structure. The notion of long-distance dependency can be formulated in at least two different ways:

(1) by a feature like in GPSGs (a Slash feature), or

(2) by a sub-type co-occurrence constraint. This constraint could emerge, for

example, from Dislog (see Chapter 3, section 3). In that case, it is a kind of meta-constraint since it operates on the predicates included in the grammar rule and not on their arguments.

Let us consider here the treatment of long-distance dependencies as a co-occurrence constraint. The pending constraint:

    pending(A,B)

can be defined and interpreted within the constraint logic programming framework in a very simple way, as can be seen below.

The domain of objects on which constraints of a CLP interpretation of Dislog operate is a domain of grammar rules (which could also be viewed in a type system as type constructor definitions, as presented in Chapter 4). Let us first consider a simple translation example of a Dislog clause into a CLP clause. A Dislog clause like:

    {(a --> a1), (b --> b1) }

where a1 and b1 denote any finite sequence of terminal and non-terminal symbols, can be translated as follows in CLP:

    a --> a1,   {pending(a, [b])}.
    b --> b1,   {pending(b, [a])}.

According to the semantics of Dislog, the constraint pending(A,B) states here that the derivation A is at the origin, and also implies, the derivation B. The general case is treated as follows. Let us consider the Dislog clause:

    { (a --> a1), (b --> b1), ..., (n --> n1) }.

It is translated into a set of CLP clauses as follows:

    a --> a1, { pending(a, [b, ..., n])}.
    b --> b1, { pending(b, [a, ..., n])}.

    ...

    n --> n1, { pending(n, [a, b, ...])}.

The constraint resolution procedure associated with the pending constraint consists in a simplification rule for the elimination of pending derivations when the co-occurrence constraint is satisfied. This simplification rule is written as follows for the first example given above:

    pending(A,B) ∧ pending(B,A) --> ∅ .

Notice that we have a symmetric treatment for the derivations A and B. Generalizing from the above simplification rule, the general simplification rule is the following, where LA, LB and LC are lists of pending derivations:

```
(pending(A, LA), pending(B, LB) --> pending(A, LC)  ) :-
   mb(A, LB),
   mb(B, LA),
   withdraw(B, LA, LC).
```

LC is the resulting pending list where B has been withdrawn from LA.

This constraint resolution mechanism can be further extended quite straightforwardly to handle linear precedence restrictions and modalities. Linear precedence constraints are dealt with independently from each other. The Dislog clause:

$$\{ (a \to a1), (b \to b1), \ldots(x \to x1), \ldots, (y \to y1), \ldots, (n \to n1) \}$$
$$\ldots, precedes(x, y) , \ldots$$

is translated into a CLP clause as follows:

```
x --> x1,
   {pending(x, [a, b, ..., ..., y, ..., n]),
        not (pending(y,[a, b, ..., x, ..., ..., n]))}.
```

The coherence control is the following:

```
pending(X, LA) ∧ not(pending(X, LA)) --> failure.
```

and the simplification rule is:

```
not (pending(Y, [A, B, ..., X, ..., ..., N] )) --> ∅
```

or, more simply, since all negations are withdrawn at each stage:

```
not (pending(_,_) -->  ∅ .
```

Let us now consider the treatment of modalities. Modality m applied to a clause allows that clause to be used any number of times, provided that the other clauses in the Dislog clause are used. The Dislog clause:

$$\{ (a \to a1), (b \to b1), \ldots, m(x \to x1), \ldots, (n \to n1) \}.$$

is translated into a CLP clause as follows:

```
a --> a1,  { pending(a, [ b, ..., m(x), ..., n])}.
x --> x1,  { pending(m(x), [ a, b, ..., ..., n])}.
```

The general simplification rule is the following:

```
(pending(A, LA) , pending(m(B), LB) --> pending(A, LA) ) :-
   mb(m(B), LA),
   mb(A, LB).
```

Notice that the occurrence of m(B) is not withdrawn from LA, so that clauses marked with modality m can be used any number of times. In this simplification rule, there is no hypothesis on the form of A which can itself be marked with modality m.

5. Conclusion

In this chapter, we have shown a different way of modelling and of implementing some linguistic constructions by means of active constraints of the constraint logic programming framework. We have first emphasized two types of constraints: boolean constraints and finite domain constraints. We have shown what were the gains in expressivity, linguistic adequacy and efficiency. Efficiency remains to be proved, however, since the available systems are generally not yet very efficient. We have concluded this chapter with the presentation of two other types of constraints which can be interpreted within the CLP framework: linear precedence constraints and the treatment of long-distance dependencies, as modelled in Dislog.

We have not shown other classes of constraints which are prominent in CLP but which seem to us to be of lesser interest and practical use for natural language processing, such as arithmetic constraints (which could be used, for example, to treat linear precedence and immediate dominance).

Active constraints are still in an early stage of development. As a consequence, they lack conception and programming methods, and it is relatively difficult to evaluate exactly when such an approach would be appropriate and how to model a problem in terms of active constraints, in particular in terms of a CSP, since boolean constraints are rather simple to use.

The formal and practical relations between finite domains and type-based systems (see, for example, Aït-Kaçi and Nasr (1986); Carpenter (1992) and Pfenning (1992)) remain to be explored in more depth. Some elements of comparison are given in section 3.3. In the same spirit, using CSP and boolean constraints within a linguistic engineering framework has to be further explored and evaluated. It seems to us that constraints could fulfil some criteria of modularity, genericity and independence from any processing strategies, criteria which are claimed to form the basis of a good linguistic engineering tool.

Chapter 6

Parallel Logic Programming for Language Processing

Parallel logic programming emerged in the past decade as a new field in logic programming and is now a domain under active research and development. Several types of methods and strategies for dealing with parallelism and concurrency have been specified and implemented for logic programs on parallel and sequential machines. On sequential machines, parallelism is simulated on a single physical processor by sharing processing time and memory space between the different processes. This allocation and the order in which clauses in a program are to be considered are often defined *a priori* at the time the program is compiled. It is then managed by a supervisor at execution time.

Parallel logic programming has several advantages over standard logic programming. From the point of view of procedural semantics, parallelism improves efficiency (on machines which can support real parallelism, i.e. multiprocessor machines) and ensures completeness. Completeness is indeed ensured because all solutions to a query are searched in parallel. Thus, for example, the risk of entering into an infinite loop at a certain stage of a proof procedure leading to failure or interruption (as it would be the case in Prolog, for example, when there is a stack overflow), is eliminated since the different processors working in parallel are autonomous. The other advantage to using parallel processing, is that less attention has to be paid *a priori* to control issues when programming and that, consequently, programs are more declarative. However, in order to guarantee acceptable efficiency, some elements related to control are often included into parallel languages.

Parallel processing is of much importance for natural language processing. There are indeed often relatively independent tasks which can be executed in parallel. A simple example is morphological agreement. Agreements in gender, number, case, person and tense are independent from each other and can be processed in parallel. For a grammar rule to be applicable in a given situation, all stipulated agreements must be satisfied. Parallel processing of these agreements detects agreement failures much earlier than in conventional logic programming. Another more elaborate example is the parallel treatment of the active constraints presented in the previous chapter, which form independent systems.

Parallel systems and languages are not yet widely used. However, parallel language implementations and programming methods are sufficiently developed at this stage to show that parallelism can be used and is very useful in a number of situations, and that it is going to play a crucial role in the development of various applications.

In this chapter, we first present the basic principles of parallel logic programming. Then, in section 2, we focus on one of the main parallel languages: Parlog. We illustrate its concepts by means of simple natural language processing examples. Section 3 introduces a more comprehensive treatment of parsing in Parlog, including the treatment of feature-based systems.

1. Introduction to Parallel Logic Programming

In this section, we present the basic notions of parallel logic programming. Concepts presented here extend those introduced in chapter 1. In this chapter, we first present the different types of non-determinism, and associated types of parallelism. Subsequently, we introduce the notion of the *guarded Horn clause*, aspects of synchronization between processes and the problem of shared variables between processes. Finally, we survey different available parallel logic programming languages.

1.1 And- and or- non-determinisms

Kowalsky (1979) discusses two kinds of non-determinism in logic programming:

(1) non-determinism in the choice of a clause in a definition composed of more than one clause,

(2) non-determinism in the order in which the goals in the body of a given clause are executed.

These two levels of non-determinism can be fully taken into account by a parallel system: all possible choices are treated as parallel (or concurrent) processes. These two levels define two types of parallelisms:

(1) *or-parallelism*: unifying a goal with several clauses at the same time, as opposed to clause-by-clause unification, starting with the first clause as is the case in Prolog,

(2) *and-parallelism*: selecting all the goals in the body of a given clause and executing them in parallel.

As an illustration, let us consider the following grammar for noun phrases:

```
(1)  np(G,N,X,Y) :-
        det(G,N,X,X1),
        noun(G,N,X1,Y).
(2)  np(G,N,X,Y) :-
        det(G,N,X,X1),
        adj(G,N,X1,X2),
        noun(G,N,X2,Y).
(3)  np(G,N,X,Y) :-
        proper_noun(G,N,X,Y).
```

In a parallel environment, a call to np will result in:

(1) a parallel execution of the three definitions given above for np (or-parallelism) and

(2) for each clause, a parallel execution of the goals in its body (and-parallelism).

In a real situation, since machines do not have an infinite number of physical processors (or even a sufficiently large number of them), each processor treats several goals. To realize real parallelism, when a physical processor is in charge of several goals, then it treats them in a random way and allocates each of them either a fixed or a variable processing time and memory space. If the goal has not been proven within the allocated time, then its current state is saved in the list of active goals and it will be activated again later, according to the policy of that physical processor. Notice that different physical processors in a given machine may be tuned differently. The way goals are treated in parallel on a physical machine is thus transparent to the programr and a given program may be executed in a number of different ways. In the remainder of this chapter, we use the term *processor* to designate a physical processor, independent of the way it is taken into account in a given physical machine. A *process* is associated with each goal to be proved.

Although there are several strategies, a parallel system works roughly as follows on the example given above. When there is a call to np, three processes are activated in parallel in an attempt to unify the call with the heads of the three clauses of the definition of np. If there is a success in the unification of the call with the head of a clause, then as many processes as there are goals in its body are activated to treat these goals in parallel. For a given clause, the processes stop either when all the goals have been fully proven or as soon as one of the goals in the body results in a failure. For example, if unification with the three np heads succeeds, then six processes working in parallel are activated to treat the bodies of these three clauses. Then, for example, if in the second clause the call to adj fails, then this second clause fails and its associated process is no longer active.

The following diagram shows how and when processes are activated. Elements on an horizontal line are all excecuted in parallel:

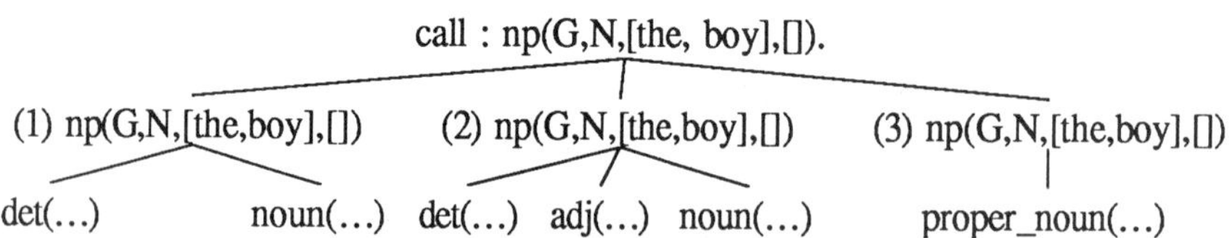

This diagram is a snapshot of the system when unification has succeeded on the three heads and when the goals of the different bodies of these clauses are being considered. It should be noticed that the three heads do not necessarily require exactly the same amount of time to be processed and that, consequently, some bodies may be activated before others. Similarly, if goals such as adj or noun are not terminal nodes, then their unification with corresponding clauses will trigger new parallel processes. As can be seen, the number of parallel processes can grow very rapidly. Some useful comparison can be made at this level with breadth-first strategies since they also have to manage a large number of alternatives, but in a sequential mode.

From this example, the reader can make a first evaluation of the gain in efficiency. In a clause of the form:

$$A :- B_1, B_2, ..., B_n.$$

if B_i is evaluated to false, it results in a failure of the clause A. A Prolog machine will evaluate sequentially the goals B_1 to B_{i-1} before evaluating B_i. A parallel Prolog machine will evaluate all the goals in parallel and therefore the position of B_i in the body of A has no effect *a priori* on the processing time. On a real parallel machine, where all goals are executed in parallel at the same time, the gain in efficiency is the processing time of B_1 to B_{i-1}.

Another example is the following, from Yang (1987). Consider the following naive sort algorithm:

```
sort(X,Y)  :-
    permutation(X,Y),
    in_order(Y).
```

where Y is the sorted list X; permutation(X,Y) generates all the permutations Y of X and in_order(Y) is true if Y is sorted in increasing order. The two clauses permutation(X,Y) and in_order(Y) are executed in parallel and they share a common variable Y. The two goals are synchronized, i.e. as soon as a portion of Y has been produced by permutation(X,Y), in_order(Y) starts running. When in_order(Y) is running, the production of a given permutation is stopped as soon as the increasing ordering is violated. Thus, the useless computation of that permutation is avoided as soon as it is detected that Y is not ordered. The same philosophy as in Prolog is used, namely generate and test, but the generate and the test levels overlap as much as possible at the level of control strategy.

This can be illutrated on a diagram. Suppose we have the following execution:

```
<-   sort([3,2,7,4],Y).
```

step 1 : permutation([3,2,7,4],   Y) starts producing Y : Y = [4|_]
         in_order([4|_]) is true,

step 2 : Y becomes : [4,7|_],   in_order([4,7,|_]) is true

step 3 : permutation produces for Y : [4,7,2|_],
    in_order([4,7,2|_]) fails and permutation stops or produces another
    ordering.
Finally, the DCG grammar:

    np --> np, pp.

    np --> det, noun.

    pp --> preposition, np.

which would result in an infinite loop in a top-down parsing strategy in Prolog, becomes a linear resolution problem in parallel programming since the two n p clauses will be executed in parallel and any execution of the left-recursive call n p in the first rule also triggers a parallel execution of the two n p clauses. We no longer have an SLD-resolution since the linear resolution strategy restriction is no longer considered. Notice that there is no risk *a priori* of entering into an infinite loop due to the left recursion of np because the parallel system stops as soon as one solution has been found.

While or-parallelism is relatively simple to handle since these clauses do not share any data, and-parallelism is more complex. We can distinguish three cases, presented here in order of increasing complexity:

(1) *restricted and-parallelism*, where the different goals have no shared variables,

(2) *stream and-parallelism*, where processes associated with the goals to prove in parallel communicate by a sequence of data items. These processes are executed concurrently and they alternatively play the role of producer and consumer of these data items,

(3) *full and-parallelism*, where there are no restrictions on the production of values for variables.

Parallel languages and their related implementations may differ substantially at this level. These differences affect the expressive power, the efficiency and, to a certain extent, the completeness of the system. Expressive power is affected, for example, in case (1), where goals may not share variables. Efficiency is affected in case (3) where very complex communication procedures between processors have to be established in order to preserve the declarative semantics of the program and the property of soundness. A possible procedure is the following.

When a variable shared by more than one goal in a clause is bound to multiple solutions from different or-branches, a consistency check occurs. All the nodes which are not compatible are withdrawn from the tree. Finally, completeness may be affected when all the solutions to a problem are not fully evaluated in parallel, as in case (2). However, as shall be seen, in Parlog programming techniques can be adapted to circumvent limitations imposed by this approach.

1.2 Guarded Horn clauses

The non-determinism implemented as or-parallelism can be further divided into two types of or-parallelism. This division is motivated both by efficiency reasons and by the difficulty of managing backtracking in a parallel system. We distinguish:

(1) *don't care non-determinism*, where alternative clauses in an or-tree are not treated any further after one solution is found. The system commits to the clause whose head matches first with the call the others are desactivated.

(2) *don't know non-determinism*, where all the clauses are fully processed, even if one has already succeeded.

Case (2) guarantees completeness whereas case (1) produces only one solution. This latter case is very often used, however, because it is much more efficient. To overcome the limitations of this approach, new programming techniques have been developed (as shall be seen in the presentation of Parlog given in section 2) and the notion of the *guarded Horn clause* has been introduced. Roughly speaking, guarded Horn clauses permit the postponement of the commitment to a given clause in an or-tree by requiring that the head and the guard of the clause succeed before any such commitment.

The principle of a guard originates from CSP languages (Hoare 1978) which include the notion of guarded commands. Clark and Gregory (1981) define a relational language which incorporates don't care non-determinism. This language is based on guarded Horn clauses, defined as follows. A guarded Horn clause is of the form :

$$A \leftarrow G_1, G_2, ..., G_m : B_1, B_2, ..., B_n. \quad (n, m \geq 0)$$

where A is the head of the clause; $G_1, G_2, ..., G_m : B_1, B_2, ..., B_n$ is the traditional body of the clause; the symbol ':' is the commit operator; it is the same as the comma, i.e. the *and* operator, but it has a special meaning for control:

- *sequential operator* : goals after ':' cannot be evaluated until all the goals before ':' have been successfully evaluated. The B_i are called the *body* of the clause and the G_i are the *guard*.

- *commited choice operator*: if all the goals of a guard are successfully evaluated, then the system commits itself to that clause and all the other alternatives to that clause are discarded.

A parallel logic programming language based on guarded Horn clauses includes the following control strategies:

(1) at the level of and-parallelism, all goals inside a guard on the one hand and all goals in the body on the other hand are evaluated in parallel with the restriction that the guard is evaluated sequentially before the body.

(2) at the level of or-parallelism, unification of the call with the heads of several clauses is treated in parallel. Then, the guards of those clauses for which unification has succeeded are executed in parallel. The first guard which fully succeeds defines the clause to which the system commits itself (it is often called the *committed clause*).

An immediate consequence of having guarded Horn clauses is that there is no possibility of backtracking. When a clause has been selected then if its body fails, no alternative clause will be tried. There will thus be no backtracking in the body of the clause after the guard. From the definition of guards, we notice that guards play a role which has some similarities with the use of the *cut* operator in Prolog: when a guard is evaluated to true then all the other solutions at that level are discarded.

To overcome the difficulty associated with the absence of backtracking, a different programming style has to be used. This will be discussed in section 2. The introduction of guarded Horn clauses permits the avoidance of the incremental communication of data between goals due to different types of non-determinism.

1.3 Synchronization of processes

The different goals in the body and the guard of a clause often share variables. Shared variables, which may be unified to different values in different goals depending on the resolution paths, is a very complex problem in parallel systems. As we have seen above, limiting non-determinism, without affecting the declarative semantics of programs, is a way of limiting that complexity. In this section we briefly survey different strategies for sharing information.

In a situation where a variable is shared by several goals, synchronization is characterized in terms of producer and consumers: a goal will be the producer of one or more values (in case of backtracking) for a variable and other goals will be the consumers. Consumers remain suspended until the producer has at least partly constructed the result. Programs can be either annotated or non-annotated from the producer-consumer's perspective. Conery (1983) and DeGroot (1984) describe complex algorithms which can dynamically analyse dependencies among variables and variable occurrences at run-time. The order of evaluation of goals is determined according to these dependencies. DeGroot proposes a method for compiling clauses into an execution graph so as to facilitate the dependency analysis.

In some other parallel logic programming languages, variables are annotated as being *read-only* or *write-only* variables. An attempt to write on a read-only variable occurrence suspends the process. The same happens when there is an attempt to read a write-only variable, although this case might be more flexible. Data flows are thus better controlled than in Prolog. In other languages, communication channels are directly specified. In both cases, the logical specifications of the status of variables or of the relations between their different occurrences in a clause remain declarative.

Finally, a simpler solution that partially solves the problem is to introduce in parallel languages the possibility of indicating that two goals have to be executed sequentially. For example, following Parlog's syntax, in:

    A <- B, C & D, E.

The symbol & is a logical operator which requires C and D to be executed sequentially, i.e. C before D. Then, the occurrence of a variable shared by C and D will automatically confer the status of a producer to C with respect to that variable and the status of a consumer to D.

1.4. Parallel logic programming languages

In this section we briefly mention the most important parallel logic programming languages, from the point of view of either their theoretical interest or their availability on the market and their quality as a programming language. A more detailed presentation of parallel languages in logic programming and of their implementations can be found in Shapiro (1988).

IC-Prolog was one of the earliest parallel languages (Clark and McCabe 1979). The stream and-parallelism is implemented and instead, of using or-parallelism, IC-Prolog has a standard backtracking strategy. Delta Prolog (Pereira and Nasr

1984) has almost identical features but it incorporates a distributed backtracking system. A parallel implementation of the Warren Abstract Machine (Warren 1983) has been developed by (Butler *et al.* 1986). In a program, annotations specify which goals are executed by and- or by or-parallelism, but if there is and-parallelism, only one solution is computed.

The most widely used parallel logic programming languages, which offer a good trade-off between efficiency, expressive power and completeness are Parlog (Gregory 1987; Conlon 1989), GHC and Concurrent Prolog. They have a lot of principles in common. In Parlog, synchronization and shared variables are implemented by means of the specification of input and output variables, identified by mode declarations. These declarations are compulsory for each variable present in the head of each definition. This type of declaration enables the compiler to generate more efficient code and allows better control of data flows. Parlog includes a guard specification which can contain any type of clause.

In GHC, there is no distinction betwen input and output variables. GHC has a special, weak form of unification, *sus-unification*, that suspends a process if there is an attempt to bind a call variable to a non-variable term. Roughly speaking, call variables are always 'more instantiated' than called variables (the input variables of Parlog). As a consequence, output results are implemented by variables (never by structured terms) in the head clause. They receive values by means of an assignment procedure given in the body of that clause. This approach is quite difficult to implement efficiently. So far, GHC has been restricted to FGHC (Flat GHC) in which guards only contain primitive clauses (i.e. not referring to other clauses defined by the programmer) and sus-unification is only used for testing the call with the head of the candidate clause.

In Concurrent Prolog, the input and output modes are not defined once and for all at the level of the definition. They are specified in each call via annotations. This offers more flexibility to the programmer and increases reversible uses of programs, which is quite difficult in Parlog. Concurrent Prolog has a unique goal suspension mechanism which occurs when an attempt is made to bind a read-only variable to a non-variable term. Similarly to GHC, Concurrent Prolog has a weak notion of guard, which only contains primitive relations. Finally, when an attempt is made to unify a call to the different clauses of a definition, local environments for variables are created for each clause, so that bindings remain local. Only when a commitment is made are the variable bindings transferred to the original call.

In the remainder of this chapter, we present Parlog in detail because it embodies all the basic principles of parallel logic programming and because there exist several implementations of it on small machines which run satisfactorily for small size applications.

2. An Introduction to Parlog

In this section we present and illustrate the different concepts of Parlog by means of natural language processing examples.

2.1 Mode declarations

The input mode declaration is represented by the symbol *?* in the variable mode declaration of the clause. For example, when describing lexical entries, suppose we want to say that they can only be read. We then have to define them as follows:

```
mode lexicon(category?, word?, morphology?).
lexicon(noun,car,[sing]).
lexicon(verb,has,[3,sing,present]).
lexicon(det,the,[sing]).
```

The input mode is basically for the transfer of data from a call to a clause: an argument position in the call must be at least as much instantiated as the same argument position in the clause. Furthermore, it is not sufficient for the call to unify with the clause: there should be no output substitutions in the unification process. In other words, the call must provide sufficient information for unification to succeed without any output substitutions on variables. For example, the following call will succeed:

```
?- lexicon(det,the,[sing]).
```

whereas the following calls will not and will result in the process being suspended:

```
?- lexicon(det,X,Morph).
?- lexicon(Cat,has, [Morph]).
```

because variables in these calls require output substitutions to produce the desired results. The process will start again when the variables concerned in the calls will be bound to terms which are sufficiently instantiated (here bound to a constant) so as to no longer require any output substitutions. In the case of a simple call as above, we have a deadlock since nothing outside the calls will add information to that call. Finally, notice that the terms used in the mode declaration (e.g. category, word, etc.) are just comments for the sake of readability; the mode may only be mentioned (i.e. just ?).

The output mode can be defined in a similar way. It is noted by the symbol ^ in the mode declaration. In the example below, there is a read-only variable argument (the word) and a write-only argument (the category). The first argument has mode input while the second has output mode:

```
mode def_cat(word?, category^).
def_cat(john, proper_noun).
def_cat(the, det).
def_cat(has, verb).
```

A call of the form :

```
?- def_cat(has,Cat).
```

will succeed and Cat will be bound to the constant v e r b. An output substitution is here possible since this second argument is declared as an output argument. The following call:

```
?- def_cat(Word, det).
```

will fail because Word is an input argument and must be bound to a constant. Parlog offers a little bit more flexibility for output modes. Indeed, the following call will succeed although the output mode argument is already bound to a constant:

```
?- def_cat(the, det).
```

In that case, output unification will be just the identity.

As can be noted, mode declarations allow programmers to control data flows very precisely without losing declarativeness. This is clearly an advantage over Prolog. This can be used in a number of situations in natural language processing where it is often desirable to have the values of some arguments percolate up in a parse tree and others which only percolate down. This has some similarities with the inherited and synthetized attributes in attribute grammars. To give an informal example of the use of these mode declarations in the natural language processing domain, consider the meta-variables in lexical functional grammars (noted as $\Downarrow$ and $\Uparrow$) (Bresnan 1982) that indicate how information on long-distance dependencies must percolate up or down in a parse

2.2 Or- and and- parallelism

Let us now examine how parallelism is realized in Parlog. In the following example:

```
mode lexicon(category?, word?, morphology?).
lexicon(noun,car,[sing]).
lexicon(verb,has,[3,sing,present]).
lexicon(det,the,[sing]).
```

a call such as:

```
?- lexicon(verb,has,[3,sing,present]).
```

initiates an *or-parallel search* on the three definitions given for lexicon. Three processes work concurrently and the first one which succeeds is selected. The solver commits itself to the selected clause. The commitment in the above example is straightforward since there is only one possible solution. This is not the case in the following example, where *definiteness* is an input argument and *word* is an output argument:

```
mode det(def?, word^).
det(def,the).
det(indef,a).
det(indef,one).
det(indef,several).
det(indef,many).
```

If we have the following call:

```
?- det(indef, Word).
```

five processes will work concurrently and the process that succeeds first will be selected by the resolver. In our case, Word can either be bound to a, one, several or many, in a completely unpredictable way.

The call to the above predicate det can be decomposed into three stages:

(1) test if unification on input and output mode variables is possible,

(2) if so, then commit to the first clause that unifies with it, and

(3) produce unifications for output mode variables.

This procedure is called in Parlog the *test-commit-output* procedure. As we have seen in section 1, the commit procedure is the most crucial one since it triggers the selection of only one clause in a definition. In the case of a clause with a non-empty body, the above procedure is decomposed into four stages:

(1) test if unification on input and output mode variables is possible on the

(1) test if unification on input and output mode variables is possible on the head of each clause,

(2) if so, then commit to the first clause that unifies with it,

(3) prepare unifications for output mode variables, and

(4) unify all input mode variables in the body with that of the head and spawn in parallel the different goals of the body.

This procedure is called the *test-commit-output-spawn* procedure.

When a clause has been selected, output unifications are realized and no binding with a call variable is ever retracted later. There will be no backtracking. This means that Parlog will always compute only one solution to a query. This illustrates the incompleteness of Parlog. However, some programming techniques permit us to avoid much of this incompleteness. Finally, it should be noted that a Parlog execution is truly non-deterministic since the output of a query is not entirely determined by the input. The order in which the different goals will be treated is indeed unpredictable *a priori*.

Parlog offers the possibility of specifying sequential search instead of or-parallelism. This is represented by the symbol ';' indicated at the end of each clause instead of the symbol '.'. In that case, Prolog search strategy is used. The above example with a sequential search becomes:

```
mode det(def?, word^).
det(def,the);
det(indef,a);
det(indef,one);
det(indef,several);
det(indef,many);
```

Then the query :

```
?- det(indef, Word).
```

will provoke the binding of Word to the word a. It should be noted that the use of sequential search does not bring any substantial gain in most situations, while some nice properties of parallelism are lost.

Let us now consider and-parallelism. In the following clause:

```
mode bird(name?).
bird(X) <-
   has_feathers(X),
   has_beak(X),
```

the three goals in the body will be executed in parallel. This means that three processes will be activated to solve the three goals in parallel. The clause succeeds if and only if the three goals succeed. These goals are completely independent from each other: they only share an input mode variable. They constitute an ideal situation for parallelism. Similarly for the following complex query:

```
?- bird(X), black(X).
```

In many cases, the different goals in the body of a clause cannot be fully executed in parallel. There is indeed a type of synchronization which is implicitly imposed by the modes of some arguments. Consider, for example, the following clause :

```
mode np(in_string?, outstring^).
np(X,Y) <-
   det(X,X1),
   adjective(X1,X2),
   noun(X2,Y).
```

with the following mode declarations for the terminal elements:

```
mode det(in_string?, outstring^).
mode adjective(in_string?, outstring^).
mode noun(in_string?, outstring^).
```

The three goals det, adjective and noun will be activated in parallel, the call to det(X,X1) has a fully instantiated input string, so it can be a priori fully solved. The situation is different for adjective(X1,X2), since X1 is free at the beginning. The process associated with adjective(X,Y) suspends till X1 is produced by the call to det(X,X1). Similarly for noun(X2,Y) whose associated process waits till X2 is bound to a value.

This example illustrates the dataflow synchronization process. As can be seen, the three goals will be fully solved in a sequential manner. We do not really have a full sequential execution of these goals, but the resolution of det(X,X1) starts before the execution of the goal adjective(X1,X2) which is suspended till X1 is bound to a sufficiently large portion of the list produced in det(X,X1). Similarly for the goal noun(X2,Y).

This synchronization can be represented on the following dataflow diagram,

This synchronization can be represented on the following dataflow diagram, where the variables indicated on the arrows represent the output variables of the process just above and the input variables of the process just below. :

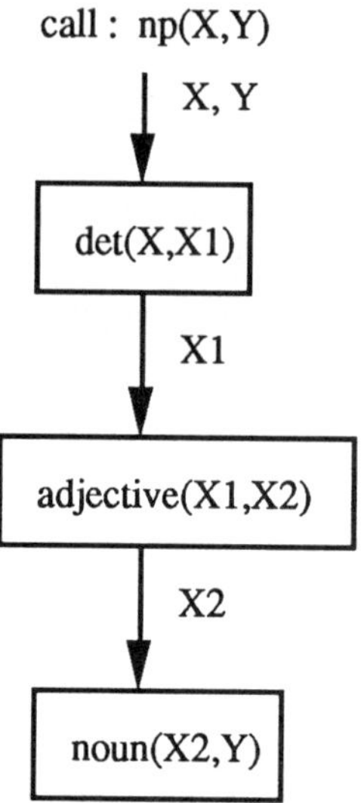

2.3 Guarded clauses

Parlog formalism incorporates the notion of guard as presented in section 1.3 above. Let us recall that a call will always commit to at most one clause in a definition and that this commitment is irreversible. This means that guards have to be placed in clauses at the most appropriate place so as to guarantee that the right choice has been made by the solver. Placing guards at the right place is entirely the programmer's responsibility. Location of guards may affect the declarative semantics of the program. It should be noted, however, that limiting backtracking is not necessarily a handicap from both operational and declarative perspectives since:

- multiple choices (and thus backtracking) may affect completeness,

- efficiency may be affected because identical computations are often done several times, and

- due to Prolog's computation rule, the clause ordering in a definition is often crucial and may affect the declarativity of the program.

since Parlog requires a body to be non-empty, the predefined predicate 'true', which is always evaluated to true is the body of the clause, e.g.:

```
bird(X)  <-
   has_feathers(X),
   has_beak(X),
   lay_eggs(X) : true.
```

A clause with no guard has an empty guard, which is always evaluated to true. Then, the only test on that clause is the unification of the head with the call.

The guard is part of the definition of the clause. It is not an added artificial part to manage control. The guard remains static and declarative and contributes to the declarative semantics of the program.

Guards must obey some informal principles to weaken as much as possible the irreversibility of the commitment process. A first property is called the *sufficient test property*. In a clause of the form:

```
Head <- Guard : Body.
```

if, for a given call C, unification with the head succeeds and the guard is evaluated to true, then the body will also be evaluated to true. This principle permits an improvement of completeness, since commitment to a clause will never lead to a deadlock because of the falsity of the body.

A second principle is called the *minimum guard principle*. To avoid useless computations before the commitment decision is taken, the guard should be as small as possible. The smaller the guard, the earlier the commitment will be made and so the earlier the non-selected clauses will be discarded. It is particularly advisable to avoid as much as possible recursive calls in the guard of a clause. Notice that in a program with several definitions calling each other, having non-minimal guards has a multiplicative effect on the decrease of efficiency.

A third principle, called the *safe guard property*, forbids guards to attempt to bind any input mode variable of the call. The reason behind this restriction is that guards may not succeed and the clause may not be selected, so no input variable should be affected at this point by the guard.

Let us now consider an example that illustrates the notion of guards and the above programming principles:

```
% lexicon
   mode det(?,^).
det([the|L],L).
```

```
  mode det(?,^).
det([the|L],L).
det([a|L],L).
  mode pn(?,^).
pn([edith|L],L).
pn([john|L],L).
  mode num(?,^).
num([two|L],L).
num([three|L],L).
  mode poss(?,^).
poss([my|L],L).
poss([her|L],L).
  mode n(?,^).
n([dog|L],L).
n([friends|L],L).
  mode v(?,^).
v([sees|L],L).
v([seen|L],L).
v([talks,to|L],L).
  mode aux(?,^).
aux([has|L],L).
  % grammar
  % s level has two input variables: the sentence and the empty list
mode s(?,?).
 s(X,Y) <- np(X,X1), vp(X1,Y).
mode np(?,^).
np(X,Y) <- pn(X,Y) : true.
np(X,Y) <- det(X,X1) : n(X1,Y).
np(X,Y) <- num(X,X1) : n(X1,Y).
np(X,Y) <- poss(X,X1) : n(X1,Y).
mode vp(?,^).
vp(X,Y) <- v(X,X1) : np(X1,Y).
vp(X,Y) <- aux(X,X1) : v(X1,X2), np(X2,Y).
```

This grammar will evaluate to true a call of the form :

```
?-  s([edith,talks,to,three,friends],[ ]).
```

Let us first look at the lexical entries. They have one input mode argument

[word | sequence of words]
the sequence of words possibly being the empty list. So, any call variable will be more instantiated than the first argument of any lexical entry, and the input unification will succeed, the variable L being instantiated to the sequence of words. This first argument will only be read and it will not really be bound to any output value. The second argument only contains that variable L. Since L is unknown before unification, it must be an output mode variable.

Let us now consider the grammar. Guards have been placed so that they follow the sufficient test property. Indeed, when a guard is evaluated to true, the body of the corresponding clause is:

- either necessarily evaluated to true if the sentence is recognized by the grammar,

- or evaluated to false if the sentence is not recognized by that grammar.

Because of the test-commit-output-spawn procedure of Parlog, this grammar is treated in a deterministic way. Notice that guards have been kept minimal, following the minimal guard principle. Notice also, as mentioned in section 2.2 above, the goals in the guards or bodies with more than one goal are executed in parallel, but remain suspended until their input arguments are instantiated. From the point of view of and-parallelism, the execution of this grammar is mostly sequential.

The position of guards may be affected by a change in the form or in the contents of the definition. To illustrate this point, let us now make a few changes to the above grammar. If we add morphological features to the grammar, it becomes more restricted: the guards need not be changed. We have the following grammar:

```
% lexicon
mode det(in?,out^,number^).
det([the|L],L,_).
det([a|L],L,sing).
mode pn(in?,out^,number^,gender^).
pn([edith|L],L,sing,fem).
pn([john|L],L,sing,masc).
mode num(in?,out^,number^).
num([two|L],L,plu).
num([three|L],L,plu).
```

```
num([three|L],L,plu).
mode poss(in?,out^,number^,gender^).
poss([my|L],L,sing,_).
poss([her|L],L,sing,fem).
mode n(in?,out^,number^).
n([dog|L],L,sing).
n([friends|L],L,plu).
mode v(in?,out^,number^,person^).
v([sees|L],L,sing,3).
v([seen|L],L,sing,3).
v([talks,to|L],L,sing,3).
mode aux(in?,out^,number^,person^).
aux([has|L],L,sing,3).
  % grammar
mode s(in?,out?).
s(X,Y)  <- np(X,X1,N),  vp(X1,Y,N,3).
mode np(in?,out^,number^).
np(X,Y,N) <-    pn(X,Y,N,G) : true.
np(X,Y,N) <-    det(X,X1,N) :
                n(X1,Y,N).
np(X,Y,N) <-    num(X,X1,N) :
                n(X1,Y,N).
np(X,Y,N) <-    poss(X,X1,_,G) :
                n(X1,Y,_).
mode vp(in?,out^,number^,person^).
vp(X,Y,N,P)  <- v(X,X1,N,P) :
                np(X1,Y,_).
vp(X,Y,N,P)  <- aux(X,X1,N,P) :
                v(X1,X2,N,P),
                np(X2,Y,_).
```

If we now increase the coverage of the grammar by adding prepositional phrases and di-transitive constructions, we have to revise the positions of guards in the whole grammar. Adding a grammar rule may affect the whole grammar. This is significantly different from the updating of grammars in standard Prolog.

We now have the following new lexical entries and grammar rules:

```
mode prep(in?,out^).
prep([to|L],L).
prep([at|L],L).
mode pp(in?,out^,number^).
pp(X,Y,N) <- prep(X,X1), np(X1,Y,N).


% new verb phrase grammar rules, same mode declaration
vp(X,Y,N,P) <- v(X,X1,N,P),
               np(X1,Y,_) : true.
vp(X,Y,N,P) <- aux(X,X1,N,P),
               v(X1,X2,N,P),
               np(X2,Y,_) : true.
vp(X,Y,N,P) <- v(X,X1,N,P),
               np(X1,X2,_),
               pp(X2,Y,_) : true.
vp(X,Y,N,P) <- aux(X,X1,N,P),
               v(X1,X2,N,P),
               np(X2,X3,_),
               pp(X3,Y,_) : true.
```

The guard in the last two rules can be made a little more minimal, taking into
account the derivation rule of s. Indeed, Y in that rule will always be bound to
the empty list. Since vp is the last element in the derivation of s, its output
argument will always be bound to the empty list. With this constraint in mind,
we can revise the above rules for vps as follows:

```
vp(X,Y,N,P) <-    v(X,X1,N,P),
                  np(X1,Y,_) : true.
vp(X,Y,N,P) <-    aux(X,X1,N,P),
                  v(X1,X2,N,P),
                  np(X2,Y,_) : true.
vp(X,Y,N,P) <-    v(X,X1,N,P),
                  np(X1,X2,_),
                  not(X2 = [ ] ) :
                  pp(X2,Y,_).
vp(X,Y,N,P) <-    aux(X,X1,N,P),
                  v(X1,X2,N,P),
                  np(X2,X3,_),
```

```
        np(X2,X3,_),
        not(X3 = [] ) :
        pp(X3,Y,_).
```

To further illustrate how fragile grammar descriptions can be, notice that if we add the following derivation rule for s:

```
   s(X,Y)  <-  np(X,X1,N),
               vp(X1,X2,N,3),
               adverb(X2,Y).
```

then the above improvement will no longer remain applicable since X2 will no longer necessarily be the empty list, and only the general rules with maximal guards and empty bodies will remain appropriate.

2.4 Concurrency between processes

Or-parallelism allows for a concurrent treatment of the different clauses in a definition. When several clauses in a definition are possible candidates, the clause which is selected can be any of these possible clauses and the selection is unpredictable. This selection must not be viewed as a fully random process, but the unpredictability of the clause selection can be used to simulate a kind of weakly random clause selection.

2.4.1 Count It Out

We first illustrate concurrency by a game, Count It Out, which uses all the power of concurrency. This game is particularly difficult to implement in Prolog because it requires a complete revision of Prolog's control strategy. This game is presented by Saint-Dizier (1989b). We summarize it here and show the advantages of using concurrency.

The basic game

For the purpose of readability, we consider a slightly simplified version of the game. Let us consider four numbers, X1, X2, X3, and R. The game Count It Out consists of combining X1, X2 and X3, using the standard arithmetic operations (+, -, *, /) to obtain R as a result. The numbers X1, X2 and X3 must be combined in that order but must not be used more than once. For example, if we have the four numbers

   2, 4, 5

(2 + 4) * 5

The program that resolves this game is invoked with the call:

```
count(X1,X2,X3,R).
```

and the one that carries out the operations between X1, X2 and X3 and stores the result in Op is called with:

```
operation(X,Y,Z,Op).
```

The definition of the predicate operation is the following, where we have not included the division to avoid the treatment of real numbers:

```
mode  operation(nb1?,nb2?,nb3?,result?,op^).
operation(X,Y,Z,R,[X,'+',Y,'+',Z])  <-   R is X+Y+Z : true.
operation(X,Y,Z,R,[X,'+',Y,'-',Z])  <-   R is X+Y-Z : true.
operation(X,Y,Z,R,[X,'-',Y,'-',Z])  <-   R is X-Y-Z : true.
operation(X,Y,Z,R,[X,'+',Y,'*',Z])  <-   R is X+Y*Z : true.
operation(X,Y,Z,R,[X,'*',Y,'+',Z])  <-   R is X*Y+Z : true.   % etc.
```

Notice that, since we do not have any backtracking, we have to enumerate all the possible solutions with appropriate guards.

The main program is then the following:

```
mode  count(in1?,in2?,in3?,total?).
count(X1,X2,X3,R)  <-
        operation(X1,X2,X3,R,Op),
        write1(Op).              % printing order
mode  write1(in?).
write1([L|S])  <-  write(L),
                 tab(2),  write1(S).
write1([])  <-  nl.
```

In most cases it is not possible to find a combination of numbers X1, X2 and X3 that gives exactly R. If this happens, we can either abandon the game, saying there is no solution, or attempt to find a solution as close as possible to R, with a number either greater or smaller than R.

Finding an approximate value

A strategy for finding an approximate value is to restart the program with R1= R - 1 and R1 = R + 1 working concurrently. The program is the following, and approximate is the main call:

approximate is the main call:

```
  mode  operation(nb1?,nb2?,nb3?,result?,op^).
  operation(X,Y,Z,R,[X,'+',Y,'+',Z])  <-   R  is  X+Y+Z  :  true.
  operation(X,Y,Z,R,[X,'+',Y,'-',Z])  <-   R  is  X+Y-Z  :  true.
  operation(X,Y,Z,R,[X,'-',Y,'-',Z])  <-   R  is  X-Y-Z  :  true.
  operation(X,Y,Z,R,[X,'+',Y,'*',Z])  <-   R  is  X+ Y*Z  :  true.
  operation(X,Y,Z,R,[X,'*',Y,'+',Z])  <-   R  is  X*Y+Z  :  true.   % etc.


  mode  count(in1?,in2?,in3?,total?,op^).
  count(X1,X2,X3,R,Op)  <-
          operation(X1,X2,X3,R,Op).
  mode  write1(in?).
  write1([L|S])  <-  write(L),  tab(2),  write1(S).
  write1([])  <-  nl.


  mode  approximate(in?,in2?,in3?,result?).
  approximate(X1,X2,X3,R)  <-
          count(X1,X2,X3,R,Op)  :
          write('Result  found  with  a  total  value  of:  '),
          write(R),  nl,  write1(Op).
  approximate(X1,X2,X3,R)  <-
          R1  is  R - 1,  not(count(X1,X2,X3,R,Op))  :
          approximate(X1,X2,X3,R1).
  approximate(X1,X2,X3,R)  <-
          R1  is  R + 1,  not(count(X1,X2,X3,R,Op))  :
          approximate(X1,X2,X3,R1).
```

A call such as:

```
  <- approximate(2,  3,  7,  14).
```

produces the following response:

```
  Result  found  with  a  total  value  of:  13
  2  *  3  +  7
```

The three clauses in the definition of approximate work concurrently. The
first one deals with the case in which there is an exact solution whereas the last
two treat the case in which the result needs to be either decremented or
incremented by 1. These calls contain in their guard a call to:

```
  not(count(X1,X2,X3,R,Op))
```

the solution which is closest to the number R initially given. This program is difficult to write in Prolog. Indeed, if the first clause fails, the second one will always be selected. Thus an approximate solution will always be less than R.

This program is not optimal: a solution may indeed be computed several times, by combination of increments and decrements. A way to overcome this problem is to assert the unsuccessful attempts and to include a control in the guard of each clause.

2.4.2 A concurrent implementation of free-word order with precedence constraints

Suppose we have a free-word order language. We want to be able to produce any possible surface realization from a given list of words. For example, from the list:

    [a,b,c,d]

we want the system to produce, for example, the following string :

    [a,d,c,b].

A technique to construct *a priori* any possible realization is to have several predicates working concurrently. Such a technique can be implemented by the following program, where free(A,Store,B) is defined as follows: B is any permutation of the list A, Store is a working argument which is empty at the start and at the end of the process:

```
mode  free(in?,inempty?,out^).
free([L|L1],Rest,[L|Constr])  <-   free(L1,Rest,Constr).
free([L|L1],Rest,Constr)  <-   free(L1,[L|Rest],Constr).
free([],L,Constr) <-
          not(L = []) : free(L,[],Constr).
free([],[],[]).
```

The first two clauses of the definition free work concurently: commitment can be made on either the first clause or the second one. In the case of the first clause, the first element is appended as the head of the result list, while in the case of the second clause, it is put in the store Rest to be used in a later stage. The basic idea is very simple: a list is traversed, its elements are either appended to the output list or put in the store to be appended later to that list. The third clause treats the case in which the input list is empty: when the store is not empty it becomes the new input list. The last clause is the termination condition. Notice that it may lead to an infinite loop if the second and the third condition. Notice that it may lead to an infinite loop if the second and the third clauses are the only committed ones.

A call to the program above has the following form:

```
<- free([a,b,c,d,e],[ ],P).
```

A possible result can be the following:

```
P = [a,c,e,b,d].
```

If we now want to impose some linear precedence constraints, we can keep the concurrency but have a guard that makes precedence checkings before constructing any string. The definition becomes:

```
free_restr(Inlist,Store,Result,Before,After).
```

where Result is constructed from Inlist with the constraint that Before linearly precedes After. The program is then the following:

```
mode  free_restr(in?,inempty?,out^,before?,after?).
free_restr([After|L1],Rest,[After|Constr],Before,After)  <-
                    not(in(Before,Rest)),
                    not(in(Before,L1))  :
                free_restr(L1,Rest,Constr,Before,After).
free_restr([L|L1],Rest,[L|Constr],Before,After)  <-
                    not(L = After)  :
                free_restr(L1,Rest,Constr,Before,After).
free_restr([After|L1],Rest,Constr,Before,After)  <-
                    in(Before,L1),
                    not(in(Before,Rest))  :
                free_restr(L1,[After|Rest],Constr,Before,After).
free_restr([L|L1],Rest,Constr,Before,After)  <-
                    not(L = After)  :
                free_restr(L1,[L|Rest],Constr,Before,After).
free_restr([],L,Constr,Before,After)  <-
                    not(L = [])  :
                free_restr(L,[],Constr,Before,After).
free_restr([],[],[],_,_).


mode  in(element?,in_list?).
in(A,[A|_]).
in(A,[B|C])  <-
        not(A = B):
```

For example, a call such as:

```
<- free_word_restr([a, b, c, d, e], [ ],L,d,a) .
```

produces the following response:

```
L = [b,c,d,e,a]
```

Notice that in this program the concurrency remains the same modulo the satisfaction of the constraint. The first and the third clauses compete when After is the head of the call and the second and fourth clauses compete when After is not the head of the call. Similarly, sets of linear precedence constraints can be implemented: all these constraints have to be specified in the guard. This approach is a nice way of implementing in a very direct way the *immediate dominance principles* of the ID/LP system. Notice however that this system will produce only one solution since there is no backtracking. The solution may, however, differ from one execution to another since the order in which processes are activated is non-deterministic.

2.5. A treatment of alternative solutions

As we have seen it in the last sections, the committed choice strategy prevents the system from backtracking. This strategy is mainly motivated by efficiency reasons. In section 2.3 of this chapter, we gave some general programming principles in Parlog which permit the avoidance of commitments that lead to failure.

In some cases, using relatively long guards may not, however, be sufficient to recognize or generate strings according to a certain grammar. Let us, for example, consider the following grammar, where non-terminal symbols are written in capital letters and terminal symbols are written in small letters:

```
A --> a, A /  a / a, B / a, C.
B --> b, C.
C --> c, C / c, D / c.
D --> d, D / d, B.
```

All the derivations of A start with a terminal element a, therefore it is not sufficient to have a in the guard. The only solution that would not lead to wrong choices would be the following, written in DCG style:

```
A --> a, A : true.
A --> a : true.
A --> a, B : true.
A --> a, C : true.
```

```
A --> a, C : true.
```

This solution, however, has several shortcomings. First, efficiency is affected because guards are maximal, and may contain recursive calls as, for example, in the first rule. Next, the second clause in these rules competes with the three others and nothing can prevent it from being selected since the guard finds just a symbol a in the head of the string of symbols being processed, as in the guards of the other rules. Finally, guards are not evaluated before the string of symbols has been fully traversed. This weakens the role of guards.

A more appropriate solution in Parlog is to represent this grammar as a finite state automaton, with two final states a and c, corresponding to the rules:

```
A --> a.
C --> c.
```

in the grammar above. Since this automaton is non-deterministic, a possible representation of its transitions consists in giving for each node the list of its immediate successors. For example, a has a, b and c as immediate successors. This is represented by the following predicate:

```
prod(node, list of immediate successors).
```

The corresponding Parlog program is the following:

```
mode  prod(from?,to^).
prod(a,[a,b,c]).
prod(b,[c]).
prod(c,[c,d]).
prod(d,[d,b]).


mode final(final_state?).      % declaration of final states
final(a).
final(c).
```

These descriptions can then be interpreted by means of the following procedure:

```
parse([list of symbols to parse]).
```

which succeeds if the string of symbols is recognized by the automaton. The program is the following :

```
mode  parse(inlist?).
parse([A,B|L]) <-
      prod(A,C),  in(B,C) :
      parse([B|L]).
```

```
mode in(element?,in_list?).
in(A,[A|_]).
in(A,[B|C]) <-
      not(A = B):
      in(A,C).
```

The first clause of parse traverses the string of symbols and checks whether contiguous symbols are valid successors. The second clause treats the last symbol of the string and checks whether it is a final state. Notice that in this program, the guard is minimal and contains only a control on the validity of the successor of the current symbol with respect to the described automaton, and not on the correctness of the full string. The use of the parallel operator in the first clause between the call to prod and to in is possible since the mode definition of in requires its second argument, namely C, to be an input mode argument. Thus, the execution of in will be suspended till C is sufficiently instantiated.

This technique will be used in the examples of section 3 of this chapter to treat grammars with a high degree of non-determinism and in which guards cannot really be minimized.

2.6   The producer consumer schema

Parallel languages allow programmers to express synchronization between processes. They also allow the specification of message exchanges between these processes in a simple way. A message can be, for example, a data structure which is only partially instantiated in the beginning and which is filled in step by step by each process.

The producer consumer that we present in this section goes beyond the competition between processes that we have presented in section 2.4. We present here simple synchronization techniques which permit the suspension of a process till another process has completed its work, or has done a specified part of it. These processes can be viewed as independent machines which communicate by means of messages. These messages can moreover be considered as objects. It is only the content of these messages which determines and triggers the suspension of a process.

Let us now examine step by step the construction of synchronization mechanisms between processes. The example presented here is simple, but it covers all the facets of the mechanisms we want to present. Let us consider again the formal language given in section 2.5. We have the following description, the formal language given in section 2.5. We have the following description, under the form of a finite state automaton:

```
mode prod(from?,to^).
prod(a,[a,b,c]).
prod(b,[c]).
prod(c,[c,d]).
prod(d,[d,b]).
mode final(final_state?).        % declaration of final states
final(a).
final(c).
```

and the procedure in(A,B) which is true if the element A is in the list B:

```
mode in(element?,in_list?).
in(A,[A|_]).
in(A,[B|C]) <-
        not(A = B) :
        in(A,C).
```

Let us now consider a first producer consumer schema. Given a string to parse, a simple schema is to have a producer produce the list of pairs of adjacent symbols from the string to parse, and to have the consumer consume them in the order they are produced if and only if there exists for each pair a corresponding valid arc described in the finite state automaton. When a final state is encountered, then the consumer signals that it has completed its work. If the producer has fully traversed the string, then the string is recognized by the grammar.

For example, let us consider the string:

```
[a, a, b, c, c, c, d, b, c]
```

which is recognized by our finite state automaton. The producer produces the following list of pairs:

```
(a,a),
(a,b),
(b,c),
(c,c),
etc.
```

while the consumer checks to ensure that, for each of these ordered pairs there is a corresponding production. The communication between the two processes is realized by means of a data structure :

which describes the different sequences of adjacent symbols in the string to parse.

A first strategy is to produce the set of arcs on the one hand and to control the arcs on the other hand. The consumer starts working as soon as there is an arc available. Then, if the producer runs faster than the consumer, it will complete its work before the consumer and the latter will have terminated the controls some time after. If the consumer runs faster than the producer, it will suspend till new arcs are produced.

Let us define two predicates:

```
prod1([input string of symbols],[orderet set of arcs])
```
and
```
cons1([ordered set of arcs to control]).
```
The call for the above example is then the following:

```
<-  prod1([a, a, b, c, c, c, d, b, c], P), cons1(P) .
```

It succeeds and produces the following set for the variable P which is shared by the two processes and which is bound step by step (as can be seen if you use the 'view' option of your Parlog system) to the list of arcs being produced and checked:

```
P   =[arc(a, a), arc(a, b), arc(b, c), arc(c, c), arc(c, c), arc(c, d),
            arc(d, b), arc(b, c)|final(c)]
```

The program is the following:

```
mode  prod1(instring?,outpair^).
prod1([A,B|C],[arc(A,B)|D])  <-
                   prod1([B|C],D).
prod1([A],final(A)).

mode  cons1(inpair?).
cons1([arc(A,B)|D])  <-
                   prod(A,T),
                   in(B,T),
                   cons1(D).
cons1(final(A))  <-   final(A) : true.
```

Notice the mode of arguments. The argument of cons1 is in mode input. Thus, it will remain suspended till it is instantiated (at least partly). On the other hand, the very same argument is an output mode argument of the producer, hand, the very same argument is an output mode argument of the producer, which will be instantiated step by step while traversing the string to parse.

In this first example, the only synchronization which occurs is the suspension of the consumer until some new arcs are produced. In the case where the producer runs faster than the consumer, which is probable since its code is shorter, the producer completes its work much faster than the consumer. If the consumer detects an arc which is not recognized by the finite state automaton, then it stops (fails). The string to parse is incorrect with respect to that automaton and the producer has done some useless work by producing the arcs that come after the non-recognized arc.

Let us now write a more complex synchronization procedure. The producer produces an arc, then it pauses while the consumer checks for the validity of the arc. If the arc is valid, then the consumer returns a message to the producer, e.g. 'done', and the producer produces a new arc. The consumer remains suspended till that arc has been produced. So, at a given moment either the producer or the consumer works. To handle this synchronization, we add to the arc data structure a new field that contains the message of the consumer:

```
arc(A,B,Message).
```

A possible call is then the following:

```
<-  prod2([a, a, b, c, c, c, d, d, b, c], P), cons2(P) .
```

and the system's response is:

```
P  =  [arc(a, a, done), arc(a, b, done), arc(b, c, done),
        arc(c, c, done),  arc(c, c, done), arc(c, d, done),
        arc(d, d, done), arc(d, b, done), arc(b, c, done)|final(c)]
```

The program is the following:

```
mode  prod2(instring?,outpair^).
prod2([A,B|C],[arc(A,B,Resp)|D])  <-
                cont(Resp)  &  prod2([B|C],D).
prod2([A],final(A)).
mode  cons2(inpair?).
cons2([arc(A,B,Resp)|D])  <-
                prod(A,T),
                in(B,T)  :
                Resp = done, cons2(D).
cons2(final(A)) <-    final(A)  :  true.
mode cont(response?).
```

The producer prod2 includes in its guard a control on the response Resp of the consumer. The predicate cont(Resp) is declared as having an input mode argument. Thus it provokes the suspension of prod2 till Resp is instantiated. To avoid the recursive call to go on running before the response of the consumer is produced, a sequential operator & is required. Notice that it is not possible to use a guard (which includes a certain idea of sequentiality between the guard and the body) instead of the sequential operator, as in:

```
prod2([A,B|C],[arc(A,B,Resp)|D]) <-
                 cont(Resp)  :  prod2([B|C],D).
```

because the test-commit-output-spawn procedure will be stopped at the commit level till Resp is instantiated. Since it is blocked at that level, the output level will never be reached, no arc will ever be produced, and therefore the consumer will never start working. Using the sequential operator permits the realization of the output level.

The consumer cons2 now has a guard, which was not necessary (but possible) in the previous program. It is indeed only when the validity of the arc has been established that the consumer is allowed to produce the response 'done'. As soon as Resp is bound to 'done', the suspension of the predicate cont is revoked and it resumes production. The process can be represented by the following diagram:

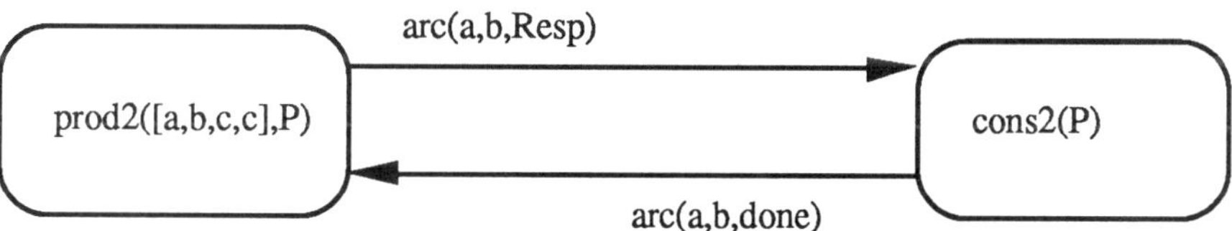

This strategy can be extended to several producers, each of them processing a different string of symbols, and calling a single or any number of consumers. In that case, messages must bear the identification of the producer so as to avoid any confusion between different strings of symbols being parsed at the same time.

Finally, let us have the list inclusion control (in) as a separate process which is also synchronized with the consumer.

```
mode  prod3(instring?,outpair^).
prod3([A,B|C],[arc(A,B,Resp,T)|D]) <-
                 cont(Resp) &  prod3([B|C],D).
```

```
prod3([A],final(A)).
mode cons3(inpair?).
 cons3([arc(A,B,Resp,T)|D]) <-
              prod(A,T),
              in(B,T,In) :
              cont(In),
              Resp = done,  cons3(D).


cons3(final(A))   <-    final(A) : true.


 mode in(element?,in_list?,response^).
 in(A,[A|_],in).
 in(A,[B|C],In) <-
        not(A = B):
        in(A,C,In).
```

The same technique is used as with the previous program: cons3 is suspended till in finds a solution. The result is characterized by the production of an 'in' message. The communications between these three processes can be represented on a diagram as follows:

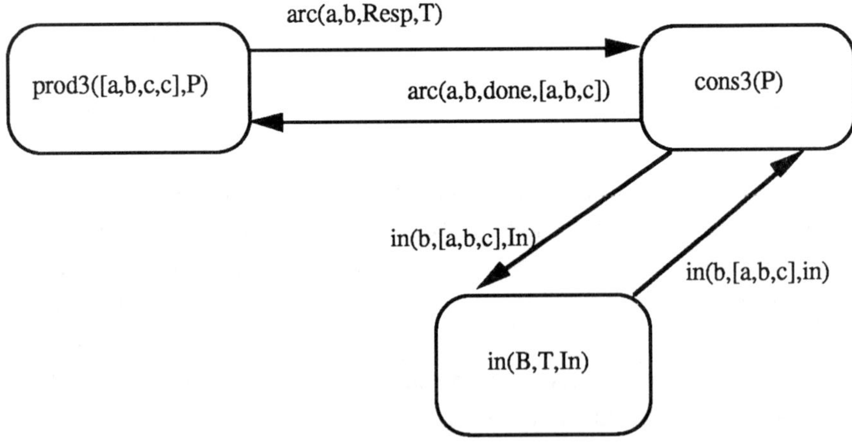

3. Towards more complex natural language systems

3.1 A parallel top-down parser

We now present a more elaborate top-down parser which makes use of parallelism at different levels.

The grammar presented in section 2.3 of this chapter is a standard DCG incorporating guards to prevent the system from making incorrect commitments which cannot be revised later by backtracking. As we have seen, this approach has some limitations, including the following:

- the size of the guard, which is often the whole derivation,

- the fragility of the description which often entails revising the location of guards in all the rules when the grammar is updated.

The technique presented in section 2.5, where alternative solutions are given in a list, avoids these problems. The drawbacks of this latter approach with respect to the former are relatively minor: the grammatical descriptions are less direct (an intermediate data-structure is needed) and there is some overhead processing due to the necessity of using a meta-interpreter.

Let us now introduce the grammar. It is represented by means of the following predicate:

```
grammar(Left-hand Part, [list of possible right-hand parts]).
```

Each right-hand part is itself a list of grammar symbols. Here is a toy-grammar, which does not include any morphological or syntactic control for the sake of readability:

```
mode grammar(form?, expansions^).
grammar(sentence(X,Y),
        [[noun_phrase(X,X1), verb(X1,Y)],
         [noun_phrase(X,X1), verb_phrase(X1,Y)]]).
grammar(noun_phrase(X,Y),
        [[determiner(X,X1), noun_expression(X1,Y)]]).
grammar(noun_expression(X,Y),
        [[noun(X,Y)], [adjective(X,X1), noun_expression(X1,Y)]]).
grammar(verb_phrase(X,Y),
        [[verb_expression(X,X1), noun_phrase(X1,Y)]]).
grammar(verb_expression(X,Y),
```

```
[[verb(X,Y)], [adverb(X,X1), verb(X1,Y)]]).
```

The associated dictionary is represented by the following predicate:

```
dictionary(Syntactic category, in-list of words, out-list of words).
```

Here is a toy-dictionary:

```
mode dictionary(form?,In?,Out^).
dictionary(verb,[likes|L],L).
dictionary(determiner,[the|L],L).
dictionary(determiner,[a|L],L).
dictionary(noun,[boy|L],L).
dictionary(noun,[girl|L],L).
dictionary(noun,[car|L],L).
dictionary(adverb,[quickly|L],L).
dictionary(adjective,[big|L],L).
dictionary(adjective,[small|L],L).
```

Let us now consider the parser. The main call is :

```
parse(input structure to parse, syntactic tree).
```

For example, to the call:

```
<- parse(sentence([the, boy, likes, a, girl], []), P) .
```

The system will respond:

```
P = sentence(noun_phrase(determiner(the),
                         noun_expression(noun(boy))),
             verb_phrase(verb_expression(verb(likes)),
                         noun_phrase(determiner(a),
                         noun_expression(noun(girl)))))
```

The meta-interpreter is the following:

```
mode parse(sentence?, parse^).
parse(Form, F1(F2)) <-
  Form =.. [F1,[F2|L],F3] ,
  dictionary(F1,[F2|L],F3) :
  true.
parse(Form, Parse) <-
  grammar(Form, Expansions) :
  expansions_parse( Expansions, ParseList),
  Form =.. [F1|_],
  Parse =.. [F1|ParseList].
```

```
    % treatment of the list of expansions
    % two expansions, selection of the first one
  mode expansions_parse( expansions?, parselist^).
  expansions_parse( [Expansion1, Expansion2], Parse) <-
    one_expansion_parse(Expansion1, Parse) :  true .
    % selection of the second one
  expansions_parse([Expansion1, Expansion2], Parse) <-
    one_expansion_parse( Expansion2, Parse) :
    true.
    % case where there is only one expansion
  expansions_parse([Expansion], Parse) <-
    one_expansion_parse( Expansion, Parse).


    % treatment of a given expansion
  mode one_expansion_parse( expansion?, parselist^).
  one_expansion_parse( [Form1, Form2], [Parse1, Parse2]) <-
    parse(Form1,Parse1),
    parse(Form2,Parse2).
  one_expansion_parse([Form], [Parse]) <-
    parse(Form,Parse).

  mode member(?, ?).
  member(H, [H|T]);
  member(X, [H|T]) <-
            member(X, T).
```

This program can be generalized to take into account two types of extensions:
(1) lists of expansions of more than two different expansions and (2) expansions
with more than two symbols. Instead of directly decomposing the lists, a
recursive call would traverse the structures in such a generalization.

3.2 Processing features in parallel

In section 2.1 of Chapter 4, we presented a parser that uses a simple feature
system in a flexible and efficient way. In a grammar rule, feature-value pairs
occurring in the different symbols in a rule can often be processed almost
independently of each other. For example, the control on gender agreement can be
done independently of the control on agreement in number in a language like

French. Similarly, control on the inclusion of the subject NP's semantic features into the selectional restrictions of the verb (with respect to its potential subject) can be realized independently of the morphological controls between these two constituents. Since these controls can be processed independently, it is natural to execute them in parallel.

In this section we propose an implementation in Parlog of the program given in section 2.1 of Chapter 4. As will be seen, the linguistic characterizations remain unchanged and only a few superficial, syntactic changes are introduced. In particular, in order to avoid the use of the operator ':' which represents the right-most limit of a guard in Parlog, we represent a feature-value pair by a list:

[feature ID, associated value]

It is interesting for the reader to notice the differences between the two programs. In Parlog, the cut symbol is replaced by a more comprehensive set of constraints: the logical specification is thus more explicit and does not take advantage of the behaviour of the cut. The definition of in is also changed because variables can be in either the input or the output mode, but not both. Finally, notice also that guards are kept minimal, to guarantee a good degree of parallelism in the body of the clause.

A call to the program is the following:

```
<- s(Synt, [the, worker, drinks, a, very, warm, coffee], [ ]) .
```

The system's response is:

```
Synt  =  s(np(det(the), n(worker)),
            vp(v(drink),
               np(det(a),
                  ap(adverb(very),  a(warm)),
                  n(coffee))))
```

and the program is as follows:

```
% lexicon
mode det(^,^,?,^).
det(det(the), [[number, sing]], [the|L],L).
det(det(a), [[number, sing]], [a|L],L).

mode n(^,^,?,^).
n(n(car), [[number, sing], [sem , [vehicle]]], [car|L],L).
n(n(worker), [[number, sing],[sem , [hum]]], [worker|L],L).
```

```
n(n(coffee),  [[number,sing],  [sem,  [liquid]]],  [coffee|L],L).


mode  v(^,^,?,^).
v(v(sing),  [[number,  sing],[tense ,pres],  [sems ,  [hum]],
            [semo ,  [nhum]],[scat ,  [np]]],  [sings|L],L).
v(v(drink),  [[number,  sing],  [tense ,  pres],  [scat,  [np]],
            [sems ,  [hum]],  [semo ,  [liquid]]],  [drinks|L],  L).
v(v(drive),  [[number,  sing],  [tense ,  pres],  [scat,  [np]],
            [sems ,  [hum]],  [semo ,  [vehicle]]],  [drives|L],  L).


mode  a(^,^,?,^).
a(a(warm),  [[number,  sing],  [sem,  [liquid]]],  [warm|L],L).
mode  adverb(^,^,?,^).
adverb(adverb(very),  [],  [very|L],L).


  % Grammar
% s --> np, vp.
mode  s(^,?,^).
s(s(NP,VP),X,Y)    <-
   np(NP,T1,X,X1),
   extract(T1,number,V1),
   extract(T1,  sem,S),
   vp(VP,T2,X1,Y),
   extract(T2,number,V1),
    extract(T2,sems,S).
% np --> det, n.
mode  np(^,^,?,^).
np(np(Det,N),  T,X,Y)    <-
   det(Det,  T1,X,X1),
   n(N,  T2,X1,Y) :
   unify(T1,T2,T).
% np --> det, ap, n.
np(np(Det,A,  N),  T,X,Y)  <-
   det(Det,  T1,X,X1),
   ap(A,  T3,X1,X2) :
   n(N,  T2,X2,Y),
```

```
        unify(T1,T2,T),
        unify(T3,  T2,  _).


% vp --> v, np.
mode vp(^,^,?,^).
vp(vp(V,NP),  T1,X,Y)  <-
        v(V,T1,X,X1),
      extract(T1,scat,Scat),
      Scat = [np],
      np(NP,  T2,X1,Y).
% ap --> a.
mode ap(^,^,?,^).
ap(ap(A),T1,X,Y)  <-
        a(A,T1,X,Y) : true.
ap(ap(Adv,Adj),T1,X,Y)   <-
        adverb(Adv,_,X,X1)  :
        a(Adj,T1,X1,Y).


% unification procedure
% identical sets
mode  unify(?,?,^).
unify( Featureset, Featureset, Featureset).
unify([],F,F).
unify(F,[],F).
% same feature same value
unify([[Feature1,Value1]|Rest1],  [[Feature1,Value1]|Rest2],
        [[Feature1,Value1]|Result]) <-
      unify(Rest1,Rest2,Result) : true.
% same feature different value
unify([[Feature1,Value1]|Rest1],  [[Feature1,Value2]|Rest2],Result)
        <- not(Value1 = Value2) :
            fail.
% different features
unify([[Feature1,Value1]|Rest1],  [[Feature2,Value2]|Rest2],Result)
    <-   not(Feature1 = Feature2),
        unify([[Feature1,Value1]],Rest2,NewRest2),
```

```
unify(Rest1,[[Feature2,Value2]|NewRest2],Result) :
true.


%  extraction of features
mode  extract(^,^,^).
extract(T1,Nom,Val)  <-  in(Nom,Val, T1).


%  set membership, with a  decomposition of the feature-value pair
mode  in(featname?,value^,in_list?).
in(Feat,Val,[[Feat,Val]|_]).
in(Feat,Val,[B|C])  <-
        not([Feat,Val] = B):
        in(Feat,Val,C).
```

The reader can check on his machine (for example with the tracer) that there is a large number of processes that run in parallel (or that virtually run in parallel). There is parallelism involved at the level of the grammar rules and at the level of the agreement controls, in particular for the traversing of the lists of feature-value pairs.

It is also interesting to note that the call to grammar symbols and to agreement controls in the left-hand part of the grammar rules can be written in any order. The mode of the arguments provokes suspensions of those calls which do not yet have enough information at the level of their input mode variables. These calls resume working as soon as their input mode variables are sufficiently instantiated. It is thus the control on data-flow which specifies when the different calls can be executed.

Since failure of any one process immediately provokes failure of the whole rule, the use of parallelism also solves the problem of determining an optimal ordering of the different agreement controls in a grammar rule.

4. Conclusion

In this chapter, we have presented the main facets of parallel processing and have shown how it can be used for natural language processing. For that purpose, we have presented Parlog in detail and have introduced the main techniques of interest to language processing, illustrating them by means of simple examples.

Although parallel logic programming techniques are not yet well established, we have introduced in this chapter, by means of examples, some of the differences between Prolog and Parlog and also some techniques and programming methods which could be used to overcome some of the limitations (for example, backtracking) imposed by a language like Parlog.

Parlog has an object-oriented extension, Parlog++, which is presented in the next chapter. The association of parallelism and object-oriented programming permits us to better organize the linguistic descriptions while keeping most of the advantages of parallelism. To illustrate the association of these two paradigms, several examples presented in this chapter are extended in the next chapter.

There is now a very important research and development effort aimed at specifying and implementing parallel logic programming languages on average-size machines such as work stations. It is now possible to efficiently simulate parallelism on these machines. For those machines which have more than one processor, the experience is even more interesting. Another approach, which is more complex from a running system point of view, is the use of several machines which cooperate to execute in parallel different parts of a given problem.

We really do believe that parallelism, among other major techniques such as active constraints, will play a major role in making the construction of large-size natural language processing systems feasible.

Chapter 7

Object-Oriented Logic Programming for Natural Language Processing

The goal of this chapter is to present the basic concepts of object-oriented logic programming (OOLP hereafter) and to show how it can be used in an appropriate way for natural language processing. This chapter reformulates and extends in different formal and practical directions the elements presented in Chapter 4 about feature structures and type-based logic programming.

Basically, OOLP and object-oriented programming (OOP) more generally, have been motivated by the need to have a more modular approach, closer to specification levels, for large projects involving several types of data and programming languages. OOP develops tools to represent heterogeneous knowledge and environments integrating different kinds of programming languages. These tools also allow a better manipulation of large knowledge bases, with better security checks. In this framework, a great attention is devoted in particular to the specification of different forms of inheritance: multiple, with defaults, etc. These forms of inheritance are particularly useful in language processing applications where syntactic and semantic concepts usually have several levels of abstraction and of specialization. Finally, we will show that objects lend themselves very well to processing on distributed and parallel systems.

In this chapter, we first introduce OOLP by means of a standard language shared by several OOLP languages. The proof procedure associated with OOLP is presented and an application of OOLP to modelling *situation semantics* concepts is presented. In section 2, we present the foundations of Parlog++, the object-oriented extension of Parlog (see Chapter 6), a more advanced OOLP language that includes a more sophisticated inheritance system, a message-passing system between objects and a full parallel treatment of queries. In section 3, we show how parsers can be designed in object-oriented parallel logic programming (noted as OOPLP) and we exemplify them in Parlog++. This section establishes a bridge with Chapter 6 where parallel logic programming techniques were introduced. To conclude this chapter, in section 4 we present a more elaborate application of OOLP within the domain of machine translation.

1. An Introduction to Object-Oriented Programming

The basic notion of OOP is the notion of encapsulation: data and procedures that manipulate them are grouped together in a unique structure: the object. Implementation details are hidden from programmers, and access and manipulation of data are realized by means of a set of operations called the interface to the object. Compared to typed structures, as presented in Chapter 4, objects are not simply data structures, but they also contain procedures, related to these data-structures. In Chapter 4, we presented examples where clauses encoding controls were associated with data-types, but their role was substantially different from procedures with objects, as we shall see below.

Data related to a given action being often related to that precise action, an object is not characterized by its structure and form but by its behaviour. This is a way to realize the well-known phenomenon of data abstraction. The only way to communicate with an object is by invoking a procedure (also called a *method*) in its interface. The call to a procedure is made through a request, often called a *message*. In several OOP systems, if the object itself cannot execute the request, it can delegate it to another object which can. This allows for the specification of very flexible inheritance mechanisms.

1.1 Different classes of languages with objects

Structurally speaking, we have three basic types of OOP :
- languages which only offer abstraction and encapsulation facilities such as Ada and Modula-2,
- languages which organize objects in classes and instances, as in Simula and Smalltalk-80,
- languages fully based on the notion of object enriched by the notion of inheritance, as in Planner, Plasma and Parlog++.

From a conceptual and modelling perspective, we have three main points of view:
- a *structural* point of view where the object defines a model for its data and the operations which can be performed on these data,
- a *conceptual* point of view, where the object is a unit of knowledge at a certain level of abstraction and complexity,
- an *actor* point of view where the object is considered as an autonomous and active entity.

1.2 Constructing and structuring objects

Objects can be characterized according to three dimensions: classes and instantiation capabilities, various forms of inheritance, including multiple and non-monotonic inheritance, and message processing. A class can be viewed as an object with a high degree of genericity, as a prototype. The distinction between objects and classes in the literature is not always easy to make. These points are presented in the next three sub-sections where the notion of class and object are introduced.

1.2.1 Classes and instances

A class is the description of a family of objects with the same data-type and behaviour. Each class has (1) a static component, the data and (2) a dynamic component, the procedures or methods. Although there are several notational variants in the literature on OOLP, a general form of a class can be the following:

```
class( <class name>,
          data_field(<list of variables or data-structures involved>
          methods : <sequence of clauses local to the object> ).
```

For example, let us consider the following simple class that treats the preterite
form of verbs in English:

```
class( tensed,
          data_field([Verb, Verb_root,
                        Pres_3term, Pret_term, Past_part]),
          methods: present( [Verb]),
                        present3([Verb, Pres_3term] ),
                        preterite([Verb_root, Pret_term]),
                        participle([Verb_root, Past_part])   ).
```

The name of this class is tensed. Its data field is composed of five structures:
   - Verb is the verb itself,
   - Verb_root : the verbal root for preterite and participle,
   - Pres_3term : the regular termination of the third person singular,
   - Pret_term : the preterite form termination, and
   - Past_term is the termination of the participle form.

The method field is composed of four clauses relating to the following:
   - present, for regular verbs,
   - present third person singular, (e.g. sleep - sleeps), and
   - preterite and
   - participle forms.

In this example, we have not treated the problem of list concatenation for the
sake of readability. Methods composed of facts are just represented as a list of
Prolog terms. In this example, because of its simplicity, we do not distinguish
between the name of a method on the one hand and the program associated with
it on the other. In more complicated cases, such a distinction could be made by
using a top-level predicate which simply calls the underlying programs (see
section 2).

   A method section can contain clauses with non-empty bodies and local
variables (i.e. variables not referred to in the data-field section) as in the
following example:

```
class(np,
    data_field([Syn_Tree,  Input]),
    methods :
  np(Input,Output,Syn_Tree)  :-
                            proper_noun(Input,Output,Syn_Tree).
  np(Input,Output,np(Det,N))  :-  det(Input,Y,Det),
                            n(Y,Output,N).
  proper_noun([john|X],X,pn([john])).
  proper_noun([ann|X],X,pn([ann])).
  proper_noun([edith|X],X,pn([edith])).
  det([the|X],X,det([the])).
  det([several|X],X,det([several])).
  n([car|X],X,n([car])).  etc... ).
```

Let us now consider the instantiation of a class. An instance of a class is
simply an instantiation of its variables (or of some of its variables). The method
section is not affected. Instances are associated with their class by the
instance_of relation, called the instantiation relation. For example, we could
define the following instances for the class tensed:

```
  class( data_field([sleep, slep, s, t, t]) ) instance_of tensed.
  class( data_field([work, work, s, ed, ed]) ) instance_of tensed.
```

For verbs accepting more than one type of termination in one of the tenses
considered here, we need to introduce two objects:

```
  class( data_field([dream, dream, s, ed, ed]) ) instance_of tensed.
  class( data_field([dream, dream, s, t, t]) ) instance_of tensed.
```

We could also have included a list of possible terminations and have a more
complex method section. The above four examples of instances are also
subclasses of the class tensed. They cannot however be further decomposed into
subclasses since all the variables of the tensed class have been instantiated. In
that case we use the term *instance*, otherwise, we use the term *subclass*.

For a more linguistically adequate description of verb morphology, we could
also define classes of verbs that behave in the same way (one level of
instantiation) and then define the set of verbs for each of these classes (a lower
level of instantiation). This three-level organization requires a certain form of
inheritance. This is introduced and exemplified below. More generally, object-
oriented programming permits programrs to define in a simpler and more flexible

way parametrized and generic modules of programs that correspond to a certain facet of an object in the world or to a certain task which has its own autonomy and internal logic.

1.2.2 Standard inheritance

Inheritance allows the introduction of several levels of abstraction. Classes can be hierarchically organized: an object can be related to other objects or to sub-classes (also called *specializations*). Similarly, classes may have super-classes. Sub-classes of a given class inherit all of the variables and methods of that class. A sub-class may be created for two different reasons:

(1) to enrich a class by new variables and/or methods to account for a more specific class of objects,

(2) to substitute a new definition for an inherited definition, which is no longer appropriate.

Let us consider the example above and create two sub-classes, one treating the regular verbs and the other the irregular verbs. The top-level class is defined as follows:

```
class( tensed,
       data_field([Verb, Verb_root, Pres_3term]),
       methods : present( [Verb]),
                 present3([Verb, Pres_3term] ) ).
```

The regular verb class is defined as follows:

```
class( reg_tensed,
       data_field([ ]),          % can be omitted since it is empty
       methods : reg_preterite([Verb_root, ed]),
                 reg_participle([Verb_root, ed])   )
    subclass_of  tensed.
```

and the irregular verb class is the following:

```
class( irreg_tensed,
       data_field([Pret_term, Past_part]),
       methods : preterite([Verb_root, Pret_term]),
                 participle([Verb_root, Past_part])   )
    subclass_of  tensed.
```

Definitions of instances of classes are defined as follows:

```
class( data_field([sleep, slep, s, t, t]) ) instance_of  irreg_tensed.
class( data_field([work, work, s]) ) instance_of  reg_tensed.
```

```
class( data_field([dream, dream, s]) ) instance_of   reg_tensed.
class( data_field([dream, dream, s, t, t]) )
                                instance_of   irreg_tensed.
```

Notice that in the above the instances of regular verbs have three variables whereas the instances of irregular verbs have five variables. The reason is that the reg_tensed sub-class does not have any variables in addition to those it inherits from its super-class, whereas the irreg_tensed class has two variables which are added to the variables it inherits from its super-class. To facilitate understanding, we assume that inherited variables are always appended to the front of the variables already present in the class under consideration. Thus, the irreg_tensed class has the following ordered set of variables:

```
data_field([Verb,  Verb_root,
                    Pres_3term,  Pret_term,  Past_part])
```

Inheritance is expressed here by the subclass_of relation. There is a similar inheritance for the methods of the tensed verb object.

When inheriting variables from a super-class data_field, variable renaming operations may take place if corresponding variables are referred to in the two classes with different names. Similarly, variables in the super-class may be instantiated if these variables are instantiated in the sub-class.

Inheritance in OOLP can be interpreted from at least the following three perspectives:

- The point of view of *set inclusion*: inheritance describes an inclusion relation, the elements of a subclass being included into the elements of their super-class. In other words, the set of objects associated with (or included in) a class is the union of the sets of objects associated with its sub-classes and with the class itself.

- The *logical* point of view: if an object is an instance of a class then it is also an instance of any super-class of that class. In our example, we can say that:

$$\text{irreg\_tensed}(X) \;\Rightarrow\; \text{tensed}(X).$$

- The *conceptual* point of view, where inheritance indicates a type of specialization or a degree of genericity.

In the inheritance form that we have considered so far, we made two hypotheses:

(1) inheritance uniformly applies to all aspects of objects: data and methods,

(2) inheritance is the same for all instances of the subclass_of relation.

This situation is, however, somewhat simplistic and does not necessarily correspond to the way knowledge is structured in real applications. Most classes and objects can indeed have several super-classes; they can also exhibit a certain degree of irregularity (exceptions) with respect to their ancestors. This is the reason why it is often necessary to deal with exceptions on the one hand and with multiple inheritance on the other hand.

1.2.3 Treating exceptions in inheritance

In a number of situations, sub-classes exhibit irregularities with respect to their parent class. This does not, however, alter the fact that they are basically sub-classes of that class. Treatments of exceptions can take several forms depending on where the exception is located.

The general rule for treating exceptions to inheritance is based on the notion of 'local preference'. It can be stated as follows : if a sub-class has a method with the same identifier as a method defined in the parent class and if it is defined differently, then, by default, the method in the sub-class is preferred for that sub-class and the corresponding method in the parent class is not inherited.

This can be illustrated by the following hierarchy of classes, describing lexical entries with their related phrasal constructions (other methods being omitted):

```
class( noun,
     data_field( [ ] ),
     methods : in_derivations([(np --> det, noun),
                               (np --> det, adjective, noun, ...])  ).
class( proper_noun,
     data_field( [ ] ),
     methods : in_derivations([(np --> proper_noun )]) )
   subclass_of   noun.
class( pronoun,
     data_field( [ ] ),
     methods : in_derivations([(np --> pronoun) ])  )
   subclass_of   noun.
```

In this example, the in_derivations facts associated with the proper noun and the pronoun are preferred to the in_derivations fact that would normally be inherited from the class noun. This does not however forbid inheritance of other methods from that class.

It should also be noticed that the symbols det and adjective refer to other classes, accessible to the present class (see *delegation mechanism* in section 2.2).

A second situation arises when a method with the same identifier, but with different definitions which are *a priori* compatible, is present in a class and in its parent class. In that case, the class keeps its definition and inherits the definition from the parent class. The operator subclass_of then has an argument that specifies which methods are compatible and must co-exist in the sub-class:

```
subclass_of([compatible(<method  identifier>)]).
```

This situation can be illustrated by the same example as above for adjectives. Here is the general class describing adjectives:

```
class(adjective,
      data_field( [ ] ),
      methods : in_derivations([(ap --> adjective)] ) ).
```

and here is the class that describes scalar adjectives :

```
class(scalar_adjective,
       data_field([  ]),
       methods : in_derivations(([ap --> adverb, adjective]),
                 (comparative_form --> [as], adjective, [as]), ...] ) )
    subclass_of([compatible(in_derivations)])    adjective.
```

The scalar_adjective class inherits from the in_derivations method of the adjective class. The result of the inheritance is the following class:

```
class(scalar_adjective,
      data_field( [ ] ),
      methods : in_derivations([(ap --> adjective)] ).
                in_derivations([(ap  --> adverb, adjective),
                (comparative_form --> [as], adjective, [as]), ...] )).
```

A third situation that may arise is called *differential inheritance*. In that situation, a sub-class inherits from its parent class a subset of the definitions of a method. The above definition of the subclass_of operator can then include the specification of those definitions which must not be inherited for a given method. It is noted as follows:

```
subclass_of([compatible(<method identifier>)-[<list of definitions not inherited>]).
```

The list of definitions not inherited contains these definitions in full to avoid any ambiguity. It is clear that this method is usable only when that list is relatively small. From the example above, we can define the sub-class of implicit superlative adjectives (e.g. worse, perfect, excellent) as follows:

```
class  imp_super_adjective,
     data_field([  ]),
     methods : in_derivations([(np --> [the], adjective)]) )
  subclass_of([compatible(in_derivations) -
               in_derivations(([ap --> adverb, adjective]))])
     scalar_adjective.
```

This more subtle specification of inheritance allows us to block phrases such as *very worse*. After inheritance, the resulting class is the following:

```
class(imp_super_adjective,
     data_field([  ]),
     methods : in_derivations([(np --> [the], adjective)])
               in_derivations([(ap --> adjective)]  ).
               in_derivations([  (comparative_form -->
                              [as], adjective, [as]), ...]  )).
```

To end this section, let us note that the argument compatible we have added to the operator subclass_of to deal with exceptions can also be added with the same meaning to the operator instance_of defined above.

1.2.4 Multiple inheritance

Multiple inheritance occurs when a class inherits from several super-classes. Inheritance proceeds in a monotonic way as long as methods from the super-classes do not conflict. Here are the different multiple inheritance situations:

- the methods coming from the different super-classes have different identifiers,
- methods with the same identifier in the different super-classes have identical definitions,
- methods with the same identifier in the different super-classes have different definitions and the result of inheritance is the disjunction of the two definitions (then several clauses will describe the definition of the method in the lower clause).

There is no inheritance conflict for the first two cases. In the third case above, there is no conflict when the different definitions of a given methods are compatible. The only problem that arises is related to control: when multiple inheritance leads to a choice of definitions which are accessible from different sources then there is the problem of selecting which one to execute. This problem is often resolved in OOP by imposing a standard, predetermined search order. The first definition of the method which can be used is selected. In some cases it is difficult to impose *a priori* a fixed search order which may not be adequate for all inheritance situations. In logic programming, it is a simple matter to allow multiple inheritance and there is no need to specify a predetermined search order for multiple inheritance, since it is not required that there be a single definition for a method. The different definitions are considered one after the other, via backtracking.

A conflict arises, however, in the third case above, when the definitions of the super-classes are incompatible. In that case, a meta-level expressing inheritance preferences, for example, must be specified. Let us further refine the subclass_of operator as follows:

```
subclass_of([inheritance_pref(
                  <list of sorted set of names of classes>)].
```

where the <list of sorted set of names of classes> contains the different classes from which the sub-class will inherit in the decreasing preference order. This sorted set has some similitudes with the set of clauses in a definition in Prolog, where the reading order of clauses indicates the order in which clauses will be considered by the Prolog system.

A further refinement of the subclass_of operator that complements its previous definition is to allow the specification of several parents in a single unit:

```
subclass_of(...)   [<list of parents>].
```

where the <list of parents> is an unordered list of parent classes of the current class.

Let us consider the following example of a nominalized verb which inherits both from the class verb and from the class noun:

```
class(verb,
      data_field( [Word, Morphology, Subcat, Thematic_roles] ),
      methods : subcat(Subcat, obligatory),
                derivations([( vp --> verb, np), (vp --> verb)] ) )
      subclass_of   tensed.    % see definition above
class(noun,
      data_field( [Word, Morphology ] ),
      methods : subcat(Subcat, optional),
                derivations( [ ( np --> det, n),
                             (np --> det, adj, n)] ) ).
```

```
class(nominalized_verb,
      data_field( [ ] ),
      methods :  derivations([ (np --> det, n, [by], np) ] ) )
     subclass_of([inheritance_pref([noun])])     [verb, noun].
```

In this example, we have stated that, in the case of inheritance conflict in the multiple inheritance, the methods to be inherited by the class nominalized_verb from the class noun should have priority over those to be inherited from the class verb. However that class verb can be related to the object nominalized_verb for some other types of data such as event structure or subcategorization not present in the class noun. As a consequence, the class nominalized_verb inherits:

```
    subcat(Subcat,  optional)
```
rather than:
```
    subcat(Subcat,  obligatory)
```
There is no conflict for variables, nominalized_verb inherits of all of them. The derivation method in the nominalized_verb class includes a new grammar rule. This rule is, however, not incompatible with the ones it inherits from the class noun; the result is thus these three grammar rules.

Besides these conventional inheritance schemas, more subtle inheritance mechanisms established for each method, for example, are presented in section 2.2 which is devoted to an introduction to Parlog++.

1.2.5 Class composition

Class composition translates into OOP the lexical semantics relation *part-of*. Class composition allows the description of a class as comprising of a set of other classes. For example, we can say that the class np comprises of the classes det, noun and adjective. A particular type of class composition is realized by the introduction of class variables within the methods. These variables are then instantiated at the object level. Consider the following class np:

```
    class( np
          data_field( [Const1, Const2, Const3] ),
          methods : derivations([ (np --> Const1, adj, noun),
                                  (np --> Const1, noun ),
                          Const2,
                          Const3 ] ) ).
```

and the class then represents a definite determiner:

```
class(definite_det,
      data_field([  ]),
      methods : det([the]) ).
```

Then, if we define the object:

```
object(definite_np,   data_field([definite_det, adjective, noun]) )
                 instance_of   np.
```

as being an instance of an np composed of a definite determiner, then the variable Const1 is replaced via instantiation by the method section of the class definite_det. Similarly, the variables Const2 and Const3 can be replaced respectively by the methods section of the classes adjective and noun.

If we want to be able to directly state the class composition structure at the level of the class and not at the level of an object, instantiation of that class, we can define a relation composed_of as follows:

```
A composed_of [A1, A2, ..., An]
```

which will trigger inclusion of all the elements of the Ai into A, including variables, in the order the Ai are given and in the order in which they appear in each Ai. We could then have, for example, the following statement:

```
class( np
       data_field( [Const1, Const2, Const3 ] ),
       methods : derivations([ (np --> Const1, adjective, noun),
                               ( np --> det, noun ),
                               Const2,
                               Const3 ] ) )
       composed_of   [definite_det, noun, adjective].
```


1.3. Semantics of object-oriented logic programming

In this section we briefly outline the formal semantics of OOLP languages and show that there is a well-founded basis for understanding OOLP programs. OOLP should not be viewed as a notational variant of logic programming, rathre, it introduces concepts and features in objects which are not needed and explained in basic logic programming approaches, which are entirely based on the semantics of relations. We will in this section show how OOLP can be mapped into logic programming, taking into account the characteristics of its specific features. The results presented in this section are most of the time general to the whole OOLP paradigm. They are based on the formal semantics defined by McCabe (1992) for the language *L&O* (standing for *Logic and Objects*).

Conventional object-oriented programming does not have, in general, a strong mathematical basis. It is often viewed as a modular approach to programming which allows for a higher level use of data structures and programs. OOLP takes a particular view of objects which fits well with the formal framework of logic programming. In OOLP, an object is characterized by a set of data and procedures that we know to be true of it. A complete OOLP program is usually composed of many objects, whereas a conventional logic program is only composed of a single global set of true facts and rules to derive new facts. In OOLP, the different objects and the facts they contain may be completely independent, weakly linked (via calls from an object to another) or strongly linked (when there is inheritance from one object to another). In OOLP, we are more concerned with the relationships between relations viewed as a whole rather than with individual tuples of relations.

Adequate rules of inference for OOLP, based on the resolution principle, can be defined. One of the most interesting results of OOLP is that OOLP programs are still first-order logic programs. It is indeed possible to map OOLP programs into first-order clauses, in a sound and complete way, and, conversely, it can also be shown that logic programs can be embedded into OOLP programs.

1.3.1 A proof theory for OOLP

For a given OOLP program, in order to be able to determine all the instances of a given query which are logical consequences of that program, we need to introduce a number of inference rules which will allow the derivation of new queries from old ones. The proof procedure is then an extension to the standard logic programming proof procedure which takes into account the specific features of OOLP.

We can consider OOLP as the specification of a collection of labelled programs. Each label represents an object. An OOLP program is then a sequence of labelled clauses of the form:

    L : Clause.

where L denotes a label and C denotes a clause. Similarly, a query is a labelled goal:

    ?- L1 : Goal.

The goals in the body of a clause as well as the subgoals in a goal need not necessarily be marked by the same label. They may indeed refer to other objects. As a consequence, every subgoal that can arise in a proof procedure is associated with a label which defines where the clauses are that would allow the resolution of that subgoal.

The introduction of a system of labels requires a clear treatment of references, and in particular a clear definition of the environment (i.e. the set of objects) in which the system is working to allow for the construction of correct proofs. For that purpose, in a similar way to the L&O system, let us define two keywords that will allow the system to better navigate in the label system. The self keyword has a value which is independent of the current proof context: it denotes the label of the query being solved. It can be viewed as a kind of reference point. The super keyword is used to bypass any local definitions of a predicate and to use only those definitions which are inherited. Whichever super-class has the appropriate definition of the predicate will be used to construct the proof. Notice that we do not need to know which of those super-classes has the correct definition.

In order to handle the self keyword we need to assign labels to every subgoal: the explicit or actual label, used by the proof, and the self label. This can be represented by subscripting the actual label with the label self noted S:

$$L_S : G [\theta].$$

where θ is the actual computing substitution. We also note:

H :- B in L.

to denote that H :- B is in the class associated with the label L. Notice that a label may contain variables if the object has input variables that characterize it (as those defined in the data_field in the examples above). An initial OOLP query is a labelled subgoal. An OOLP derivation is a sequence of subgoals starting with an initial OOLP query such that each subgoal is derived from the previous one using one of the inference rules given below. Finally, an OOLP proof is a derivation which is terminated by the empty query.

1.3.2 OOLP inference rules

The four following inference rules are related to the distribution of labels in the subgoals of a goal.

The first rule permits the binding of the different variables that are defined in the labels (or in the data_field):

$$L_S : A[\theta], \; L_S\theta : B\theta[\sigma] \vdash L_S : (A, B)[\theta,\sigma].$$

The second rule treats the disjunction of goals :

$$L_S : A[\theta] \vdash L_S : (A \, ; B)[\theta].$$

and

$$L_S : B[\theta] \vdash L_S : (A \, ; B)[\theta].$$

The third inference rule introduces the treatment of a labelled negated subgoal:

$$not(L_S : A[\theta]) \vdash L_S : not(A\,)[\theta].$$

Finally, the fourth rule captures the notion that explicit labelled subgoals retain their explicit labels:

$$M_M : A[\theta] \vdash L_S : (M : A)[\theta].$$

Then, given a subgoal having the form of a labelled predication, it can be reduced in two ways:

- by replacing the label, to consider another class, or

- by replacing the predication as in conventional logic programming.

In the replacement procedure, two strategies are possible: either a clause of the normal class or an inherited clause from a parent class is used. In that second case, the `super` keyword is used. This latter case must also take into account the different treatments of exceptions that may be attached to inheritance, as explained in section 1.2.3.

1.4. Towards modelling concepts of situation semantics in OOLP

In this section we further illustrate the concepts presented above through a modelling in OOLP of some relatively simple concepts of *situation semantics* (Barwise and Perry 1986; Barwise 1989). Situation semantics introduces concepts under a form relatively similar to abstract structured data-types with labelled fields; it is thus of much interest to attempt to model it by means of an OOLP approach. It should also be noticed that, although situation semantics is well known for its ability to describe discourse situations, it can represent a large variety of situations in different domains. Situation semantics has received in the past a very accurate computer interpretation in logic programming with types and constraints called CIL, Complex Indeterminates Language (Mukai and Yasukawa 1985; Mukai 1991). The presentation and the modelling of situation semantics given here is partly based on CIL; however, it is implemented in a different way. We now introduce some concepts of situation semantics and their implementation step by step.

1.4.1 Basic constructions

Situation semantics postulates two levels of descriptions:

- *states of affairs*, which are static situations, noted s, s', ...,

- *events*, which are dynamic situations, noted e, e', ...

Three general types of entities are also introduced:

- *individual entities*, noted a, b,c,...,

- *relations*, noted r, r', ...,

- *space-time locations*, of places and times, represented by pairs of the form:

$\langle p, t \rangle$.

A relation of arity n is represented as follows :

$\langle r, x1, x2, ..., xn \rangle$

where the xi are variables denoting individual entities.

From relations are defined *situation types*. A situation type enables us to represent the way things stand in a situation without any reference to a place or to a time. A situation type is an extensional relation s between constituent sequences $\langle r, x1, x2, ..., xn \rangle$ and $\{ 0, 1 \}$ (denoting, for example, false and true respectively). It is noted:

$\langle \langle r, a, b \rangle, 1 \rangle$

$\langle \langle r', a, b, c, d \rangle, 0 \rangle$.

A *state of affairs* is a situation type with a space-time location. It is noted as follows:

$\langle \langle p, t \rangle, \langle \text{situation type} \rangle \rangle$.

A state of affairs s is part of another state of affairs s' if s and s' have the same space and time location and if the type of s is contained in the type of s'.

State of affairs are static situations, that hold throughout some stretch of time. We need also to be able to represent changes; this is realized by means of abstract objects called *courses of events*. A course of events is a triple $\langle l, y, i \rangle$ where l is a space-time location, y is a relation of any arity and i is 0 or 1. Two courses of events are compatible if the situation types assigned to each of them are compatible for any common space-time location defined from their respective domains.

Finally a *structure of situations* M is a collection of courses of events. The following example is a structure of situations composed of two courses of events e1 and e2:

e1: at $\langle p1, t1 \rangle$: biting, Jackie, Molly; yes.

e2: at $\langle p1, t2 \rangle$: injured, Molly, yes.

1.4.2 Indeterminates

Let us now abstract over events and introduce the notion of event type. Instead of introducing event types as an equivalence class of events, situation semantics introduces some purely abstract set-theoretic entities that stand for individuals, locations and relations. An event type will be then exactly as a course of events except that it contains one or more abstract entities called *indeterminates*. Let us note:

- §a, §b, ..., individual indeterminates that represent abstract individuals,
- §r, §r', ..., relation indeterminates,
- §l, §l', ..., space-time location indeterminates.

Given an event type E of the form:

E(§a, ..., §r, ..., §l, ...),

a function f assigning real individuals, relations and locations to some of the indeterminates in E is called an *anchor* for E (this is a kind of partial interpretation function). Then, an anchor can be viewed as a way to construct new event types from existing ones, the new event types being sub-types (in the formal sense) of the original event type. An anchor defined for all indeterminates of an event type E is called a *total anchor* for E.

We can, for example, define an event type to represent in a generic way a hungry, enthusiastic Prolog programer:

in E : at §l : programmer, §a, Prolog ; yes

                     enthusiastic, §a ; yes

                     hungry, §a ; yes.

All the information represented in such an event type must of course be coherent. Anchors must also respect the coherence of the event type. For example in the relation:

give §a §b

the anchor must assign different individuals to §a and §b. Event types may be more or less abstract depending on the number of indeterminates they contain. An event type with only one indeterminate is called an *object type*.

Indeterminates can be complex. In particular they can be embedded into different event types. A complex indeterminate is defined recursively as follows:

- every basic indeterminate is an indeterminate,
- if §x is an indeterminate and E(...,§x, ...) is an event type, then <§x, E> is an indeterminate.

Finally, let us introduce the notion of *indexed event type*. The goal of an indexed event type is to allow us to classify mental states. Similarly to sentences, mental states allow people to perceive, know, guess, believe, etc. different things. An indexed event type is an event type which is classified and with which is associated a label that identifies its 'role' or 'purpose'. One of the simpler examples is the notion of *located individual* indexed by the symbol LI:

LI := at <§p, §t> : present §a; yes.

The role *individual* focuses on §a and represents it as a specific indeterminate that represents an individual:

§i = <§a, LI >

let also §h be the role that focuses on the *space-time location* of LI:

§h = <<§p, §t>, LI >.

Then, these two roles can be used to construct more complex representations such as the *hitting* event type:

E' = at §h, hitting §i, §a' ; yes.

Other indexed event types and roles can be defined in a similar way for other concepts. For example, here is the representation of the role of a speaker §a uttering §b :

speaker = <§a, D >

D = at <§p, §t> : speak, §a ; yes

                              utter, §a, §b ; yes.

Similarly for the notion of the object of attention:

t = < §b, OBJ-ATTN >

OBJ-ATTN = at §h : pay attention to §i, §b ; yes.

which uses the roles §h and §i defined above.

1.4.4 Constraints on representations

Situation semantics introduces constraints on the structure of the world. These constraints control the creation of state of affairs. Situation semantics postulates several classes of constraints that may partly overlap:

- necessary constraints are necessary relations that hold among properties and relations defined in state of affairs, e.g. a woman is a human,

- nomic constraints which are inviolable patterns, also called natural laws,

- conventional constraints which arise from implicit conventions that hold within a community of living beings,

- conditional constraints are constraints which hold in certain conditions, whether they be necessary, nomic, conventional or of any other kind,

Here is now the way that the necessary non-conditional constraint of stating
that:

Who eats an object touches this object.

is represented by:

E: at <§p, §t> : eat, §a, b§ ; yes.

E': at <§p, §t> : touch, §a, §b ; yes.

and:

for all <§p, §t> : IMPLY E, E' ; yes.

1.4.5 Representing situation semantics concepts by means of classes

Concepts of situation semantics lend themselves very easily to an OOLP
modelling. Entities, relations and space-time locations are represented by
constants; states of affairs and events are labels, also represented by constants.
Relations can be represented by facts, possibly including variables. Situation
types can be represented in two ways. The simplest way is to only assert those
situation types which are true and to leave the others unspecified. The negation
as failure rule under the closed world assumption will allow us to deduce the
falsity of any other situation type. However, this approach does not entirely
captures the meaning of situation types. A more appropriate way to represent
them is to have a specific argument that represents the truth value 0 or 1. Then,
when querying a structure of situations, we need a meta-level of interpretation to
construct proofs only based on those situations which are true.

States of affairs and courses of events do not raise any particular
representational problems. Indeterminates are represented by logical variables,
complex indeterminates are represented at two levels. In <§x, E>, §x is
represented in the data_field section whereas E is either an entire method or a
portion of it, as we shall see it below.

Let us now express the examples given in the above sub-section in OOLP.
The first example:

e1: at <p1,l1> : biting, Jackie, Molly; yes.

is represented as follows:

```
class(e1,
     data_field([  ]),
     methods : biting(jackie,  molly,  at(p1,t1),  true) ).
```

As can be seen in this example, the space-time location and the truth value are directly incorporated into the predicate that represents the action of biting. This solution is the simplest from a representation point of view, but it may not be the best one since the different types of information are all represented at the same level, namely the predicate. It is necessary to attach in a certain way the space-time information to the predicate itself. A solution consists of defining an operator, e.g. at, that will bind the space-time information to the remainder of the predicate:

```
class(e1,
     data_field([ ]),
     methods : biting(jackie, molly, true) at loc(p1,t1) ).
```

Notice that we cannot define a special field in the object that would encode the space-time location information for the entire object since the different methods in a class may be located differently in space and/or time.

The example above is completely instantiated. We can define a more abstract class that represents the action of biting by using indeterminates, which we represent by means of logical variables as follows:

```
class(e1,
     data_field([A, B, P, T ]),
     methods : biting(A, B, true) at loc(P,T). ).
```

An anchor will then consist of the definition of a set of substitutions of constants for some of the variables in that class. Under the instantiation operation the relation class-subclass is established.

The next example:

in E : at §1 : programmer, §a, Prolog ; yes
                enthusiastic, §a ; yes
                hungry, §a ; yes.

allows us to create a class with several methods which are all facets of what we want to say about Prolog programmers:

```
class(e,
     data_field([ A, P, T ]),
     methods : programmer(A, prolog, true) at loc(P, T).
               enthusiastic(A, true) at loc(P, T).
               hungry(A, true) at loc(P, T). ).
```

This class talks about a certain programmer A at a certain space-time location loc(P,T) and, besides asserting that he is a Prolog programmer, it also asserts that he is enthusiastic and hungry.

Since all classes have a name, there is no difference in our representations between an event type and an indexed event type. The role of located individual LI presented above:

LI := at <§p, §t> : present §a; yes.

is represented as follows:

```
class(li,
     data_field([A,  P,  T]),
     methods :  present(A, true) at loc(P,T). ).
```

Complex indeterminates can be represented by classes, where the indeterminates that characterizes the role at stake is specified alone in the data_field section. The class referred to (here LI) is represented as a part of that role. We can thus represent the notion of an individual as follows:

```
class(individual,
     data_field([A]),
     method : present(A) at _ ).
```

Similarly for the definition of a space-time location at which someone is present:

```
class(space_time,
     data_field([P,  T]),
     method : _ at loc(P,T) ).
```

We now have all the tools to represent the examples given at the end of section 1.4.3 where roles are used to construct more complex representations. The operator composed_of given in section 1.2.5 is used to establish a binding relation between different classes. The *hitting* event type is represented as follows:

```
class(hitting,
     data_field([I,  H,  B]),
     method :  hitting(A,B) at H.
               I at H.
               B at H. ).
  composed_of([individual, space_time, individual]).
```

Similarly, we can also represent the object of attention by the following class:

```
class(obj_attn,
     data_field([I,  H,  B]),
     method : pay_attention_to( I, B) at H.
              I at H. ).
```

The representation of constraints in OOLP is more delicate. Classes indeed represent sets of data structures and definitions which have their internal cohesion. As we have seen it, there are only two types of relations between classes: the class-subclass relation and the class composition relation. Constraints of the form:

A woman is a human.

can easily be represented by the introduction of an additional class-subclass relation between the class describing humans and the class describing women, if it does not already exist. However, a constraint such as:

Who eats an object touches it.

introduces, as we have seen it in section 1.4.4, an implication between the eating and the touching. If we have a class that describes the action of eating and another class that describes the action of touching, it is not possible directly to state that one class implies the other. The problem can partly be solved by weakening the meaning of the implication a little bit. The action of touching can then be included into the conditional part of the definition of the action of eating, at the same place and time:

```
class(eat,
     data_field([A, B, P, T]),
     method :  eat(A,B) at loc(P,T) :- touch(A, B) at loc(P,T). ).
```

which indicates that the action of touching an object is a necessary condition to the action of eating that object.

2. Object-Oriented Logic Programming and Concurrency

In this section we present the combination of OOLP and concurrency. The OOLP approach we consider here is based on the notion of actor and message exchanges (Shapiro and Takeuchi 83). Objects are activated by means of requests which have the form of messages, and objects communicate with each other also by means of messages. These messages trigger executions in the corresponding objects. Furthermore, the formalism associated with message exchange allows for the specification of inheritance in a more direct way, i.e. directly in the object.

OOLP is of much interest for *concurrent logic programming*. Notions of encapsulation of data and programs, state changing and stream manipulation allows for the removal of some of the weaknesses of concurrent logic programming where the only structure is the predicate.

Concurrent logic programming is also of much interest to OOLP. Concurrent logic programming makes available simple ways of expressing synchronization and concurrency within and between objects. Most concurrent logic programming languages also offer committed choice non-determinism, which is often the most appropriate strategy for OOLP. Finally, concurrent logic programming allows communication between processes; thus it allows for various types of communication between objects, by means of partially instantiated messages, making the system more powerful and easier to use.

In this section, we study a precise OOLP language that offers concurrency: Parlog++, which is an OOP extension to Parlog, presented in Chapter 6. This language has almost all the features of OOLP and offers a parallel logic programming framework that supports concurrency. Besides concurrency, Parlog++ also offers a more refined inheritance system than the inheritance procedures presented in the previous section.

2.1 An introduction to Parlog++

We now present the features of Parlog++; this presentation owes much to Davidson (1991). Concurrent logic programming and OOLP systems usually have the following characteristics:

- an object is viewed as a process which calls itself recursively (to maintain it 'active') and which has an internal state stored in unshared variables,
- communication between objects is based on the instantiation of variables in messages,
- an object becomes active when it receives an appropriate message, otherwise it remains suspended,
- an object instance is created by process reduction,
- a response to a message is characterized by the binding of a shared variable in a message.

In Parlog++, the basic idea is that an object is viewed as a process which remains suspended till it gets an activating message to process. This can roughly be summarized by the following Parlog program, where obj is an abstract object:

```
mode obj( ?, ? ).
obj( [Input_message| Next], Current_state) <-
  action1_obj(Input_message, Current_state, New_state) :
  obj(Next,  New_state).
obj( [Input_message| Next], Current_state) <-
  action2_obj(Input_message, Current_state, New_state) :
  obj(Next,  New_state).
etc...
obj( [ ], [ ] ).
```

The object obj has one input message stream, its first argument, and one state variable, the second argument. The state variable may originate a message which will be executed by another object in the current program. We have mentioned two different possible actions that could be triggered depending on the input message. This abstract example shows that an object could:

(1) try in parallel different actions triggered by a given message and

(2) process in parallel, and simultaneously, different messages.

Let us now introduce the main features of the language Parlog++. A Parlog++ class can be summarized as follows, in a kind of BNF form:

```
< class name > .
< variable  declarations >
{ initial   <actions> }
clauses
   < clauses >
{ code
   < predicates >  }
end.
```

Sections between curly brackets are optional. Initial, clauses, code and end are reserved keywords. A Parlog++ class begins with a name and then the variables of the class that define streams and states if any are declared. These variables, as we shall see later, can be made visible or invisible to the user (i.e. the user may or may not have access to their contents). The optional initial section contains clauses which must be executed before the clauses section. The clauses section receives and produces streams corresponding to messages. It also contains the clauses that process these messages. The general form of a clause in that section is the following:

```
< input message > => < actions to execute > <action separator>
```

The set < actions to execute >, is a Parlog clause body, possibly containing Parlog++ operations, while <action separator> is either the symbol '.' to indicate OR-parallel search between the different clauses or the symbol ';' to realize a sequential search. The code section contains the code used in the clauses of the clause section. This code section is private to the object. This can be very useful for structuring programs. Finally, the description of the class is terminated by the symbol end.

A clause is activated by the unification of the input message with its message part, occurring before the symbol =>. If the unification succeeds and if the guard (if any) is true, then the clause body is executed. Clauses may have their own local variables.

Let us consider a very simple example of an object that represents a lexicon:

```
lex1.
clauses
   last =>  end.
   lex(the, Cat) => Cat = det.
   lex(a, Cat) => Cat = det.
   lex(book, Cat) => Cat = noun.
   lex(has, Cat) => Cat = verb.
   lex(pages,Cat) => Cat = noun.
end.
```

Input messages are of the form:

```
lex( <word >, Cat)
```

and the object returns a value for Cat, if the word is in the object. For example, to the call:

```
lex(book, C).
```

Parlog++ responds:

```
C = noun.
```

The message

```
last => end.
```

ends the work-suspend cycle of the object. Unification attempts for an input message on the different messages lex is done in parallel. This object is very simple; let us make it a little bit more realistic by introducing lists of lexical items of the same category in a single clause rather than having a long enumeration:

```
lex1.
clauses
   last => end.
   lex(W, Cat) => in(W,[a,the,some,several]) : Cat = det.
   lex(W, Cat) => in(W,[car,truck, table, plate]) : Cat = noun.
   lex(W, Cat) => in(W,[has,sees,becomes,talks]) : Cat = verb.
code
mode in(?,?).
   in(A,[A| _]).
   in(A,[B|C]) <- not(A = B) : in(A,C).
end.
```

This example shows two new elements. First, in the clauses section, clauses have a guard which has to be true (as in any Parlog clause) to ensure commitment to that clause and to allow for the remainder of the body to be executed. Notice that this example follows the well-formedness conditions given in Chapter 6, section 2.3, in particular the sufficient test property. This example also shows how a code section is realized.

Streams are represented by means of variables. Variables can also represent states. Variables can be visible to the user or invisible. Declarations are made as follows:

```
B visible output stream variable:  B ostream
B visible input stream variable:  B istream
B visible state variable: B state
```

Invisible variables are declared in a special section starting with the predefined symbol invisible:

```
invisible   A ostream, B istream.
```

Finally, the output of a message into an appropriate stream is represented by the symbol '::'. For example, if Error is declared as an output stream variable, the operation:

```
Error :: 'unknown word'
```

the term 'unknown word' will send along the output stream Error. Parlog++ contains a few more predefined operators which can be found in Davidson (1991).

2.2 Inheritance between objects

Parlog++ does not have a direct inheritance mechanism that would permit an object to inherit from the clauses and the data of another object. However, it has a mechanism which links objects and in effect achieves what is usually realized by an inheritance mechanism. This mechanism is called *delegation* or *message forwarding*. Delegation permits an object that cannot handle a particular message to pass it on to another object which can either process it or pass it on to another object that can.

This allows an object to delegate some tasks to other objects. Delegation is completely hidden to the user. This mechanism permits the use of OOP with all its power in Parlog++.

Delegation is realized by means of two elements:

- output stream variables of an object are declared in the invisible section,
- the objects onto which messages are passed are declared in the initial section, the goal being to start activating them. This activation is also invisible to the user.

Let us now consider the following example representing a few lexical items according to the type/subtype relation. We define two 'top-level' (or root) concepts, service and vehicle with a few general syntactic and semantic features:

```
service1.
clauses
   semantics(service,Sem) => Sem = public.
   pred(service,P) => P = [public-offer].
end.


vehicle1.
clauses
   last => true.
   string(vehicle,S) => S = vehicle.
   cat(vehicle,C) => C = noun.
   number(vehicle,N) => N = singular.
   semantics(vehicle,Sem) => Sem = means_of_transp.
   pred(vehicle,P) => P = vehicle(X).
end.
```

We can further define subtypes of these two types. These subtypes naturally inherit the properties of their hyponyms. This inheritance is realized by means of the delegation mechanism, which works in the reverse order to inheritance since sub-types delegate actions to their hyponyms (i.e. subtypes in a taxonomy relation). Here are the objects associated with 'means of transportation' (object transp1), 'car' and 'intercity':

```
transp1.
invisible  Hyponym ostream
initial   vehicle1(Hyponym).
clauses
  last => true.
  cat(S,C) =>
      in(S,[car,automobile,truck,van,lorry,train]):
      Hyponym :: cat(vehicle,C).
  number(S,N) =>
      in(S,[car,automobile,truck,van,lorry,train]):
      N = singular.
  semantics(S,Sem) =>
  in(S,[car,automobile,truck,van,lorry,train]):
            Hyponym :: semantics(vehicle,Sem).
  pred(S,P) => in(S,[car,automobile]): P = [car].
  pred(S,P) => in(S,[truck,van,lorry]): P = [truck].
  pred(S,P) => in(S,[train]): P = [train].
code
 mode in(?,?).
  in(A,[A|B]).
  in(A,[B|C]) <- not(A = B) : in(A,C).
end.


intercity1.
invisible Hyponym ostream, Ser ostream
initial transp1(Hyponym), service1(Ser).
clauses
  last => true.
  cat(intercity,C) => Hyponym :: cat(train,C).
  number(intercity,N) =>
        Hyponym :: number(train,N).
  semantics(intercity,Sem) =>
        Hyponym :: semantics(train,Sem).
```

```
    pred(intercity,P) =>   Hyponym :: pred(train,P1),
    Ser :: pred(service,P2),  P = and(P1,P2).
  end.


  car1.
  invisible  Hyponym ostream
  initial   vehicle1(Hyponym).
  clauses
    last => true.
    string(car,S)  => S = [car,automobile].
    cat(car,C)  => Hyponym :: cat(vehicle,C).
    number(car,N) => N = singular.
    semantics(car,Sem) =>
              Hyponym :: semantics(vehicle,Sem).
    pred(car,P) => P = car(X).
  end.
```

Let us consider the intercity example. It refers to two objects, transp1 and service1. It is therefore the hyponym of two distinct objects and is subject to multiple inheritance from both of these objects. Output streams and hyponym objects are declared as follows:

```
  invisible Hyponym ostream, Ser ostream
  initial  transp1(Hyponym),  service1(Ser).
```

In the clauses section, there are explicit calls to the hyponym objects. For example, the stream variable Hyponym allows a call to the object transp1:

```
  Hyponym :: semantics(train,Sem).
```

Hyponym is thus instantiated to the message sent to the object transp1. This message is directly forwarded to the clauses in the clauses section of the latter object. Notice that the message sent to an object need not be the same as the current message (here semantics). In this application, we have simply kept the same names since they were the most appropriate ones.

Similarly, the output stream variable Ser allows direct access to the object service1 which can process another set of messages.

Finally, it should be noted that the predicative representation produced under transp1 by the message pred(S, P) is simply a constant. It is indeed not possible to produce an output result that contains a free variable. This is, however, a minor limitation of the language.

Monotonic multiple inheritance can easily be realized as shown in this example. Delegation in Parlog++ is particularly flexible since it is specified clause by clause and only those clauses for which inheritance is relevant are subject to delegation. Consequently, different clauses may inherit from different objects. This is usually not possible or very hard to realize with type-based systems such as those presented in Chapter 4.

Finally, the treatment of exceptions is straightforward: the clause that handles an exception does not contain calls to any other object. Let us consider the example of the intercity object. Suppose we do not want it to inherit from the semantics of means of transportation (transp1). Then, we simply do not have any inheritance specification, as in the following reformulation:

```
intercity1.
invisible Hyponym ostream, Ser ostream
initial transp1(Hyponym), service1(Ser).
clauses
  last => true.
  cat(intercity,C) => Hyponym :: cat(train,C).
  number(intercity,N) =>
      Hyponym :: number(train,N).
  semantics(intercity,Sem) =>
      Sem = [intercity_service].
  pred(intercity,P) => Hyponym :: pred(train,P1),
  Ser :: pred(service,P2), P = and(P1,P2).
end.
```

The example presented here can easily be extended to a larger lexicon. However, despite clear enhancement in modularity, loss of efficiency can become a serious one for real-size lexicons on a machine that does not support real parallelism.

3 Parsing in Parlog++

Let us now examine a parsing system in which an object describes a type of phrase: NPs, VPs, APs, etc. For the sake of readability, we incorporate lexical items into objects. The parsing strategy is directly realized by the delegation mechanism: the sentence object sentence1 delegates the processing of the subject np to the object np1, and the processing of the verb phrase to the object vp1. Similarly the processing of the verb phrase entails the delegation of the np or pp to the objects np1 or pp1 respectively . The strategy is thus top-down.

There are different ways of writing these objects. In this section, we propose a solution which is relatively remote from the DCG style. In section 4, we present another implementation which is closer to the DCG style. Let us now consider the different objects. The sentence object is written as follows:

```
sentence1.
invisible To_file1 ostream, To_file ostream
initial np1(To_file1), vp1(To_file).
clauses
  last => true.
  s(X,Y,R) => To_file1 :: np(X, X1,R1),
              To_file :: vp(X1,Z, R2) :
              Y = Z,
              R = s(R1, R2).
end.
```

In the message s(X,Y,R), X is the input string of words to parse, Y is the output string and R is the resulting syntactic tree. The guard includes both the treatment of the np and of the vp.

The vp object is then defined as follows:

```
vp1.
invisible To_file1 ostream, To_file ostream
initial pp1(To_file1), np1(To_file).
clauses
  last => true.
  vp(X,Y,R) =>  in2(X,X1,verb,W1) ,
                To_file1 :: pp(X1,Z,R1) :
                Y = Z,
                R = vp(verb(W1),R1).
  vp(X,Y,R) => in2(X,X1,verb,W1) ,
               To_file :: np(X1,Z,R1) :
               Y = Z,
               R = vp(verb(W1),R1).
```

```
code
 mode  in(?,?).
  in(A,[A|B]).
  in(A,[B|C])  <-  not(A = B) : in(A,C).
 mode  in1(?,?).
  in1(Word,Cat)  <-   in(Word, [has,comes,looks]) :
                            true.
 mode  in2(?,^,?,^).
  in2([W|X],X,Cat,W)  <-  in1(W,Cat).
 end.
```

After the recognition of a verb (here either has, comes or looks), the recognition of the complement, an np or a pp, is done in parallel and concurrently. The position of the guard ensures that the commitment is made only after either the np or the pp has been recognized (this is, however, not fully respected in some versions of Parlog++ where the operation A :: B is systematically evaluated to true, independently of the result of the evaluation of B).

The objects related to the pp and the np are the following. They share common clauses in the code section, which is given in full here to facilitate understanding:

```
pp1.
invisible To_file2 ostream
initial np1(To_file2).
clauses
   last => true.
   pp(X,Y,R)  =>  in2(X,X1,prep,W1)  :
                  To_file2 :: np(X1, Z ,R1),
                  Y = Z,
                  R = pp(prep(W1),R1).
code
 mode  in(?,?).
  in(A,[A|B]).
  in(A,[B|C])  <-  not(A = B) : in(A,C).
 mode  in1(?,?).
  in1(Word,Cat)  <-   in(Word, [at,on,to,with,from]) :
                            true.
```

```
mode  in2(?,^,?,^).
  in2([W|X],X,Cat,W)  <- in1(W,Cat).
end.


np1.
clauses
  last => true.
  np(X,Y,T)  =>  in2(X,Z,proper_noun,W) :
                 Y = Z,
                 T = proper_noun(W).
  np2(X,Y,T)  =>  in2(X,X1,det,W1),
                  in2(X1,Z,noun,W2) :
                  Y = Z1,
                  T = np(det(W1), noun(W2)).
  np(X,Y,T)  =>   in2(X,X1,det,W1),
                  in2(X1,X2,adj,  W2),
                  in2(X2,Z,noun,W3) :
                  Y = Z,
                  T = np(det(W1), adj(W2), noun(W3)).
  np(X,Y,T)  =>  in2(X,X1,det,W1),
                 in2(X1,X2,noun,W2),
                 in2(X2,Z,adj,W3) :
                 Y = Z,
                 T = np(det(W1), noun(W2), adj(W3)).
code
 mode  listword(?,^).
  listword(proper_noun, [john, mary, ann]).
  listword(det,[the,a,several,some]).
  listword(noun,[book,car,computer,window]).
  listword(adj,[big,expensive,fast]).
 mode  in(?,?).
  in(A,[A|B]).
  in(A,[B|C]) <- not(A = B) : in(A,C).
 mode  in1(?,?).
  in1(Word,Cat) <-  listword(Cat,  A),
                    in(Word, A) : true.
```

```
mode in2(?,^,?,^).
  in2([W|X],X,Cat,W) <- in1(W,Cat).
end.
```

The treatment of the pp is relatively simple: commitment is made when a preposition is found. The treatment of nps entails parallel and concurrent treatment of the different forms of nps.

The np1 object can be further elaborated upon by introducing noun complements as follows:

```
np1
invisible To ostream
initial pp1(To).
clauses
  last => true.
  np(X,Y,T) =>
                in2(X,Z,proper_noun,W) :
                Y = Z, T = proper_noun(W).
np(X,Y,T) =>
                in2(X,X1,det,W1),
                in2(X1,Z,noun,W2),
                To :: pp(Z,U,R1) :
                Y = U,
                T = np(np(det(W1), noun(W2)),
                        R1).


  np(X,Y,T) =>
                in2(X,X1,det,W1),
                in2(X1,Z,noun,W2),
                not(in2(Z,Z3,prep,_)) :
                Y = Z, T = np(det(W1), noun(W2)).
  np(X,Y,T) =>
                in2(X,X1,det,W1),
                in2(X1,X2,adj,  W2),
                in2(X2,Z,noun,W3),  not(in2(Z,Z3,prep,_)) :
                Y = Z,
                T = np(det(W1), adj(W2), noun(W3)).
```

```
np(X,Y,T)  =>
                in2(X,X1,det,W1),
                in2(X1,X2,noun,W2),
                in2(X2,Z,adj,W3),  not(in2(Z,Z3,prep,_))  :
                Y = Z,
                T = np(det(W1), noun(W2), adj(W3)).


code
<same as above>
end.
```

Control on the existence of a preposition is necessary to avoid wrong
commitments. It is not very elegant, however, and shows the limits of the
approach.

Finally, an object can call itself recursively. We can incorporate a recursive call
into the object **pp** as follows:

```
pp1.
invisible To_file1 ostream, To_file2 ostream
initial np1(To_file2), pp1(To_file1).
clauses
   last => true.
   pp(X,Y,R)  => in2(X,X1,prep,W1)  :
                To_file2 :: np(X1, Z ,R1),
                To_file1 :: pp(Z, T, R2),
                Y = Z,
                R = pp(pp(prep(W1),R1), R2 ).
   pp(X,Y,R)  =>  not(in2(X,X1,prep,W1) ):
                R = [].
code
<same as above>
end.
```

In this example, the contents of the clauses directly reflect the grammar rules
describing the syntax of PPs.

4. Machine Translation within OOPLP

In this section we present in detail an application of OOPLP to machine translation. We first show how a general architecture can be designed, and then focus on the problem of efficient feature percolation and cooperation between the source language and the target language processors. As we shall see, the modular approach of OOPLP is well adapted to the standard organization of a machine translation system.

4.1 A basic translation system

Without commiting ourselves to any precise theoretical or methodological approach, we may represent a simple machine translation system as follows:

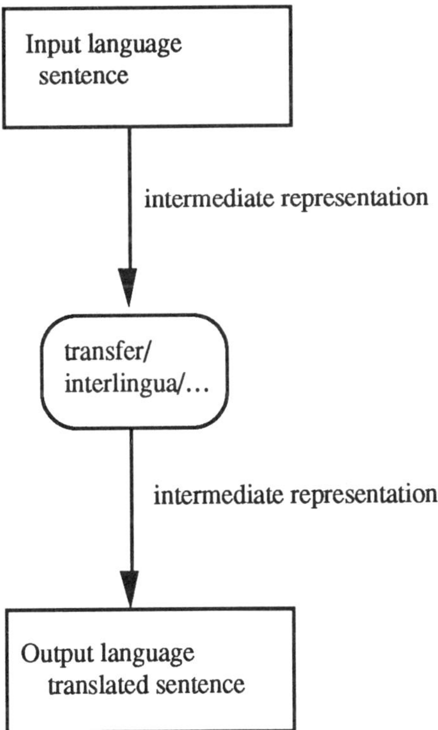

Let us assume that the intermediate representation produced in this example is based on a predicate-argument representation, embodying the notion of domain restrictor. Let us also suppose that this representation can play the role of an interlingua representation. In the following program, we have a translation system from French to English. The names of predicates and constants are given in French, which is the language adopted here for the interlingua (translation into English is given in the English lexical entries). To make the program more readable and relatively small in size, let us focus on the translation of simple NPs.

The principal element in the architecture of the program is the transfer/interlingua module that governs on the one hand a parser and on the other hand a generator for the target language. This module acts as a supervisor:

```
interlingua.
  invisible To ostream, To1 ostream
  initial npfr(To), npeng(To1).
clauses
  last => true.
  trans(In,Out) => To :: np(In,Y,T),
                   To1 :: np(T,Out),
                   write('Translation of '), write(In), nl,
                   write('  into '), write(Out), nl.
end.
```

The main call is trans(In,Out) in which a sentence is given in In and the result is produced in Out. The French NP parser is the following:

```
npfr.
clauses
  last => true.
  np(X,Y,T) =>
              word(X,Z,F,proper_noun,W) :
              Y = Z, T = arg(quant([]),restr([W])).
  np(X,Y,T) =>
              word(X,X1,feat(G,N),det,W1),
              word(X1,Z,feat(G,N),noun,W2) :
              Y = Z, T = arg(quant(W1),restr([W2])),
              write(T).
```

```
np(X,Y,T) =>
                word(X,X1,feat(G,N),det,W1),
                word(X1,X2,feat(G,N),adj,  W2),
                word(X2,Z,feat(G,N),noun,W3) :
                Y = Z,
                T = arg(quant(W1),restr([W3,[W2]])),
                write(T).
np(X,Y,T) =>
                word(X,X1,feat(G,N),det,W1),
                word(X1,X2,feat(G,N),noun,W2),
                word(X2,Z,feat(G,N),adj,W3) :
                Y = Z,
                T =  arg(quant(W1),restr([W2,[W3]])),
                write(T).
code
 mode  word(?,^,^,?,^).
  word([jean|X],X,feat(masc,sing),proper_noun,jean).
  word([marie|X],X,feat(fem,sing),proper_noun,marie).
  word([un|X],X,feat(masc,sing),det,un).
  word([une|X],X,feat(fem,sing),det,une).
  word([plusieurs|X],X,feat(_,plu),det,plusieurs).
  word([livre|X],X,feat(masc,sing),noun,livre).
  word([voitures|X],X,feat(fem,plu),noun,voitures).
  word([grand|X],X,feat(masc,sing),adj,grand).
  word([rapide|X],X,feat(_,sing),adj,rapide).
end.
```

In this object, the main calls are np(X,Y,T) where X is the input string of
symbols, Y is the output string of symbols and T is the resulting semantic
representation. That representation constitutes the input data for the English NP
generator. It is forwarded to the English generator by the supervisor. The
generator, which uses the same technique as in Chapter 4, is the following:

```
npeng.
clauses
last => true.
  np(arg(quant([]),restr([W])),X)  =>
                word([A|_],Z,F,proper_noun,W) :
```

```
            X = [A].
np(arg(quant(W1),restr([W2])),X)  =>
            word([A1|_],X1,feat(N),det,W1),
            word([A2|_],Z,feat(N),noun,W2)  :
            X = [A1,A2].
np(arg(quant(W1),restr([W3,[W2]])),X)  =>
            word([A1|_],X1,feat(N),det,W1),
            word([A2|_],X2,feat(N),adj,  W2),
            word([A3|_],Z,feat(N),noun,W3)  :
            X = [A1, A2, A3].
code
 mode  word(^,^,^,?,?).
   word([john|X],X,feat(sing),proper_noun,jean).
   word([mary|X],X,feat(sing),proper_noun,marie).
   word([a|X],X,feat(sing),det,un).
   word([several|X],X,feat(plu),det,plusieurs).
   word([book|X],X,feat(sing),noun,livre).
   word([cars|X],X,feat(plu),noun,voitures).
   word([large|X],X,feat(sing),adj,grand).
   word([fast|X],X,feat(sing),adj,rapide).
end.
```

In this object, the main call is np(T,X), where T is the input intermediate representation (produced by the French parser) and X is the English translation, which is then printed out by the supervisor.

4.2 Using OOPLP synchonization mechanisms to limit percolation of lexical information

Recent work in computational linguistics show the central role played by the lexicon in language processing, and in particular by the lexical semantics component. Lexicons are no longer a mere enumeration of feature-value pairs but tend to show increasing intelligent behaviour. This is the case, for example, for generative lexicons (Pustejovsky 1991) which contain, besides complex feature structures, a number of rules for creating new definitions of word-senses such as rules for type coercion. As a result, the size of lexical entries describing word-senses has substantially increased. These lexical entries become very hard to be used directly by a natural language parser or generator because their size and complexity allow little flexibility.

Most natural language systems consider a lexical entry as an indivisible whole which is percolated up in the parse/generation tree. Access to features and feature values at grammar rule level is realized by more or less complex procedures (Shieber 86, Johnson 88). The complexity of real natural language processing systems makes such an approach very inefficient and sometimes linguistically inadequate. In this section, we propose a dynamic treatment of lexical data and of lexical feature propagation within a machine translation (MT) framework.

A MT system can be viewed as a set of producer-consumer pairs. The central pair is composed of (1) a parser which produces fragments of intermediate representations from a sentence of the input language, and (2) a generator which consumes these representations to produce a sentence in the target language. The parser is tuned to send minimal information and the generator can ask the parser to produce more if required. Other elements such as lexicons and grammars can also behave as producers with respect to their associated parsers or generators.

Lexicons and grammars are activated when information is required; the parser is always active when there is a sentence to parse. When it is asked for more information by the generator, it suspends its current work to produce the required information. Finally, the generator suspends till it has sufficient information to go on working. This global schema can be represented as follows:

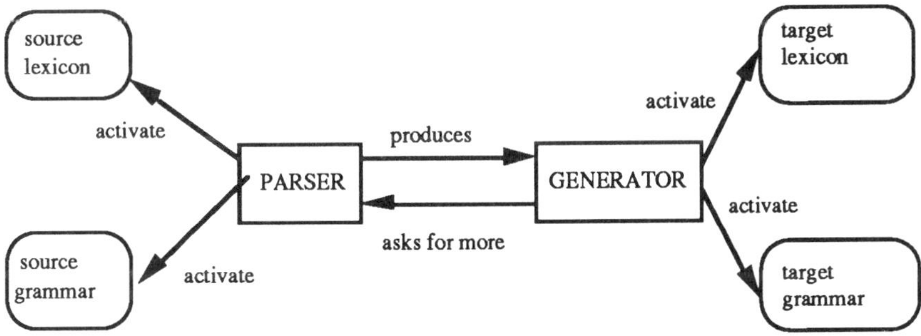

From an architectural point of view, the lexicons and grammars can have various forms. For the sake of understandability, let us say that the general form of these components is based on unification grammar. They contain the usual lexical and grammatical information.

The motivations for this approach are twofold. The first motivation is obviously efficiency. When translating a sentence, only small portions of the lexical entries corresponding to the words of the surface sentence being processed are used. It is preferable to delay this global percolation and to extract the relevant information only when required. The second motivation for this approach is linguistic adequacy. Most of the information conveyed by features is often linguistically relevant (and thus used) very locally in a parsing/generation tree. For example, in:

John opened the door.

the aspectual value of the verb *open* is only relevant at the level of the VP category, i.e. the level of the maximal projection of the verb. There is no reason to have a more or less specified aspectual feature at lower levels, e.g. V^1 and V^0 in the X-bar system.

Let us now consider the relatively simple case of *essen* versus *fressen* (to eat) as possible German translations of the verb *manger* in French. German has two different verbs for eat depending on the semantic type of the subject. If the subject is human, then *essen* is used, whereas *fressen* is used when the subject is an animal. Here is a simple portion of an object that processes sentences. The rule presented here under the message $s(X,Y,T)$ processes intransitive verb constructions of the form:

```
sentence --> proper_noun, intransitive_verb.
```

X and Y represent the difference lists as in DCGs. T is the resulting semantic representation, which has the following form here:

```
pred([<predicate name>, <predicate argument>]).
```

The program is the following. For the sake of readability, the lexicon has been incorporated into the object:

```
strans.
clauses
  last => true.
  s(X,Y,T) =>
            word(X,Z,F,proper_noun,W1),
            word(Z,S,F1,verb,W2),
            Y = S,
            T = pred([W2,W1]).
  semantics(W,Sem,Cat) =>
            word([W|_],_,feat(_,_,SSem),Cat,_),    Sem = SSem.
```

```
code
 mode word(?,^,^,?,^).
    % declaration of arguments : ? is input mode, ^ is output mode
  word([jean|X],X,feat(masc,sing,human),
      proper_noun,jean).
  word([marie|X],X,feat(fem,sing,human),
      proper_noun,marie).
  word([lola|X],X,feat(fem,sing,animal),
      proper_noun,lola).
  word([mange|X],X,feat(sing,_),verb,manger).
  word([marche|X],X,feat(sing,_),verb,marcher).
 end.
```

The message semantics is a utility which allows any other object to have
access to the semantic feature(s) of the word W of category Cat. Clearly, such a
message will be produced by the target language system in order to get,
whenever required, and only then, the necessary data. The target language
generator system is the following:

```
 starg.
 invisible To ostream
 initial  strans(To).
 clauses
  last => true.
  s(pred([W1,W2]),X)  =>
     not( W1 = manger) :          % end of guard, realizes commitment
     word([A|_],_,feat(_,SSem),verb,W1),
     X = [W2, A].
  s(pred([W1,W2]),X)  =>
     W1 = manger :
     To :: semantics(W2,SSem,proper_noun),
                            % call to the object strans
     word([A|_],_,feat(_,SSem),verb,W1),
     X = [W2, A].
code
 mode  word(?,^,^,?,^).
  word([esse|X],X,feat(sing,human),verb,manger).
  word([fresse|X],X,feat(sing,animal),verb,manger).
```

```
    word([wandert|X],X,feat(sing,animal),verb,marcher).
end.
```

This example shows how specific cases, treated in parallel with more general ones, are identified. The guard permits postponement of the committed choice of the parallel system till it is evaluated to true, thus avoiding incorrect choices. In the case of W1 = manger, then the generator suspends till it gets the semantic feature value of the subject argument. This is realized by the call:

```
    To :: semantics(W2,SSem,proper_noun)
```

which is sent to the strans object and executed in parallel with other activities that the object may have. During the execution, the starg object suspends this activity. It resumes working when it gets the information back.

5. Conclusion

In this chapter, we have shown how an object-oriented programming approach could be used for modelling natural language processing systems in a modular and linguistically adequate way. We have also shown how this approach can be merged with parallel logic programming, using Parlog++ as an example. Current development of operational systems using the object-oriented approach clearly shows its relevance and feasability on a large scale.

Chapter 8

Higher-Order Logic Programming for Language Processing

The goal of this chapter is to present the basic principles of higher-order logic programming and to show what its main are features with respect to natural language processing. We consider here a relatively weak higher-order system, based on the notion of hereditary Harrop formulas, and implemented in λ-Prolog. We show how this approach introduces λ-abstractions and their related reduction operations, universal and existential quantification and implications in clause bodies, a more powerful form of unification and a more refined treatment of scoping. These properties are illustrated in section 2 by the development of a Montagovian-style grammar and by the presentation of an original treatment of filler-gap dependencies in GPSGs.

1. An Introduction to λ-Prolog

In this first section, we briefly introduce the logical foundations of higher-order logic programming. We present the language T, which is a weak higher-order system, at the basis of the logic programming language λ-Prolog. As shall be seen, λ-Prolog is a programming language which is a good compromise between expressive power and computational tractability. Next, we introduce the main features specific to λ-Prolog: universal quantification, lambda-abstraction, and the use of implication in clause bodies. This section ends with introductory programming examples. Several definitions and examples presented in this section are based on elements given byMiller and Nadathur (1986).

1.1 The language T

The higher-order logic system λ-Prolog is based on a formal language called T, which can be viewed as a subsystem of Church's simple theory of types (Church 1940) or Montague's intensional logic IL (Dowty *et al.* 1981). However, T is very weak because it does not take into account notions such as extensionality, definite descriptions, infinity and possible worlds. T mainly generalizes first-order logic by introducing stronger notions of variables, scoping and substitution.

The language T is a typed language. The notion of sorts, often used in first-order logic and the notion of functional type, is provided by the typing mechanism. Primitive types (or sorts) are o for booleans and i for first-order individuals (they respectively correspond to t and e in the Montagovian tradition). Functional types are noted:

$\alpha \rightarrow \beta$

where α and β are types. Functional types denote functions whose domain is α and resulting domain (or co-domain) β. For example:

$i \rightarrow i$

denotes the function which maps individuals to individuals.

To each type is associated a denumerable set of constants and variables. A constant or a variable forms a formula of its corresponding type. If A is of type $\alpha \rightarrow \beta$ and B is of type α, then the function application, noted (AB), is of type β. If x is a variable of type α and C a term of type β, then the λ-abstraction (also called function abstraction) λx C is a formula of type $\alpha \rightarrow \beta$.

Let us now introduce the following logical constants:

- true of type o,

- not of type o $\rightarrow$ o,

- $\vee$, $\wedge$, $\supset$ are of type o $\rightarrow$ o $\rightarrow$ o, since they map two formula of type o to a boolean,

- Π and Σ of type $(A \rightarrow o) \rightarrow o$, which respectively represent the universal and existential quantifiers. $\forall x\ P$ is an abbreviation for $\Pi(\lambda x\ P)$ and $\exists xP$ for $\Sigma(\lambda x\ P)$. These two symbols are examples of what is usually called *generalized quantifiers* (Barwise and Cooper 1981; van Benthem 1986), which introduce a relation Q between two sets of entities, represented by the formulas P and R as follows: Q P R.

The type o plays a special role in the language T. It indeed permits us to distinguish predicates from functions. A formula of type:

$$t_1 \rightarrow t_2 \rightarrow \ldots \rightarrow t_n \rightarrow o$$

is called a predicate of arity n, the ith argument of that predicate being of type t_i. Predicates permit the representation of sets and relations. A predicate of type:

$$i \rightarrow o$$

represents a set of individuals (noted $< e,t >$ in Montague grammar), whereas a predicate of type:

$$(i \rightarrow o) \rightarrow o$$

represents a set of sets of individuals (or $<< e,t >, t >$). A type of the form:

$$i \rightarrow (i \rightarrow o) \rightarrow o$$

represents a relation between individuals and sets of individuals. Finally, a predicate of type:

$$(A \rightarrow o) \rightarrow o$$

represents a set of sets of entities of type A. Formulas of type o are called propositions.

1.2 Derivability in T

Derivability in T is defined as follows. The axioms of T are the propositional tautologies and the two formulas:

$\forall x\ Bx \supset Bt$, where t is a constant, and

$\forall x\ (Px \wedge Q) \supset \forall x\ Px \wedge Q$.

The rules of inference are the following:

- modus ponens,
- universal generalization,
- substitution, and
- λ-conversion.

Let us define more precisely λ-conversion. The rules of α-conversion, β-reduction and η-expansion are taken into account in T. They are defined as follows:

α-conversion

$\lambda x\ e \Leftrightarrow \lambda y\ e[y/x]$ if y is not in e

where e[t/x] represents the substitution in e of the term t for the variable x.

β-reduction

$(\lambda x\ e1\ e2) \Leftrightarrow el\ [e2/x]$

where *el* represents the term e1 where all abstractions have been renamed by α-conversion to avoid any variable name confusion (a phenomenon called capture).

η-expansion

$e \Leftrightarrow \lambda x\ (e\ x)$ if x is not a free variable in e.

Let us now consider unification. Here is the typed λ-term unification principle, whose algorithm and its related correctness proof have been elaborated and proven by Huet (1975). Let us consider a set of constants of type C and of variables of type V. The set S of types is the smallest set containing V and the set of boolean constants. It is defined by means of the operator $\rightarrow$:

$$\alpha, \beta \in S \Rightarrow (\alpha \rightarrow \beta) \in S.$$

A substitution σ is a set of couples $<v_i, e_i>$ where v_i is a variable not bound to a λ-operator and e_i is a term; v_i and e_i are distinct but they are of the same type; e_i is closed and $i \neq j \Rightarrow v_i \neq v_j$. We can now define the application of a substitution to a term e as follows:

$$\sigma = \{\ <v_i, e_i>, i \in [1, n]\}$$

$$\sigma(e) = e\ [e_1/v_1] \ldots [e_n/v_n].$$

Two terms e_1 and e_2 of the same type are unifiable if there exists a substitution σ such that:

$$\sigma(e_1) = \sigma(e_2).$$

Contrary to first-order unification, the notion of most general unifier (i.e. a minimal unifier) does not exist for second-order unification. For example, the two terms:

(P a) and a

where P is a variable, are unifiable by the two substitutions:

$$\sigma1 = [P\ /\ \lambda x\ x\ ]\ \text{and}$$

$$\sigma2 = [P\ /\ \lambda x\ a\ ].$$

since the substitutions applied to P are the following:

$$(P\ a)[P\ /\ \lambda x\ x\ ] = (\lambda x\ x)(a) = a\ \text{and}$$

$$(P\ a)[P\ /\ \lambda x\ a\ ] = (\lambda x\ a)(a) = a.$$

The two substitutions $\sigma1$ and $\sigma2$ are not comparable, thus it is not possible to say that one of them is more general than the other.

Let us now define the notion of equality between two terms. To terms are equal if they are each convertible to the other via the operation of η-conversion. If this operation is not taken into account, then it is possible to establish more refined distinctions between terms, but these distinctions are not very relevant to our purpose. We say that a formula is in a λ-normal form if it has the form:

$\lambda x_1 \ldots \lambda x_n \ (h \ t_1 \ \ldots \ t_m)$ where n, m $\geq$ 0

and h is a constant or a variable, $(h \ t_1 \ \ldots \ t_m)$ has a primitive type A and similarly for each t_i.

1.3 Operational semantics of λ-Prolog

λ-Prolog allows for:

- the explicit specification of existential quantification (represented by the symbol sigma), at any place in a clause,
- the introduction of explicit universal quantifications (represented by the symbol pi) at any place in a clause,
- the use of λ-abstractions which can bind variables within a term (λx is noted X \) and
- the use of implication in clause bodies (noted by the symbol =>).

Let us say a few words about the operational semantics of λ-Prolog. Basically, λ-Prolog can be interpreted in a way very similar to Prolog, i.e. with the same proof procedure. The main difference is the unification algorithm, which produces different results as we have seen above. It can be shown that the unification procedure is only semi-decidable (i.e. if there is a solution, it can be found in a finite amount of time). The other difference is related to the introduction of quantification. The existential quantification does not raise any major problem *a priori* since in a Prolog goal variables are *a priori* existentially quantified. The treatment of universal quantification is slightly more complex. The technique which is usually used to solve a universally quantified goal $\forall x \ G$, amounts to choosing an arbitrary symbol c and trying to solve $G[c/x]$. If this is the case, then it is necessary to check that c does not appear as a subterm of the resolved goal G. Without this verification, an implementation is not correct. For example, to solve the goal:

$\forall x \ ((F \ x) = x)$

where F is a variable, we have two possible solutions when attempting to solve:

$(F \ c) = c$

namely:

$F = \lambda u\ u$ and $F = \lambda u\ c$.

Since the second solution contains an occurrence of c, it is not a correct solution and only the first one is acceptable.

The implication included in λ-Prolog, as in:

p :- (f => g).

has the following treatment. The clause f is added at the beginning of the program, in particular before any other possible definitions for f already present in the program. Notice that the λ-Prolog interpreter treats clauses in the order they appear in the program, as Prolog does. Then, to prove p, g has to be proven given the assertion of f. When this is done, f is withdrawn from the program.

Besides the possibility of introducing a kind of hypothesis (such as f in the above example) to prove a predicate, the use of implication introduces a notion of locality. In our example, f is indeed true only while p is being proven.

1.4 Programming in λ-Prolog

Besides the new unification capabilities that we have presented above, the facilities offered by λ-Prolog can be summarized in terms of a more refined treatment of scoping. λ-abstraction introduces a variable scope restricted to those terms in the scope of the λ-abstraction, quantifications introduce scope at the level of formulas, and the treatment of universal quantification and of the implication symbol introduces a new scope directly into the interpretation mechanism.

Programs in λ-Prolog are basically higher-order definite clauses. The notation used is based on the Lisp notation. Some Prolog equivalents may also be used in certain circumstances. Variables are written in capital letters, as in Prolog. Since the language is typed, the type of each term must be declared in the program. This is realized by explicitly defining the type of each constant, variable and predicate (some forms of type inference can also be done automatically, as in the language ML).

Here is a simple program for the concatenation of two lists:

```
type conc (list A) -> (list A) -> (list A) -> o.
conc nil X X.
conc (cons X L) Y (cons X Z) :- cons L Y Z.
```

The notation:

```
cons X Y
```

can also be written as:

    [X | Y].

We can write in λ-Prolog the predicate member in a similar way:

    type (list A) -> (list A) -> o.
    member X [X | _].
    member X [_ | L] :-
                    member X L.

The concatenation can be written in a different way, which shows how context can be used in a program instead of using term percolations (Brisset and Ridoux 1992):

    type conc (list A) -> (list A) -> (list A) -> o.
    type app (list A) -> (list A)   -> o.
    app [A|X] [A|Z] :-
                    app X Z.
    conc X Y Z :-
                    (app [] Y => app X Z).

In this program, the second argument, Y, is processed after the end of the treatment of the list X by means of the definition (app [] Y). According to the definition of the operator =>, the definition (app [] Y) is asserted at the beginning of the program for the duration of the proof. Thus, the definition of conc can be paraphrased as follows: the list X is decomposed and then stored element by element in Z. When X is empty, the call (app [] Y) is executed and Y is inserted after the elements of X in the list Z. In this example, the context, Y, is memorized by the program, in a specific clause, rather than by a term in a clause which is asserted, as it is the case in the first implementation of conc given above.

Let us now consider a program that expresses the distributivity of morphological operations on a string of words. For that purpose, we use a variable that represents a function. This is a technique which is only allowed in higher-order languages since first-order logic does not permit quantification over predicate names. Let us assume, for example, that the possible instantiations of that variable are:

    - sing_plur (singular to plural form),

    - plur_sing,

    - masc_fem, etc.

The predicate morph defined below has three arguments respectively representing the morphological operation, the input list of words and the output list of words. It is written as follows:

```
morph M  [X | Y] [(M X )| Z] :-
          morph M Y Z.
morph  M [] [].
```

The call morph (M L1 L2) can be proven if L2 is a list which represents the application of M to each element of L1. For example, the result of the call:

```
morph  sing_plur  [the,black,car]  L.
```

is L = [(sing_plur the), (sing_plur black), (sing_plur car)].

If we now have the call:

```
morph (X\ (id X X)) [the, black] L.
```

λ-Prolog evaluates it and returns the following value for L, after application of λ-reduction:

```
L = [(id the the), (id black black)].
```

Notice that, in attempting to prove:

```
morph M [luggage, car] [(sing_plur luggage), (sing_plur car)]
```

there is only one possible substitution for M, namely:

```
X\ (sing_plur X).
```

A substitution of the form:

```
X\ (sing_plur a),
```

where a is any constant symbol, would provoke a failure. In searching for higher-order substitutions, the system needs to backtrack over choices of solutions.

Let us now illustrate the use of quantification and implication. A simple ontology of a domain consists of the definition of a certain number of concepts assumed to be primitive with respect to the domain to be modelled, and a number of primitive relations taking these concepts as arguments. These concepts introduce a kind of typing. From these ontological elements, more complex concepts and relations can be constructed, following a number of construction principles which may vary from one application to another.

Let us define a few primitive concepts and relations:

```
prim_concept human.
prim_concept  tall.
prim_concept money.
prim_concept bird.
prim_concept physicalobject.
prim_concept date.
```

```
prim_concept event.
prim_relation before.   % arity of relations not given at this level
prim_relation own.
prim_relation send.
```

Let us now introduce more complex concepts and relations:

```
concept C :- prim_concept C.
concept (X\ (C1 & C2)) :-                    % association of concepts
        concept C1,
        concept C2.
concept (X\ (pi Y\ (R X Y => C X))) :-
        relation R,
        concept C.
concept (Y\ (pi X\ (R X Y => C Y))) :-
        relation R,
        concept C.


relation R :- prim_relation R.
relation (Y\  X\ (R X Y & C Y)) :-
        relation R,
        concept C.
relation (X\  Y\ (R X Y & C X)) :-
        relation R,
        concept C.
relation (X\ Y\ D\ ( pi E\ (R X Y E & date E D))) :-
        relation R,
        event E,
        date D.
```

etc.

The first definition of concept says that a primitive concept is a concept. The
second clause states that a concept can be the conjunction of any two concepts.
This statement is somewhat too powerful and should be constrained in a real
situation. For instance, human and tall can be conjoined to yield the concept of
tall humans, butdate and money, for example, do not really form a concept in our
world. The third clause allows us to define concepts that satisfy a certain
relation. For example, we can construct the following concepts:

```
X\ (human X & tall X)
```

which represents tall humans,

   Y\ (pi X\ (own X Y => money Y))

which represents the concept of money owned by someone, and

   X\ (bird X & (pi Y\ (own Y X => human Y)))

which represents the concept of birds all of which are owned by humans.

   Let us now consider the definition for relation. The first clause states that a primitive relation is a relation. The second and the third clauses permit the construction of relations with 'typed' arguments. The last clause views a relation as an event, E, and relates that event to a certain date D (this is at least a possible interpretation of this construction). From the definitions of concepts and relations, we can construct the following relations:

   X\ Y\ (own X Y & human X)

which defines the relation of a Y owned by an X which is a human;

   X\ Y\ D\ (pi E\ (own X Y E & date E D))

which defines the tuples (X, Y, D) such that X owns Y at a certain date D. In our representation, we have introduced an event E which allows us to bind the two predicates own and date and thus to establish non-ambiguously a link between X and Y on the one hand and D on the other hand;

   X\ Y\ D\ (pi E\ ((own X Y E & bird Y & date E D))

which defines the same relation as above where Y is restricted to be birds.

2. Parsing in λ-Prolog

In this section we develop more advanced examples of natural language processing in λ-Prolog. We first propose a reformulation of the DCG grammar given in section 3.2 of Chapter 2 that computes semantic forms in λ-Prolog and show that this formulation is very close to the semantic rules defined in Montague grammar. We then propose a simple interpreter of DCGs in λ-Prolog which makes use of λ-abstraction to represent difference lists. Finally, we show how the implication can be used to treat the problem of filler-gap dependencies in GPSGs in an elegant, though not fully satisfactory way.

2.1 A DCG-style grammar in λ-Prolog

Let us first consider the grammar given in section 3.2 of Chapter 2 which constructs simple first-order semantic representations:

```
                        % lexicon
    det(X, P, Q, the(X, P, Q)) --> [ the ].
    det(X, P, Q, a(X,  P, Q)) --> [ a ].
    n(X, student(X)) --> [ student ].
    n(X, computer(X)) --> [ computer ].
    v(X, Y, has(X,Y)) --> [ has ].
    a(X, Y, young(X)) --> [ young ].
                        % grammar
    s(R) --> np(X, R1, R) , vp(X, R1).
    np(X, R2, R) --> det(X, R1, R2, R), n(X, R1).
    vp(X, R) --> v(X, R).
    vp(X, Y, R) --> v(X, Y, R1), np(Y, R1, R).
    n( X, and(R, A)) --> a(X, A), n(X, R).
```

Instead of using a variable number of extra-arguments to percolate in the proof tree variables which will serve to bind arguments representing partial representations in different predicates, it is more linguistically adequate to use λ-abstractions. As a result, a single argument is needed to represent the semantic representation associated to any syntactic category. Here is the above lexicon reformulated in λ-Prolog (we have added parentheses to predicate-argument structures to facilitate reading):

```
    det (X\ P\ Q\ (the  X  P  Q)) --> [ the ].
    det (X\ P\ Q\ (a  X  P  Q)) --> [ a ].
    n (X\ student(X))   --> [ student ].
    n (X\ computer(X))   --> [ computer ].
    v(X\ Y\ have(X Y))   --> [ has ].
    a(X\ young(X)) --> [ young ].
```

The grammar is then the following:

```
    sentence X\ (P1 P2) --> np X\ P1  vp X\ P2.
    vp  (X\ Y\ (P2  P1))  --> v X\ Y\ P1,  np Y\ P2.
    np (X\ (P1 P2)) --> det X\ P1,  n X\ P2.
    np (X\ (P1 P2)) --> det X\ P1,  nadj X\ P2.
    nadj (X\ (P2 & P1)) --> a X\ P1,  n X\ P2.
```

Let us see in an example how this grammar permits the construction of semantic representations. Let us consider the sentence:

The student has a computer.

The np *the student* is represented as follows: associated to the determiner *the*, we have the representation:

    X\ P\ Q\ (the X P Q).

For the noun *student*, the representation is:

    X\ student(X)

Then, for the np *the student* we have the representation:

    X\(P\ Q\ (the X P Q) student(X)).

By λ-reduction, we obtain the representation for the subject np:

    X\ (Q\ (the X student(X) Q)).

Similarly, we have the following representation for the object np, where variables have been renamed to avoid any confusion:

    X1\ (Q1\ (a X1 computer(X1) Q1)).

Let us now construct the vp *has a computer*. Its representation is:

    X2\ Y2\ (Q1\ (a Y2 computer(Y2) Q1) have(X2 Y2)).

Notice that X1 has been bound to Y2 by unification in the vp rule. Then the λ-reduction λQ1 can be applied, yielding the following result:

    X2\ Y2\ (a Y2 computer(Y2) have(X2 Y2))

Let us now consider the sentence level. The rule for the sentence symbol requires the representation:

    X2\ (Q\ (the X2 student(X2) Q)
            Y2\ (a Y2 computer(Y2) have(X2 Y2)))

The variables X and X2 are bound by unification, then, by the λ-reduction λQ, we get the final representation:

    X2\ (the X2 student(X2) Y2\ (a Y2 computer(Y2) have(X2 Y2)))

Since there is no occurrence of Y2 outside the scope of its λ-operator, that λ-operator can be raised at the sentence level and placed at the same level as the λ-operator on X2:

    X2\ Y2\ (the X2 student(X2) (a Y2 computer(Y2) have(X2 Y2)))

Notice that a similar technique is used for associating adjectives to nouns in noun phrases. The variables associated with each predicate are bound and the two predicates are conjoined:

    nadj (X\ (P2 & P1)) --> a X\ P1, n X\ P2.

Determiners can be rewritten into logical forms, using the quantifiers of λ-Prolog. The first branch of the three-branched quantified tree formalism can also be skipped since the λ-abstraction introduces a variable at a higher level in the semantic representation. We then have the following definitions:

    det X\ P\ Q\ (Q   (iota P)) --> [the].
    det X\ P\ Q\ (pi X\   P => Q) --> [every].
    det X\ P\ Q\ (sigma X\ (P & Q) --> [a].

Let us recall that the symbols & and => are of type o -> o -> o, pi and sigma (respectively the universal and the existential quantifiers) are of type (i -> o) -> o. The symbol iota has the type (i ->o) -> i. It plays the role of a definite description operator: it picks out an individual from a description of a set of individuals. In the representation:

    (Q (iota P))

this operator picks out any individual in P. This individual may then be forwarded to Q during an evaluation phase of that semantic representation.

Notice that the grammar rules presented here and the way they contribute to constructing a semantic representation are very close to the construction rules given in Montague semantics. We do not have introduced in the grammar rules (but this could be done in a symbolic way by means of operators) the notions of intensionality (noted in Montague tradition by the symbol ^) and of interpretation function F which produces primed versions of predicates. Let us consider for example the rules S2 (for syntax) and T2 (the corresponding rule for semantics), given by Dowty *et al.* (1981) (p. 194) for the construction of a noun phrase in English composed of a determiner followed by a noun. We have the following rules (slightly simplified for a better understanding within the context of this book):

S2. If $\delta \in P_{DET}$ and $\zeta \in P_{CN}$, then $F_2(\delta, \zeta) = \delta'\zeta$ and δ' is δ except in the case where δ is 'a' and the first word in ζ begins with a vowel; here δ' is 'an'. This rule describes the combination of a determiner (element of P_{DET}) , of type << e,t >,< e,t >,t >, followed by a noun (element of P_{CN}), of type < e,t >. It simply concatenates the two words and changes the form of the determiner whenever appropriate. This is approximately what the np rule above does.

Let us now consider the semantic rule T2:

T2. If $\delta \in P_{DET}$ and $\zeta \in P_{CN}$, then $F_2(\delta, \zeta)$ translates into $\delta'(^\wedge\zeta')$. Besides the intensional symbol and the way variables are bound in our grammar, this rule exactly does the semantic combination given in the np rule. The similarities between λ-Prolog and Montague semantics should not however be pushed beyond these examples; there are indeed more complex elements in Montague semantics, such as some forms of meaning postulates which cannot easily be expressed in λ-Prolog. The intensional part is also important, since it permits us to evaluate several modal operators that cannot be expressed in λ-Prolog.

2.2 Abstracting over grammar symbols

One of the main advantages of λ-Prolog is that it provides the ability to abstract over predicate and function names. From that perspective, we can write a grammar in a DCG form and use λ-abstraction to treat the difference lists. We then define an interpreter for DCGs in λ-Prolog.

Let us consider the following grammar, where x0 represents terminal elements and xp any phrasal element:

```
x0 det [the].
x0 det [a].
x0 noun [student].
x0 noun [computer].
x0 verb [has].
x0 adjective [young].
xp_dcg np det n.
xp_dcg vp v np.
xp_dcg s np vp.


/* lambda-Prolog DCG interpretor */
    % rule composed of two x0 constituents
xp X\ Y\ (sigma Z\ (C1 X Z, C2 Z Y)) XP  :-
    xp_dcg XP C1 C2,
    x0 C1 X1,
    conc X1 Z X,
    x0 C2 X2,
    conc X2 Y Z.


    % rule composed of an x0 followed by an xp
xp X\ Y\ S\ (sigma Z\ (R X Z,  S Z Y))(F)  XP :-
    xp_dcg XP C1 C2,
    x0 C1 X1,
    conc X1 Z X,
    xp (Z\ Y\ F) C2.
```

```
    % rule composed of two xp constituents
  xp X\ Y\ (R\ S\ (sigma Z\ (R X Z,  S Z Y))(F2)(F1))   XP  :-
      xp_dcg XP C1 C2,
      xp X\ Z\ F1   C1 ,
      xp (Z\ Y\ F2)  C2.
```
etc...

A call to this program has the form:

```
xp( F [] [sentence]) s .
```

Let us examine a step in the construction of the higher-order formula that
represents the treatment of the difference list. Let us consider that we use first the
third rule above and that in that rule, R and S are both treated by the first rule of
the program. We have the following formula, where variables have been renamed
to avoid any confusion:

```
X\ Y\ (R\ S\ (sigma Z\ (R X Z,  S Z Y))
                  (sigma Z1\ (C11 X Z1,  C21 Z1 Z))
                  (sigma Z2\ (C12 Z Z2,  C22 Z2 Y)))
```

and, after λ-reduction:

```
X\ Y\ (R\ S\ (sigma Z\
          (sigma Z1\ (C11 X Z1,  C21 Z1 Z)) X Z,
          (sigma Z2\ (C12 Z Z2,  C22 Z2 Y)) Z Y)).
```

In this formula, we can see in an explicit way the distribution of X, Y and Z and
of intermediate strings such as Z1 and Z2. This DCG interpreter is a little bit
rigid, but it illustrates well another use of λ-Prolog. Of particular interest is the
interpretation of X-bar syntax in the form of DGC rules which have a very
regular, binary format. Notice that the success of a query does not depend on the
way λ-reductions are performed, e.g. as soon as possible or at the end of the
parse.

2.3 A treatment of filler-gap dependencies

Let us now show how the problem of filler-gap dependencies can be modelled in
λ-Prolog. We propose in this section a revised and adapted version of the
example proposed by Pareschi and Miller (1990). The way the implication => is
interpreted in λ-Prolog allows the specification of a mechanism that can handle
local information. This is the kind of situation typically involved in the GPSG
notion of slash non-terminal symbol which permits the treatment of filler-gap

dependencies. In GPSGs, a symbol is marked:

   S / XP

to indicate that the symbol S has an internally empty XP constituent (a gap). For example, in the construction of relative clauses we have to establish a dependency between the relative pronoun and a missing (or empty) noun phrase in the body of that relative clause. A sentence such as:

   The person whom you met is a cellist.

is analysed as:

   The person [$_S$ whom you met [$_{NP}$ _]] is a cellist.

There is a dependency between the pronoun *whom* and the empty NP. This dependency is expressed by means of a slash symbol:

   rel_clause --> [whom], s/np.

which means that after the terminal [whom], there is a sentence with a missing np. As we shall see it later, this specification is a little too permissive, since nothing is said about which np is missing (e.g. the subject np or the object np).

This rule can be implemented as follows in λ-Prolog, where the two first arguments of the symbols represent the difference lists and the third argument represents the logical formula associated with the relative clause construction:

```
rel_clause([whom| X], Y, Rel) :-
          pi X\ (np(Z, Z, Gap) => s(X, Y, REL(Gap))).
```

Let us see how the empty np is processed. The goal corresponding to the above example is:

```
?-  rel_clause([whom, you, met, is, a, cellist], [], Rel).
```

Then, the body of the clause has to be proven:

```
pi Gap\ (np(Z, Z, Gap) =>
          s([whom, you, met, is, a, cellist], [], REL(gap))).
```

Given the interpretation of universal quantification, a constant c is introduced for the variable Gap. Then, the goal succeeds if REL and Z can be instantiated to a value not containing c. The proof is realized by asserting the following clause at the beginning of the program:

```
np(Z, Z, Gap).
```

This clause will precisely treat the case of empty noun phrases. Its assertion can be viewed as making an assumption about an empty np and then checking for the parsability of the sentence. When the proof is terminated, this clause is withdrawn from the program. This guarantees that the empty np occurs only within the derivation of s. This also guarantees that only one gap will be found since the variable Z corresponding to the string position is a logic variable and can thus only be instantiated once. Finally, the variable Rel gets instantiated to the following ground λ-term:

```
X\ met(you, X).
```

To allow for multiple empty nps to appear within the derivation of s, the above rule would have to include a quantification on the gap position variable Z as follows:

```
rel_clause([whom| X], Y, Rel) :-
          pi X\ ( pi Z\ np(Z, Z, Gap) => s(X, Y, REL(Gap))).
```

The treatment given above for the gap-filler dependency is not, however, fully satisfactory for two reasons:

- the empty np can occur in any position within s, whereas the case of the pronoun requires it to appear as an object, with case accusative or, possibly dative,
- the assertion of the clause np(Z, Z, Gap) at the beginning of the program entails that this clause may be used (with the highest priority) for the derivation of s, but this does not entail that this clause will necessary be used. This approach can be contrasted with the interpretation of Dislog clauses (see Chapter 3), where the use of this clause is made compulsory, in the definition of a Dislog clause itself.

The second point cannot be treated in a satisfactory and simple way in λ-Prolog (except maybe by using a linear logic theorem prover). The first point can be solved in two ways. The solution proposed by Pareschi and Miller (1990) consists in no longer asserting an empty np but in asserting that a transitive vp is derived into a verb without any object:

```
rel_clause([whom| X], Y, Rel) :-
    pi Gap\ ((vp(Z, Z1, Tv(gap)) :- tv(Z, Z1, TV)) =>
                              s(X, Y, Rel(Gap))).
```

This solution is not very satisfactory, however, because it can solve the case of mono-transitive verbs but not the case of di-transitive ones. A more appropriate way is to mark the empty np with a case (for example, *accusative* in the case of *whom*) and to let the verb assign cases:

```
rel_clause([whom| X], Y, Rel) :-
          pi X\ (np(Z, Z, Gap, accusative) => s(X, Y, REL(Gap))).
```
with, for example, the following grammar where case is assigned:

```
vp --> v,  np(_, accusative).
s --> np(_, nominative), vp.
```
Similarly, the pronoun *who* will be related to an np with case nominative, and the pronouns *that* and *which* to an np with case accusative.

3. Conclusion

Higher-order logic programming is still in an early stage of investigation, from the language definition point of view as well as from the point of view of the definition of well-adapted control strategies. The natural language processing examples we have developed in this chapter show that this extension to Prolog offers many interesting enhancements which are worth pursuing: higher-order unification, three levels of scoping instead of just one as in Prolog, the introduction of universal quantification and of the implication in clause bodies to allow, for example, the expression of hypothesis. The introduction of λ-abstractions also offers an interesting synthesis of functional and logic programming.

λ-Prolog also enhances declarativity and linguistic adequacy (e.g. to compute semantic representations, as illustrated in section 2.1). The introduction of typing matches well with other trends in logic programming, in particular typed feature systems, although the typing proposed in λ-Prolog is more abstract and basic.

References

Abramson, H., Definite Clause Translation Grammars, in *Proc. Symposium on Logic Programming*, Atlantic City, IEEE, 1984.

Aït-Kaçi, H., Nasr, R., LOGIN: A Logic Programming Language with Built-in Inheritance, *Journal of Logic Programming*, vol. 3, pp. 185-215, 1986.

Aït-Kaci H., Podelski, A., *Is There a Meaning of Life?*, Manuscript, Paris Research Laboratory, DEC, Paris, December 1990.

Apt, K. R., de Bakker, J. W., Rutten J. J. M. M., (eds), *Logic Programming Languages, Constraints, Functions and Objects*, MIT Press, 1993.

Barwise, J., *The Situation in Logic*, CSLI Lecture Notes no. 17, Stanford University, 1989.

Barwise, J., Cooper, R., Generalized Quantifiers and Natural Language, *Linguistics and Philosophy*, vol. 4, 1981.

Barwise, J., Perry, J., *Situations and Attitudes*, MIT Press, 1983.

Blache, P., Using Active Constraints to Parse GPSG, in Proc. *COLING'92*, Nantes, 1992.

Bresnan, J., *Lexical Functional Grammars*, MIT Press, 1982.

Brown, C., Koch, G. (eds), *Natural Language Understanding and Logic Programming*, vol. 3, North Holland, 1991.

Butler, R., Lusk, E. L., Olson, R., Overbeek, R. A., A Parallel Implementation of the Warren Abstract Machine, Research Report, Computer Science Division, Argonne National Labs, USA, 1986.

Büttner W., Simonis H., Embedding Boolean Expressions into Logic Programming, *Journal of Symbolic Computation*, vol. 4, pp. 191-205, 1987.

Carpenter, B., *The Logic of Typed Feature Structures*, Cambridge Tracts in Theoretical Computer Science no. 32, Cambridge University Press, 1992.

Chomsky, N., *Lectures on Government and Binding*, Foris, GRASS series, Dordrecht, 1982.

Chomsky, N., *Barriers*, Linguistic Inquiry Monograph no. 13, MIT Press, 1986.

Church, A., A Formulation of the Simple Theory of Types, *Journal of Symbolic Logic*, vol. 5, 1940.

Clark, K. L., Negation as Failure, in *Logic and Databases*, H. Gallaire and J. Minker (eds), Plenum Press, New York, 1978.

Clark, K., Predicate Logic as a Computational Formalism, Research Monograph no. 79/59, Imperial College, London, 1979.

Clark, K., Gregory, S., A Relational Language for Parallel Programming, in *Proc. ACM Conference on Functional Programming Languages and Computer Architectures*, 1981.

Clark, K., McCabe, F. G., The Control Facilities of IC-Prolog, in *Expert Systems of the Micro-Electronic Age*, Edinburgh University Press, 1979.

Cohen J., Constraint Logic Programming Languages, *Communications of the ACM*, vol. 33, no. 7, 1990.

Colmerauer, A., Les systèmes Q ou un formalism pour analyser et synthétiser des phrases sur ordinateur, Research Report, Project TAUM, Université de Montréal, Canada, 1971.

Colmerauer, A., Un système de communication homme-machine en français, Université d'Aix-Marseille, Research Report, GIA, 1973.

Colmerauer, A., Les grammaires de métamorphose, Technical Report, Université d'Aix-Marseille, GIA, 1975.

Colmerauer, A., Metamorphosis Grammars, in *Natural Language Understanding by Computers*, L. Bolc (ed.), Lecture Notes in Computer Science no. 63, Springer Verlag, 1978.

Colmerauer, A., An Interesting Subset of Natural Language, in *Logic Programming*, K. L. Clark and S. A. Tärnlund (eds), Academic Press, 1982.

Colmerauer A., An Introduction to Prolog III, *Communications of the ACM*, vol. 33, no. 7, 1990.

Conlon, T., *Programming in Parlog*, Addison-Wesley, 1989.

Conery, J. S., *The AND/OR Process Model for Parallel Execution of Logic Programs*, PhD Dissertation, University of California at Irvine, Technical Report no. 204, Dept of Computer Science, 1983.

Cruse, A., *Lexical Semantics*, Cambridge University Press, Textbooks in Linguistics Series, 1986.

Dahl, V., Translating Spanish into Logic Through Logic, *Journal of Computational Linguistics*, vol. 7, no. 3, 1981.

Dahl, V., Abramson, H., On Gapping Grammars, in *Proc. Second Logic Programming Conference*, Uppsala, 1984.

Dahl, V., Abramson, H., *Logic Grammars*, Springer-Verlag, 1989.

Dahl, V., McCord, M.C., Treating Coordination in Logic Grammars, *American Journal of Computational Linguistics*, vol. 9, no. 2, 1983.

Dahl, V., Saint-Dizier, P. (eds), *Natural Language Understanding and Logic Programming*, vols. I and II, North Holland, 1985 and 1988.

Davidson, A., Parlog++: A Parlog Object-Oriented Language, Technical Report, Parallel Logic Programming Ltd, Twickenham, UK, 1991.

De Groot, D., Restricted AND-Parallelism, in *Proc. Fifth Generation Systems*, Tokyo, 1984.

De Groot, G., Lindstrom, G., *Logic Programming: Functions, Relations and Equations*, Prentice-Hall, NJ, 1986.

Deransart, P., Jourdan, M., Lorho, B., Attribute Grammars: Main Results, Existing Systems and Bibliography, *Lecture Notes in Computer Science no. 323*, Springer-Verlag, 1988.

Deransart, P., Maluszynski, J., What Kind of Grammars are Logic Programs ?, in *Logic and Logic Grammars for Language Processing*, P. Saint-Dizier and S. Szpakowicz (eds), Ellis Horwood, 1990.

Dincbas M., Van Hentenryck P., Simonis H., Aggoun A., Graf T., Berthier F., The Constraint Logic Programming Language CHIP, *Proc. International Conference on Fifth Generation Computer Systems*, pp. 693-702, ICOT, Tokyo, 1988.

Dowty, D. R., Wall, R. E., Peters, S., *Introduction to Montague Semantics*, D. Reidel, 1981.

Dowty, D., Thematic Proto-roles and Argument Selection, *Language*, vol. 67, no. 3, 1991.

Freuder E. C., Synthetizing Constraint Expressions, *Communications of the ACM*, vol. 21, no. 11, pp. 958–966, 1978.

Gal, A., Lapalme, G., Saint-Dizier, P., Somers, H., *Prolog for Natural Language Analysis*, John Wiley, London, 1991.

Gazdar, G., Klein, E., Pullum, G., Sag, I., *Generalized Phrase Structure Grammar*, Basil Blackwell, London, 1986.

Gazdar, G., Mellish, C., *Natural Language Processing in Prolog*, Addison-Wesley, 1989.

Gregory, S., *Parallel Logic Programming in Parlog*, Addison-Wesley, 1987.

Grimshaw, J. *Argument Structure*, Linguistic Inquiry Monograph no. 18, MIT Press, 1991.

Günthner F., *Features and Values*, Technical Report SNS-Bericht no. 88-40, Universität Tübingen, Germany, 1988.

Hathout, N., *Théorie du Gouvernement et du Liage et programmation en Logique avec contraintes: une application à l'analyse automatique du français*, PhD dissertation, University of Toulouse III, France, 1992.

Hirschman, L., Conjunction in Meta-Restriction Grammar, *Journal of Logic Programming*, vol. 3, no. 4, 1986.

Hirschman, L., Puder, K., Restriction Grammars, in *Logic Programming and its Applications*, M. van Caneghem and D. H. D. Warren (eds), Ablex, 1986.

Hoare, C. A. R., Communicating Sequential Processes, *Communications of the ACM* , vol. 21, no. 2, 1978.

Höhfeld M., Smolka G., Definite Relations over Constraint Languages. LILOG Report no. 53, IBM Deutschland, Stuttgart, Germany, 1988.

Huet, G., A Unification Algorithm for Typed λ-Calculus, *Theoretical Computer Science*, vol. 1, 1975.

Jaffar J., Lassez J. L., Constraint Logic Programming, Technical Report, Department of Computer Science, Monash University, Victoria, Australia, June 1986.

Jackendoff, R., *Semantic Structures*, MIT Press, 1991.

Johnson, M., *Attribute-Value Logic and the Theory of Grammar*, CSLI Lecture Notes no. 16, Stanford University, 1988.

Joshi, A., Tree Adjoining Grammars: How much context-sensitivity is required to provide reasonable structural descriptions, in *Natural Language Parsing*, D. Dowty *et al.* (eds), Cambridge University Press, 1985.

Kaplan, R., Bresnan, J., Lexical Functional Grammar: A formal system for grammatical representation, in *The Mental Representation of Grammatical Relations*, J. Bresnan (ed.), MIT Press, 1982.

Karttunnen, L., Features and Values, in *Proc. Coling 84*, Stanford, ACL publications, 1984.

Kasper, R. T., Rounds, W. C., The Logic of Unification in Grammar, *Linguistics and Philosophy*, vol. 13, no. 1, 1990.

Kay, M., Functional Grammar, in *Proc. 5th Annual Meeting of the Berkeley Linguistic Society*, Berkeley, USA, 1979.

Kay, M., Unification Grammars, Technical Report, Xerox, Palo Alto, CA, 1983.

Kay, M., Parsing in Functional Unification Grammar, in *Natural Language Parsing: Psychological, Computational and Theoretical Perspectives*, Chapter 7, Cambridge University Press, 1985.

Kowalski, R. A., Algorithm = Logic + Control, *Comm. of the ACM*, vol. 22, pp. 424-436, 1979a.

Kowalski, R. A., *Logic for Problem Solving*, North-Holland, Amsterdam, 1979b.

Lloyd, J. W., *Foundations of Logic Programming*, Springer-Verlag, second edition, 1987.

Mackworth A. K., Consistency in Networks of Relations, *Artificial Intelligence*, vol. 8, no. 1, 1977.

Mackworth A. K., Constraint Satisfaction, in *Encyclopedia of Artificial Intelligence*, pp. 205–211, S. Shapiro (ed.), Wiley-Interscience Publication, New York, 1987.

Maluszynski, J., Towards a Programming Language Based on the Notion two-level Grammar, *Theoretical Computer Science*, vol. 28, no. 1, 1984.

Marrafa P. and Saint-Dizier P., A Reversible Constraint-Based Logic Grammar: Application to the Treatment of Secondary Predication and Small Clauses, in *Proc. ACL Workshop on Reversible Grammars*, Berkeley, 1991, also published by Kluwer Academic Press, T. Strzakolwski (ed.), 1993.

Martin J., *Constraints on Syntactic Features*, manuscript, University of Maryland, 1992.

Matsumoto, Y. (ed.), *Natural Language Understanding and Logic Programming*, vol. 4, North Holland, 1993.

Matsumoto, Y., Tanaka, H., Hirakawa, H., Miyoshi, H., Yasukawa, H., BUP: a Bottom-Up Parser embedded in Prolog, *New Generation Computing*, vol. 1, no. 2, 1983.

McCabe, F .G., *Logic and Objects*, Prentice-Hall, Series in Computer Science, 1992.

McCord, M., Using Slots and Modifiers in Logic Grammars for Natural Language, Technical Report no. 69-80, University of Kentucky and *Artificial Intelligence*, North Holland, 1982.

McCord, M., Design of LMT: A Prolog Based Machine Translation System, *Computational Linguistics*, vol. 15, no. 1, 1989.

Mellish, C., Implementing Systemic Classification by Unification, *Computational Linguistics*, vol. 14, no. 1, 1988.

Miller, D. A., Nadathur, G., Higher-Order Logic Programming, in *Proc. 3rd Logic Programming Conference*, London, UK, E. Shapiro (ed.), Springer-Verlag, 1986.

Mukai, K., Record Algebra Model for Feature Structures, in *Unification in Grammar*, J. Wedenkind and C. Rohrer (eds), MIT Press, 1991.

Mukai, K., Yasukawa, H., Complex Indeterminates in Prolog and its Application to Discourse Models, *New Generation Computing*, vol. 3, no. 4, 1985.

Pareschi, R., Miller, D., Extending Definite Clause Grammars with Scoping Constraints, in *Proc. 7th Internationl Conference on Logic Programming*, D. H. D. Warren and P. Szeredi (eds), MIT Press, 1990.

Pereira, F. C. N., Extraposition Grammars, *American Journal of Computational Linguistics*, vol. 9, no. 4, 1981.

Pereira, F. C. N., Logic for Natural Language Analysis, SRI International Technical Note no. 275, 1983.

Pereira, F. C. N., Sheiber, S., *Prolog and Natural Language Analysis*, CSLI Lecture Notes no. 10, University of Chicago Press, 1987.

Pereira, L. M., Nasr, R., Delta Prolog: a Distributed Logic Programming Language, in *Proc. Fifth Generation Computer Generation Conference*, Tokyo, 1984.

Pereira, F. C. N., Warren, D. H. D., Definite Clause Grammars for Language Analysis: a Survey of the Formalism and Comparison with Augmented Transition Networks, *Artificial Intelligence*, vol. 13, no. 3, 1980.

Pfenning, F., (ed.), *Types in Logic Programming*, MIT Press, 1992.

Pustejovsky, J., Type Coercion and Selection, in *Proc. West Coast Conference on Formal Linguistics*, Vancouver, B.C., 1989.

Pustejovsky, J., The Generative Lexicon, *Computational Linguistics*, vol. 17, no. 4, 1991.

Pustejovsky, J., Linguistic Constraints on Type Coercion, in *Computational lexical Semantics*, P. Saint-Dizier and E. Viegas (eds), Cambridge University Press, 1993.

Radford, A., *Transformational Syntax*, Cambridge University Press, Textbooks in Linguistics, 1981.

Reiter, R., On Closed World Databases, in *Logic and Databases*, H. Gallaire and J. Minker (eds), Plenum Press, New York, 1978.

Saint-Dizier, P., An Approach to Natural Language Semantics in Logic Programming, *Journal of Logic Programming*, vol. 3, no. 4, North Holland,

1986.

Saint-Dizier, P., Contextual Discontinuous Grammars, in *Natural Language Understanding and Logic Programming II*, V. Dahl and P. Saint-Dizier (eds), North Holland, 1988.

Saint-Dizier, P., A Generation Method Based on Principles of Government and Binding Theory, in *Proc. Second European Natural Language Generation Workshop*, Edinburgh, 1989a.

Saint-Dizier, P., *An Introduction to Programming in Prolog*, Springer-Verlag, 1989b.

Saint-Dizier, P., Dislog: Programming in Logic with Discontinuities, *Computational Intelligence*, 1990.

Sells, P., *Lectures on Contemporary Syntactic Theories*, CSLI Lecture Notes no. 3, Stanford, 1987.

Shapiro, E. (ed.), *Concurrent Prolog: collected papers*, MIT Press, 1988.

Shapiro, E., Takeuchi, A., Object Oriented Programming in Concurrent Prolog, *New Generation Computing*, vol. 1, no. 1, 1983.

Shieber, S., *An Introduction to Unification-Based Grammars Approaches to Grammar*, CSLI Lecture Notes no. 4, Chicago University Press, 1986.

Shieber, S., *Constraint-Based Grammar Formalisms*, MIT Press, 1992.

Shieber, S., Uszkoreit, H., Pereira, F. C. N., Robinson, J., Tyson, M., The Formalism and Implementation of PATRII, in *Research on Interactive Acquisition and Use of Knowledge*, AI Center, SRI International, Stanford, 1983.

Smolka, G., A feature Logic with Subsorts, Lilog Report no. 33, IBM Deutschland, Stuttgart, 1988.

Smolka, G., *Logic Programming over Polymorphically Order-Sorted Types*, PhD dissertation, Universität Kaiserslautern, 1989.

Smolka, G., Aït-Kaci, H., Inheritance Hierarchies, Semantics and Unification, *Journal of Symbolic Logic*, vol. 7, 1989.

Stabler, E., *The Logical Approach to Syntax*, MIT Press, 1992.

Sterling, L., Shapiro, E., *The Art of Prolog*, MIT Press, 1986.

Van Benthem, J., *Essays in Logical Semantics*, Essays in Linguistics and Philosophy Series, vol. 29, D. Reidel, 1986.

van Emden, M. H., Kowalski, R. A., The Semantics of Predicate Logic as a Programming Language, *Journal of the ACM*, vol. 23, no. 4, 1976.

Van Hentenrick P. *Constraint Satisfaction in Logic Programming*, MIT Press,

Cambridge, Mass., 1989.

Warren, D. H. D., An Abstract Prolog Instruction Set, Technical Note no. 309, AI Center, SRI International, 1983.

Yang, R., *P-Prolog: A Parallel Logic Programming Language*, World Scientific Publishers, Singapore, 1987.

List of Abbreviations

AP: adjective phrase

BUP: bottom-up parsing

CIL: complex indeterminates language

CLP: constraint logic programming

CSP: constraint satisfaction problem

CWA: closed world assumption

DCG: definite clause grammars

Det: determiner

FAC: function application with type coercion

FOL: first-order logic

GB: government and binding theory

GG: gapping grammars

GLB: greater lower bound

GPSG: generalized phrase structure grammars

GHC: guarded horn clause (programming language)

LFG: lexical functional grammars

L&O: logic and objects

MG: metamorphosis grammars

mgu: most general unifier

MSG: modifier structure grammars

MT: machine translation

NP: noun phrase

OOP: object-oriented programming

OOLP: object-oriented logic programming

OOPLP: object-oriented parallel logic programming

PLP: parallel logic programming

PP: prepositional phrase

RGs: restriction grammars

SS: situation semantics

TAG: tree adjoining grammars

TFS: type feature structure

UG: unification grammars

VP: verb phrase

WAM: Warren abstract machine

XG: extraposition grammars.

INDEX

References of the Main Prolog versions mentioned in this book

Here are the references of the main Prolog versions used in this book. Addresses are those established in 1993. For any other information the author can be contacted at stdizier@irit.fr. Only reasonably priced or public domain systems are listed here. For more information see also the *Logic Programming Newsletter*, vol. 4-4, November 1991(*).

AAIS Prolog (on MacIntosh): Advanced AI Systems Inc. P.O. Box 39-0360, Mountain View, CA 94039-0360, USA.

BIM Prolog (on Unix): BIM, Kwikstraat 4, B-3078 Everberg, Belgium.

CLP(R): Dept of Computer Science, Monash University, Clayton, Victoria 3168, Australia.

Parlog and Parlog++ (on MacIntosh): Parallel Logic Programming Ltd, PO Box 49, Twickenham TW2 5PH, UK.

PrologIA: Case 919, Luminy, 13288 Marseille, France.

Sicstus Prolog (mainly on Unix): SICS, PO Box 1263, S-164-28 Kista, Sweden.

(*) Association for Logic Programming: Attn C. Anderson, DoC-ICSTM, 180 Queen's Gate, London SW7 2BZ, UK.